Human Emotions

Humans are the most emotional animals on earth. Almost every aspect of human cognition, behavior, and social organization is driven by emotions. Emotions are the force behind social commitments to others in face-to-face interactions and groups. But they are much more; they are also the driving force responsible for the formation of social structures, and conversely, they are the fuel driving collective actions that tear down social structures and transform cultures.

Because emotions are so central to human affairs, it should be possible to develop a general theory explaining why particular emotions are aroused in individuals and groups of individuals, with particular attention to the consequences of emotions for social relations and larger sociocultural patterns in societies. As a general theory diverse manifestations of emotions can be explained; emotions drive, for example, the friendships that people develop with each other, the commitments they make to social structures, or the acts of terrorism that are designed to strike collective fear. There is a common set of forces that can be theorized and, hence, that can explain all dimensions of emotions in human affairs. The goal of *Human Emotions* is to begin the process of developing a general theory that can be tested with data from diverse sources, ranging from the experimental laboratory through case studies in natural settings to historical accounts of how emotions affect key historical events.

This book is essential reading for undergraduate and postgraduate students researching sociology of emotions, social psychology, and contemporary social theory and is also relevant for students and researchers working in the fields of psychology and cultural studies.

Jonathan H. Turner is Distinguished Professor of Sociology at the University of California, Riverside.

Other books by Jonathan H. Turner

Patterns of Social Organization: A Survey of Social Institutions (1972)
American Society: Problems of Structure (1972)
The Structure of Sociological Theory (1974)
Inequality: Privilege and Poverty in America (1976, with Charles Starnes)
Social Problems in America (1977)
Sociology: Studying the Human System (1978)
Functionalism (1979, with Alexandra Maryanski)
The Emergence of Sociological Theory (1981, with Leonard Beeghley)
Societal Stratification: A Theoretical Analysis (1984)
Oppression: A Socio-History of Black–White Relations in America (1984, with Royce Singleton
     and David Musick)
Herbert Spencer: A Renewed Appreciation (1985)
American Dilemmas: A Sociological Interpretation of Enduring Social Issues (1985, with David
     Musick)
Sociology: A Student Handbook (1985)
Sociology: The Science of Human Organization (1986)
A Theory of Social Interaction (1988)
The Impossible Science: An Institutional History of American Sociology (1990, with Stephen P.
     Turner)
The Social Cage: Human Nature and The Evolution of Society (1992, with Alexandra Maryanski)
Classical Sociological Theory: A Positivist's Perspective (1992)
Sociology: Concepts and Uses (1993)
Socjologia Amerykanska W Poszukiwaiou Tazsamosci (1993, with Stephen P. Turner)
American Ethnicity: A Sociological Analysis of the Dynamics of Discrimination (1994, with
     Adalberto Aguirre)
Macrodynamics: Toward a Theory on the Organization of Human Populations (1995)
The Institutional Order (1997)
On the Origins of Human Emotions: A Sociological Inquiry into the Evolution of Human Affect
     (2000)
Face-to-Face: Toward a Sociological Theory of Interpersonal Behavior (2002)
Human Institutions: A Theory of Societal Evolution (2003)
The Sociology of Emotions (2005, with Jan E. Stets)
Incest: Origins of the Taboo (2005, with Alexandra Maryanski)
Sociology (2006)
On the Origins of Societies by Natural Selection (2007, with Alexandra Maryanski)

Human Emotions

A sociological theory

Jonathan H. Turner

Routledge
Taylor & Francis Group

LONDON AND NEW YORK

First published 2007
by Routledge
2 Park Square, Milton Park, Abingdon, Oxon, OX14 4RN

Simultaneously published in the USA and Canada
by Routledge
270 Madison Ave, New York NY 10016

Routledge is an imprint of the Taylor & Francis Group, an informa business

Transferred to Digital Printing 2008

© 2007 Jonathan H. Turner

Typeset in Bembo by
RefineCatch Limited, Bungay, Suffolk

British Library Cataloguing in Publication Data
A catalogue record for this book is available from the British Library

Library of Congress Cataloging in Publication Data
A catalog record for this book has been requested

ISBN 10: 0–415–42781–9 (hbk)   ISBN 13: 978–0–415–42781–4 (hbk)
ISBN 10: 0–415–42782–7 (pbk)   ISBN 13: 978–0–415–42782–1 (pbk)
ISBN 10: 0–203–96127–7 (ebk)   ISBN 13: 978–0–203–96127–8 (ebk)

To Professor Dr. med. Beat Hintermann

and the staff of Kantonsspital Liestal, Liestal, Switzerland

Contents

Figures

Tables

Preface

This book represents the culmination of thinking that began when I was an undergraduate at the Riverside and Santa Barbara branches of the University of California. I began as a psychology major at UC Riverside because I wanted to become a clinical psychologist. After a year of running rats in the laboratory, I began to have doubts that the discipline of psychology was right for me, and when I transferred to Santa Barbara, I fell under the spell of Tamotsu Shibutani in his social psychology class. At last, here was a discipline that studied the relationship among emotions, social structure, and culture. During my undergraduate years at Santa Barbara, I read widely in a special program for students who planned to become college instructors; and over a several-year period, I read not only George Herbert Mead, who had little to say about emotions, and Charles Horton Cooley, who had more to say, but I also read Freud and many more contemporary psychiatrists such as Harry Stack Sullivan. Even though my major area in graduate school at Cornell was social psychology, my heart was in theory; and moreover, I became fascinated by macro-level social processes during my three years at Cornell. Thus, for two decades I was a dedicated theorist with mostly macro interests, but that was to change in the late 1980s when, under the influence of my then colleague at Riverside, Randall Collins, I was re-introduced to the topic of emotions which once again sparked my interest in psychology and sociology. I was never quite happy with Collins's notion of "emotional energy," not because it was wrong but because it seemed incomplete. While the positive or negative valence of emotional energy is critical, the dynamics of *specific emotions* are also important in theorizing about human emotions.

As I moved back into the study of emotions in particular, and interpersonal processes more generally, I brought with me my early training in the psychoanalytic tradition – a training that was reinforced not only by Shibutani but others, such as Talcott Parsons, who also used ideas from this tradition. In my view, the standard symbolic interactionist model – for all of its other strengths – does not adequately address powerful emotions that are often repressed and transformed into new kinds of emotions. The standard approach is too cognitive, too gestalt-based. Emotions about self are powerful, and if sociocultural conditions generate intense negative feelings, repression and other defense mechanisms change the emotional dynamics. These changes, in turn, have different effects on meso- and, potentially, macro-level social structures. Thus, a sociological theory of emotions must explain how emotions are generated under sociocultural conditions operating at micro-, meso-, and macro-level levels of social reality, how these emotions target self, others, and structures at each level of social reality, how these emotions can, when negative, be transmuted by the operation of defense mechanisms, and how the emerging emotions come back and have effects on the very sociocultural conditions that generated them. The theory developed in these pages tries to address all of these issues.

Along the way over the last fifteen years, I increasingly realized that a theory of emotions must also address the biology of emotions. Indeed, I became fascinated with the brain and how emotions are generated by various subcortical systems in the brain; and the more I studied the brain, the more I wanted to understand the selection pressures that wired the human brain for emotions during the course of hominid and human evolution. Indeed, I became so fascinated that I wrote a book on the topic (Turner, 2000a).

While I became for a time somewhat obsessed with the evolution of emotions, I was still working away on a more purely sociological theory, one that emphasized the sociocultural conditions that activate these brain systems to produce specific emotions in face-to-face encounters, with an eye to understanding how variations in emotional arousal in encounters have effects on different levels of social structure and culture. I brought with me – to my critics' dismay – both my interest in the biology of emotions and the psychoanalytic emphasis on repression as a key force. And so, the theory that appears in these pages is a composite not only of various lines of purely sociological thinking but also of ideas from other intellectual traditions that, I believe, are important and that, too often, are ignored or underemphasized by sociologists.

The theory that emerges in chapters 4, 5, 6, 7, and 8 is collapsed with some pushing and shoving into seventeen abstract principles (for a preview, they are summarized in Chapter 9), but there are many dozens of additional hypotheses offered throughout the book. I have also brought to this analysis of emotions the general conceptual scheme that I now use to analyze all sociological phenomena; and while this scheme is about as minimal as it can be, the propositions only make sense by understanding some of the vocabulary and concepts in this scheme, which is summarized in Chapter 3.

I have written the book so that the topic of biology can be ignored, if the reader so desires. All that is necessary is to skip Chapter 2 where the evolutionary story of why humans became so emotional is told and where, in the appendix to this chapter, the basic neuroanatomy of emotional arousal in humans is summarized. Thus, the theory that I develop is purely sociological, but I place it in a broader context provided by evolutionary biology. This theory is still a work in progress, but it is now sufficiently developed that I feel it is time to let others see it and make suggestions for how I can improve upon the principles developed in these pages.

Jonathan H. Turner

Acknowledgments

Like all of my research at the University of California, Riverside, the research for this book has been funded by grants from the Academic Senate at the University. I am most grateful for the Senate's continued support of my work. Also, this manuscript has been prepared by my typist and friend, Clara Dean, who for almost forty years has worked with me in preparing books and articles. My only fear is that she is older than I and may retire before I do.

1   Human emotions

Humans are, to say the least, highly emotional animals. We love and hate; we fall into suicidal depressions or experience moments of joy and ecstasy; we feel shame, guilt, and alienation; we are righteous; we seek vengeance. Indeed, as distinctive as capacities for language and culture make us, humans are also unique in their propensity to be so emotional. Other animals can, of course, be highly emotional, but during the course of hominid and human evolution, natural selection rewired our ancestors' neuroanatomy to make *Homo sapiens* more emotional than any other animal on earth. Humans can emit and interpret a wide array of emotional states; and in fact, a moment of thought reveals that emotions are used to forge social bonds, to create and sustain commitments to social structures and cultures, and to tear socio-cultural creations down. Just about every dimension of society is thus held together or ripped apart by emotional arousal.

These observations seem so obvious that it is amazing that for most of sociology's history as a discipline, the topic of emotions was hardly mentioned. In recent decades, however, theory and research on emotions have accelerated in sociology and now represent one of the leading edges of inquiry in the discipline (see Turner and Stets, 2005; Stets and Turner, 2006, 2007 for reviews). There are now many theories, supported by research findings, that seek to explain emotional dynamics; and my goal in this book is to present yet another theory, although my approach attempts to integrate existing theories and research findings into a more global analysis of human emotionality.

What are emotions?

Surprisingly, a definition of our topic is elusive. Terms such as affect, senti-ment, feeling, mood, expressiveness, and emotion are sometimes used inter-changeably and at other times, to denote a specific affective state. For my purposes, the core concept is *emotion*, with other terms denoting varying aspects of emotions. What I propose, then, is a theory of human emotional arousal that seeks to provide answers to one fundamental, though com-plex, question: *What sociocultural conditions arouse what emotions to what effects on human behavior, interaction, and social organization*? Clearly, this one question is really a number of separate questions, each of which will be given a provisional answer in a series of abstract principles (see Chapter 9 for a summary). Still, I have not clearly defined by topic – emotions – nor will I be able to offer a general definition because depending upon the vantage point, the definition will vary. From a biological perspective, emotions involve changes in body systems – autonomic nervous system (ANS), musculoskeletal system, endocrine system, and neurotransmitter and neuroactive peptide systems – that mobilize and dispose an organism to behave in particular ways (Turner, 1996a, 1999a, and 2000a; as well as the appendix to Chapter 2). From a cognitive perspective, emotions are conscious feelings about self and objects in the environment. From a cultural perspective, emotions are the words and labels that humans give to particular physiological states of arousal. As Figure 1.1 outlines, Peggy Thoits (1990) sought to get around this vagueness by isolating four elements of emotions: situational cues, physiological changes, cultural labels for these changes, and expressive gestures. All of these are interrelated, mutually influencing each other, but simply denoting "elements" of emotions does not really provide a clear definition of our topic. For the present, then, a precise definition will have to elude us. We can get a better sense for the topic by outlining the varieties and types of emotions that are aroused among humans and that, as a consequence, lead them to think and act in particular ways.

Primary emotions

Primary emotions are those states of affective arousal that are presumed to be hard-wired in human neuroanatomy. There are several candidates for

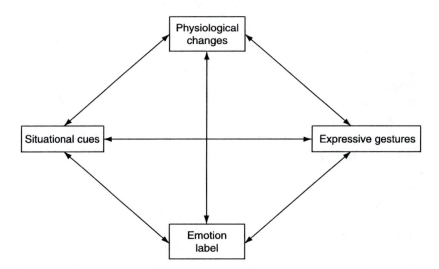

Figure 1.1 Thoits's elements of emotions.

such primary emotions, as outlined in Table 1.1 where the lists of primary emotions posited by researchers from diverse disciplines are summarized (Turner, 2000a:68–9). Despite somewhat different labels, there is clear consensus that anger, fear, sadness, and happiness are primary; and indeed, humans probably inherited these not only from our primate ancestors but from all mammals as well. Disgust and surprise can be found on many lists, and we might consider these as primary as well. Shame and guilt can be found on several lists but, as I will argue shortly, these are not primary but, instead, elaborations of primary emotions. Other emotions like interest, anticipation, curiosity, boredom, and expectancy are less likely to be primary, and in fact, they may not even be emotions at all but, rather, cognitive states.

Humans have the capacity to arouse primary emotions at varying levels of intensity, from low- through medium- to high-intensity states. Table 1.2 summarizes my conceptualization of four primary emotions and their varying levels of intensity. As I will argue in Chapter 2, natural selection probably worked on the neuroanatomy of hominids and humans to increase the range of expression of these primary emotions. With this wider range, it becomes possible to expand further the subtlety and complexity of emotional feelings and expressions which, in turn, increase the attunement of individuals to each other. The terms in Table 1.2 are, of course, cultural labels and, as such, are part of an emotion culture, but in my view, these linguistic labels for variations in primary emotions are a surface manifestation of a basic neurological capacity. They are a kind of emotional superstructure to an underlying biological substructure; and what is true of variations in primary emotions is doubly true for combinations of these emotions.

Elaborations of primary emotions

First-order elaborations of primary emotions

At some point in hominid and human evolution, natural selection worked on our ancestors' neuroanatomy to create a new level of emotionality: the capacity to *combine* primary emotions. Plutchik (1962, 1980) was one of the first researchers to posit a way to conceptualize how emotions are "mixed" to produce new emotions. For Plutchik, primary emotions are much like primary colors and can be conceptualized on an "emotion wheel," with the mixing of relatively few primary emotions generating many new kinds of emotions. The basic elements of his scheme are portrayed in Figure 1.2.

When emotions are combined, new kinds of emotions appear, just like mixing primary colors. I prefer to conceptualize this "mixing" as elaborations. Just how this elaboration is done neurologically is not so clear, but it probably involves the simultaneous activation of primary emotion centers in the subcortical parts of the brain in ways that produce new kinds of more complex emotions. In my conceptualization, a first-order elaboration of

Table 1.1 Representative examples of statements on primary emotions

Johnson-Laird/Oatley (1992)	Emde (1980)	Panksepp (1982)	Sroufe (1979)	Turner (1996a)	Trevarthen (1984)	Arnold (1960)	Osgood (1966)	Darwin (1872)	Izard (1977, 1992b)
happiness	joy		pleasure	happiness	happiness		joy quiet pleasure	pleasure joy affection	enjoyment
fear	fear	fear panic	fear	fear	fear	fight	fear anxiety	terror	fear
anger	anger	rage	anger	anger	anger	fight defensive aggression	anger	anger	anger contempt
sadness	sadness	sorrow loneliness grief		sadness surprise	sadness		sorrow		
disgust	surprise disgust shame shyness distress						amazement disgust	astonishment	surprise disgust shame shyness distress
	guilt interest	expectancy			approach		interest expectancy		guilt interest
					inhibition		boredom	pain	

	Ekman (1984)	Epstein (1984)	Arieti (1970)	Frommel/ O'Brien (1982)	Plutchik (1980)	Scott (1980)	Fehr/Russell (1984)	Gray (1982)	Kemper (1987)	Malatesta/ Haviland (1982)
	happiness	joy love	satisfaction	joy elation satisfaction	joy	pleasure love	happiness love	hope	satisfaction	joy
	fear	fear	fear tension	fear	fear	fear anxiety	fear	anxiety	fear	fear
	anger	anger	rage	anger	anger	anger	anger	anger	anger	anger
	sadness	sadness	unpleasure	grief resignation	sadness	loneliness	sadness	sadness	depression	sadness
	surprise disgust			shock	surprise disgust					
					anticipation	curiosity				interest
	appetite		appetite		acceptance					pain brownflash knitbrow

Examples of dyads

Primary
anger + joy = pride
joy + acceptance = love, friendly
acceptance + surprise = curiosity
surprise + fear = alarm, awe
sorrow + disgust = misery, remorse
disgust + expectancy = cynicism
expectancy + anger = revenge

Secondary
anger + acceptance = dominance
joy + surprise = delight
acceptance + fear = submission
surprise + sorrow = disappointment
fear + disgust = shame, prudishness
sorrow + expectancy = pessimism
disgust + anger = scorn, loathing
expectancy + joy = optimism

Tertiary
anger + surprise = outrage, hate
joy + fear = guilt
acceptance + sorrow = resignation
fear + expectancy = anxiety, dread
sorrow + anger = envy, sullenness
disgust + joy = morbidness
expectancy + acceptance = fatalism

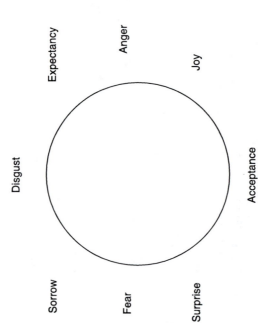

Expectancy

Anger

Joy

Disgust

Sorrow

Acceptance

Fear

Surprise

Figure 1.2 Plutchik's model of emotions.
Note
Primary, secondary, and tertiary emotions are created by "mixes" of emotions at varying distances from each other on the wheel above. A primary emotion is generated by mixing emotions that are adjacent to each other, a secondary by emotions once removed on the wheel, and a tertiary by emotions at least twice removed on the wheel.

Table 1.2 Variants of primary emotions

	Low intensity	Moderate intensity	High intensity
satisfaction–happiness	content	cheerful	joy
	sanguine	buoyant	bliss
	serenity	friendly	rapture
	gratified	amiable	jubilant
		enjoyment	gaiety
			elation
			delight
			thrilled
			exhilarated
aversion–fear	concern	misgivings	terror
	hesitant	trepidation	horror
	reluctance	anxiety	high anxiety
	shyness	scared	
		alarmed	
		unnerved	
		panic	
assertion–anger	annoyed	displeased	dislike
	agitated	frustrated	loathing
	irritated	belligerent	disgust
	vexed	contentious	hate
	perturbed	hostility	despise
	nettled	ire	detest
	rankled	animosity	hatred
	piqued	offended	seething
		consternation	wrath
			furious
			inflamed
			incensed
			outrage
disappointment–sadness	discouraged	dismayed	sorrow
	downcast	disheartened	heartsick
	dispirited	glum	despondent
		resigned	anguished
		gloomy	crestfallen
		woeful	
		pained	
		dejected	

Source: data from Turner, 1999a, b.

primary emotions involves a greater amount of one primary emotion "mixed" with a lesser amount of another primary emotion (in some unknown neurological way). The result is a new emotion that can further refine individuals' emotional feelings, expressions, and attunement.

Table 1.3 outlines the first-order elaborations for the four primary emotions outlined in Table 1.2 (Turner, 1996a, 1999a, 2000a). Thus, for example, a greater amount of satisfaction–happiness combined with a lesser amount

Table 1.3 First–order elaborations of primary emotions

Primary emotions		First-order elaborations
satisfaction–happiness		
satisfaction–happiness + *aversion–fear*	→	wonder, hopeful, relief, gratitude, pride, reverence
satisfaction–happiness + *assertion–anger*	→	vengeance, appeased, calmed, soothed, relish, triumphant, bemused
satisfaction–happiness + *disappointment–sadness*	→	nostalgia, yearning, hope
aversion–fear		
aversion–fear + *satisfaction–happiness*	→	awe, reverence, veneration
aversion–fear + *assertion–anger*	→	revulsed, repulsed, antagonism, dislike, envy
aversion–fear + *disappointment–sadness*	→	dread, wariness
assertion–anger		
assertion–anger + *satisfaction–happiness*	→	condescension, mollified, rudeness, placated, righteousness
assertion–anger + *aversion–fear*	→	abhorrence, jealousy, suspiciousness
assertion–anger + *disappointment–sadness*	→	bitterness, depression, betrayed
disappointment–sadness		
disappointment–sadness + *satisfaction–happiness*	→	acceptance, moroseness, solace, melancholy
disappointment–sadness + *aversion–fear*	→	regret, forlornness, remorseful, misery
disappointment–sadness + *assertion–anger*	→	aggrieved, discontent, dissatisfied, unfulfilled, boredom, grief, envy, sullenness

of aversion-fear generates new emotions like wonder, hopeful, relief, gratitude, and pride (see top of Table 1.3), or a greater amount of aversion-fear
mixed with a lesser amount of satisfaction-happiness generates emotions
like awe, veneration, and reverence. Similar kinds of new emotions appear
for all of the other combinations of primary emotions.

As I will argue in the next chapter, natural selection hit upon this solution
to enhancing emotionality for two critical reasons. First, as evolved apes,
humans do not have strong herding, pack, pod, or group "instincts" or
behavioral propensities; tight-knit groups are *not* natural social formations
for an ape (for monkeys, to be sure, but not apes; see Maryanski and Turner,
1992; Turner and Maryanski, 2005). Hence, by increasing hominids' and
then humans' emotionality, a new way to generate stronger social bonds
became possible; and once emotions proved to be a successful adaptation,
natural selection continued to enhance this capacity.

Second, three of the four primary emotions are decidedly negative and
work against increased social solidarity (and, if we add other primary emotions from the list in Table 1.1, the proportion of negative primary emotions
only increases). Fear, anger, and sadness are not, by themselves, emotions that

bind individuals together; and so, if emotions were to be used to forge social bonds among hominids and eventually humans, the roadblock presented by a bias of emotions toward the negative had to be overcome (Turner, 2000a). One "solution" hit upon by natural selection was to combine negative emotions with satisfaction-happiness to produce emotions that could work to create tighter-knit social bonds. For instance, wonder, hopeful, relief, gratitude, pride, appeased, calmed, soothed, relish, triumphant, bemused, nostalgia, hope, yearning, awe, reverence, veneration, placated, mollified, acceptance, and solace can all potentially forge social bonds and mitigate the dis-associative power in the negative emotions. However, other more dangerous emotions such as vengeance and righteousness are also generated by combinations of anger and happiness; and these emotions can fuel violence and disruption of social bonds. Another solution to the predominance of negative primary emotions was for natural selection to work on the neuro-anatomy of hominids and humans to combine two negative primary emotions in ways that reduce the "negativity" of each of the two emotions alone and, as a result, produce new emotions that are less volatile. Still, as the combinations of two negative emotions in Table 1.3 reveal, many of these new kinds of emotions are also highly negative, although some call attention to another's plight. For example, dissatisfied, sullenness, forlorn-ness, remorseful, and melancholy are generated by disappointment-sadness combined with a lesser amount of fear or anger, and, perhaps, these emotions would encourage supportive behaviors to re-establish social bonds. Other combinations can be used to sanction negatively those who have broken social bonds and/or violated the moral order, thus turning a negative combination into an emotional response that has some potential for re-establishing the social order. Yet, many of these emotions such as wariness, envy, repulsed, antagonism, bitterness, betrayal, jealousy, suspiciousness, and aggrieved can also work to disrupt bonds.

Second-order elaborations of primary emotions

First-order emotions alone, then, could not fully mitigate against the power of negative emotions to disrupt the social order, and so I believe that natural selection further rewired the human neuroanatomy (and perhaps our immediate hominid ancestor's) to generate what I term second-order elaborations that are a mix of *all three* negative emotions (Turner, 2000a). As Table 1.4 outlines, I see shame, guilt, and alienation as combinations of the three negative emotions. The dominant emotion is disappointment-sadness, with lesser amounts of anger and fear in different proportions. Shame is an emotion that makes self feel small and unworthy; and it generally emerges when a person feels that he or she has not behaved competently or met social norms for expected behaviors. Shame is mostly disappointment-sadness at self, followed in order of magnitude by anger at self, and fear about the consequences to self of incompetent behaviors. Shame is a powerful

Table 1.4 The structure of second-order emotions: shame, guilt, and alienation

Emotion	Rank-ordering of constituent primary emotions		
	1	*2*	*3*
shame	disappointment-sadness (at self)	assertion-anger (at self)	aversion-fear (at consequences for self)
guilt	disappointment-sadness (at self)	aversion-fear (at consequences for self)	assertion-anger (at self)
alienation	disappointment-sadness (at self, others, situation)	assertion-anger (at others, situation)	aversion-fear (at consequences for self)

emotion for social control because it is so devastating, with the result that people try to avoid behaving incompetently and violating norms. Thus, shame operates to sustain patterns of social organization and gives negative sanctions "teeth" because such sanctions activate shame, thereby motivating individuals to change their behaviors.

However, shame is so negative that it often activates defense mechanisms and repression (see Chapter 4), with the result that the repressed emotions transmute into one or more of their constituent emotions – most often anger (Tangney *et al.*, 1992) but at times deep sadness and high anxiety or fear. These transmutations of shame can, in turn, disrupt social bonds. Still, with shame as an emotional response, people will generally monitor their own behaviors and act in ways to avoid experiencing such devastation to self.

Guilt is an emotion that combines disappointment-sadness with fear about the consequences to self and anger at self for violating moral codes. Unlike shame, guilt tends to be confined to specific actions and, unless chronic, does not attack a person's whole self (Tangney and Dearing, 2002; Tangney *et al.*, 1996a, b, 1998). People see that they have committed a "moral wrong" and are generally motivated to change their behavior so as to avoid experiencing guilt (Turner and Stets, 2005). Yet, if guilt is chronic and is activated in violation of powerful moral codes, such as the incest taboo, it too may be repressed, thereby making it more likely that one of its constituent primary emotions will surface – typically in the case of guilt, intense fear and anxiety but also depression. Still, guilt like shame mitigates the power of each of the three negative emotions from which it is built and, in fact, creates an emotion that makes people aware of moral codes and willing to abide by them in order to avoid experiencing guilt.

Alienation is the third of these second-order elaborations and is, once again, mostly disappointment-sadness, anger at a situation or social structure, and fear about the consequences of not meeting expectations in this structure. Alienation does not promote high sociality, but it does transform negative emotions into a withdrawal response, reducing the level of commitment to, and willingness to participate in, social structures. Such an emotion does not promote solidarity, to be sure, but it does reduce the disruptive power of anger and, hence, is less disruptive than anger alone. Alienation is, as we will see, an important emotion in understanding how commitments to social structures and cultural codes are lowered.

Just when hominids could experience shame, guilt, and alienation is impossible to know. The evidence suggests that chimpanzees, with which we share 99 percent of our genes, do not experience guilt and shame as humans do (Boehm, n.d.(a)), and so these emotions may be relatively late evolutionary arrivals and, hence, may be uniquely human. These are particularly important emotional capacities for several reasons. First, as noted above, they mitigate against the power of any one of the three negative emotions to disrupt social relations and, in fact, transform these negative emotions in ways which, if not repressed, increase social solidarity. Second, they cause individuals to self-monitor and self-sanction themselves when they behave inappropriately and/or violate moral codes. Third, they operate as a motive force behind individuals' efforts to repair breaches of social relations or violations of moral codes. And, fourth, they plug individuals into the culture of groups – its norms and its moral codes – and thereby provide the emotional energy behind efforts to conform to these moral codes. Without shame and guilt, social control would be difficult for a weak-tie primate, but once shame and guilt emerge as emotional responses, individuals become more attuned to each other, to the demands of social structures, and to the dictates of culture (Turner, 2000a). Indeed, without guilt and shame, human sociopaths would be far more common, and the viability of social structure and culture to control human behavior would be reduced.

By reading across and down Tables 1.2, 1.3, and 1.4, the words denote the range of human emotions.[1] While we cannot precisely define what an emotion is, at least in generic terms, we can be highly specific about the affective states that are aroused by human neuroanatomy. Humans can experience this complex of approximately one hundred emotions with relative ease. If you doubt this, turn off the sound on a movie or television drama and, in most cases, you will be able to read the emotions expressed in face as well as body countenance, movement, and juxtaposition to keep track of the story line. If you add to this the inflections, fillers, and pitch of voice (as would be the case if you watched a movie in a language that you did not know), you would do even better in understanding what was going on. As I will argue in Chapter 2, the first hominid language was that of emotions. Emotions reveal both phonemes and syntax, and like a spoken language, the "language of emotions" unfolds in terms of phonemes strung together by a grammar. Some of this grammar is hard-wired because certain emotional expressions seem universal, particularly those marking primary emotions

1 For other classifications of the range and ndiversity of emotions by sociologisdts, see: Kemper (1987) and Thamm (1992, 2004, 2006).

(Ekman, 1973a, b, 1982, 1992a, b, c; Ekman and Friesen, 1975; Ekman *et al.*, 1972). Once we move to first-order and second-order elaborations, however, culture probably has a greater effect on the expression of emotions, just as it does for spoken language (since the vocabulary and grammar of languages differ). Yet, the earlier and more primal "language of emotions" is hard-wired. We learn the language of emotions long before spoken language, and like spoken language, humans learn it within a window of neurological opportunity that passes by the age of 11 or 12. Once this window is closed, individuals will have difficulty reading the emotions of others or expressing their states of physiological arousal through auditory or body language.

Explaining human emotional responses

The study of the biology behind human emotions provides a means for exploring topics that are of interest to most sociologists – that is, the effects of culture and social structure on emotions and cognitions as these affect behavior and interaction among individuals (and, by extension, social structure and culture). Sociologists have an almost primal fear response to efforts seeking to bring biology into sociological explanations, soon followed by an anger response at those who would be willing to incorporate biology into sociology. The fear goes back to purported "racism" of earlier efforts to talk about biology and to misguided views that incorporating biology into sociology is inherently reductionist and would, therefore, reduce sociology to psychology or biology.

It is possible, of course, to explain emotions in purely sociological terms – that is, by emphasizing the relationships among interaction, social structure, culture, and emotions – but this analysis misses an important dynamic: the biological dimension of emotions. The Standard Social Science Model, as proposed by John Tooby and Leda Cosmides (1992), goes something like this: human behaviors are learned and hence are not innate; the biology of the brain endows humans with the capacity for culture which, more than anything else, determines behaviors; the human genome does not reveal sufficient variation to account for the variations in social behaviors and in diverse societies; culture, therefore, explains most variation in societies; and thus, emergent features of human societies cannot be understood by psychological and biological forces. Elements of this argument are often used to avoid examining the biology of humans, and while it is true that emergent phenomena of interest to sociologists cannot be wholly explained by psychology and biology, some understanding of biology as it affects cognition and emotions can add a great deal to sociological explanations.

In the sociology of emotions, the Standard Social Science Model often is expressed in social constructionist terms (see Turner and Stets, 2005:2–4). Emotions are social constructions, defined by culture through learned vocabularies of emotions. To some extent, this argument is true because the words that we use to denote emotions (as in tables 1.1 through 1.4 in this chapter) are part of a culture in which English is the dominant language. But most social constructionist arguments go further: the biology of emotions is so diffuse and generalized that it cannot explain the nature of emotional arousal; only culture, social structure, and context can do so. In this book, I try to develop a theory that explains how specific emotions are aroused under generic social structural and cultural conditions, but this is not a social constructionist argument except in the weak sense that the specific language of emotional expression in a particular society is cultural, just as auditory or spoken language is. For, just as English and Spanish are different in their respective vocabularies and grammars, so are emotional languages. Yet, the capacity to naturally learn an emotional language at an early age is hard-wired. In my view, then, the neurological capacity for emotions is much more specific and hard-wired than social constructionists would accept. More than primary emotions are hard-wired; over the next decades, ever more evidence will appear, I believe, documenting the specific neurosystems responsible for specific emotions, including first-order and second-order elaborations. Whether these are the "modules" posited by Cosmides and Tooby is not so much an issue as the biological fact that humans' emotional capacities evolved as natural selection rewired the human brain. True, while culture and social structure provide the conditions under which various types of emotions are aroused and, conversely, are reproduced or changed by emotional arousal, the biology of emotional responses cannot be ignored.

If we know more about the selection pressures that led to the rewiring of the primate brain to make humans so emotional, we will be able to develop more robust theories of human emotions. We do not need to be reductionists in exploring biology and evolution; we only need to be open-minded about what an evolutionary analysis of emotions can tell us about the topics that are of most interest to sociologists – interaction, social organization, and culture. Because it is so obvious, at least to me, that most emotions have a hard-wired basis that evolved over several million years during hominid and, then, human evolution (Turner, 2000a), the analysis of emotions can provide an opportunity to abandon our fears and anger about biology and see what a biological perspective can add to our sociological understandings. This is my goal in the next chapter and its appendix that reviews some of the key neurological details of the body systems generating human emotions. I have written this book so that it is easy to skip Chapter 2 and move on to more comfortable terrain for sociologists in Chapter 3, but I invite skeptics to see what biology might add to sociologists' understanding of human emotions.

As a sociological theorist, my goal is to provide abstract propositions on the cultural and social structural conditions under which specific emotions are aroused during the course of interaction with what effects on the socio-cultural arrangements that generated them. Understanding the biology of human emotions does not obviate this sociological mode of analysis; on the contrary, it adds a great deal to our understanding of the sociology of emotions.

2 Why did humans become so emotional?

The analysis of "human nature" became unfashionable in the early decades of the last century because it was so speculative. Today, we have much better empirical and analytical tools to explore what is basic to human biology, as distinct from what is cultural and learned. Of course, there is very little that is wholly biological, or cultural for that matter. Indeed, at biological conception when the egg and sperm meet, interaction effects between genotypes and emerging phenotypes, on the one side, and the social and physical environment, on the other, begin and never end. The womb is an environment that is affected by the larger sociocultural environment, and so there is very little about humans and their actions that is not simultaneously sociocultural and biological. Still, if we are to gain extra purchase in understanding human emotionality, we should try to discover the reasons why hominid and human neuroanatomy was rewired not only for emotions but other behavioral propensities as well. Culture and social structure certainly constrain how these propensities are expressed, but we must also recognize the converse: cultural and social structural arrangements are also constrained by human biology. How, then, should we enter this tricky terrain and try to ferret out what we can call, in a weak moment, human nature?

We can begin by recognizing that humans are primates, and that, in reality, *Homo sapiens* are just an evolved ape that happens to have a very large brain (relative to body size which, in general, is correlated with brain size). The size of the human brain, relative to our bodies, is enormous, but we must avoid the conventional "wisdom" of the Standard Social Science Model (Tooby and Cosmides, 1992). This model argues that the larger brain allowed for culture which, in turn, obviates biologically driven behavioral propensities. Instead, we need to recognize that humans are the end point in the sixty million years of primate evolution; and for eight of the last ten million years, the primate brain did not grow and, hence, culture did not represent a significant survival strategy. Indeed, humans are remnants of what, in reality, was one of the great evolutionary failures: the dramatic decline in the number of species of apes over the last sixteen million years, especially compared to our monkey relatives that constitute the vast majority of primate species. We can learn from monkeys' success in seeing why apes began to go extinct and in assessing how our hominid ancestors beat the odds. A larger brain and culture may have helped hominids escape the fate of most apes that had to adapt to open-country savanna. But, long before the neocortex began to grow and before culture was to increase fitness, other fitness-enhancing changes in hominids' anatomy and neuro-anatomy had occurred. These changes are as much a part of "human nature" as culture.

Cladistic analysis: clues about humans' basic nature

The primate family tree

One approach to understanding human nature is to examine our closest living relatives in the primate family tree. The three great apes (orangutans, chimpanzees, and gorillas) are closest to humans, while a fourth set of ape species (gibbons and siamangs) are not as closely related to humans and, hence, are not considered great apes. This family tree of all extant apes is outlined in Figure 2.1. Since humans share 99 percent of their genetic material with the common chimpanzee (and slightly less with the bonobo chimpanzee), chimpanzees should rightly belong to the family Hominidae and, more significantly, to genus *homo*. But, people like to think of them-selves as somehow unique, and so the fiction that we are so different from our closest living relatives is maintained even in most scientific classifications of the primates.

The structure of ape and monkey societies

Alexandra Maryanski (1986, 1987, 1992, 1993, 1994, 1996a, b, 1997) conducted a pioneering study some years ago employing what is termed in biology, cladistic analysis. The basic methodology of cladistic analysis is used in other disciplines, such as linguistics where scholars examine contempor-ary "families" of a language to determine what the root language of all languages in this family was like (Maas, 1958). Similarly, in cladistic analysis, comparison of what is common to closely related species can yield great insight into the nature of the last common ancestor to these species (Platnick and Cameron, 1977; Andrews and Martin, 1987; Jeffers and Lehiste, 1979). This is, in essence, what Maryanski did in her examination of primate social structures in terms of the strength or weakness of the social ties among age and sex classes. By reviewing the research literature on social ties among species of primates, Maryanski was able to portray their respective social structures. Then, taking those tie patterns common to all extant species of apes, she was able to reconstruct the likely structure of the last common ancestor to all living apes, including humans. Another feature of cladistic analysis is to have a control group consisting of another set of species that are closely related to those under investigation but that are not part of the same

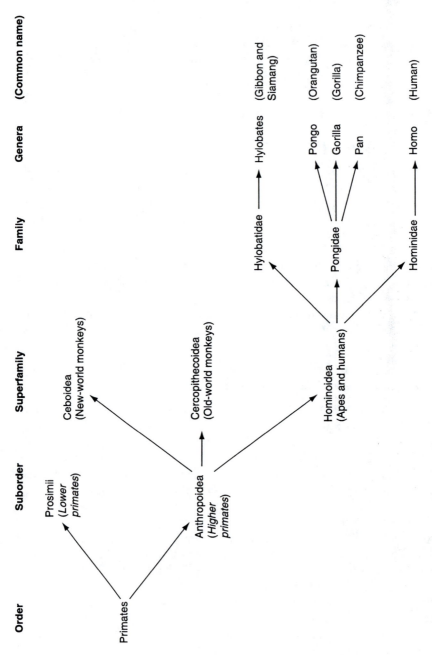

Figure 2.1 Simplified traditional family tree for living primates.

family as the one under investigation. In this study, the obvious choice was the social structure of monkeys that are the closest relatives (aside from humans) to present-day apes, as can be seen in Figure 2.1. By comparing the data on apes with those on monkeys, it is possible to see if there is something unique about ape social structure.

At times with Maryanski (Maryanski and Turner, 1992; Turner and Maryanski, 2005) and at other times alone (Turner, 2000a), I have summarized the findings and then used them to tell the story of hominid and human evolution. I will present the truncated version of this story, with the most recent and more elaborate story to be found in Turner and Maryanski (2005:85–122). The basic conclusion from Maryanski's cladistic analysis is that monkeys reveal tight-knit social structures revolving around dominance hierarchies among males and matrilines among related females, whereas apes evidence much more loosely structured communities composed mostly of weak ties among adults. These dramatically different types of social structures between apes and monkeys are generated by (1) the transfer patterns of males and females at puberty, (2) the pattern of ties between and among males and females, and (3) the basic unit that organizes ape and monkey societies.

The transfer patterns are critical because they are the exact opposite among species of apes and monkeys. In monkey societies, males transfer out of their natal group at puberty and migrate to new groups and, for many, enter into competition along the dominance hierarchies typical of all monkey groupings. In contrast, female monkeys stay in their natal groups and form strong-tie matrilines among related females (mothers, daughters, aunts, female cousins). Apes, on the other hand, reveal the opposite pattern: at puberty, females leave their natal group – and, indeed, in most cases their natal community – and migrate to a new community, never to return (and, except for chimpanzees, males also leave the natal group among all other species of apes). As a result, matrilines among biologically related females cannot form because the related females have all dispersed to other communities. As a result, all females in an ape community have migrated from other communities and are, in essence, strangers to each other. The same is true for males, again except for chimpanzees where bonds between brothers and other male friendship networks can persist within a community for a lifetime. Some apes, such as gorillas and chimpanzees, evidence dominance hierarchies in which males compete for control of local groups, while others like the gibbon/siamang and orangutan do not reveal such hierarchies.

The result of these transfer/migration patterns is dramatic. With females leaving at puberty, one basis of strong ties so evident of monkeys (matrilines) is destroyed for apes. The continuity of the group is thus broken, and this lack of continuity is reinforced by differences in the basic unit organizing apes and monkeys. For monkeys, it is the local group or troop, revolving around dominance hierarchies and female matrilines. For apes, it is the larger regional community that can be over many square miles, with groups being highly unstable as individuals move in and out of foraging parties within the larger community. Despite these fluid and constantly changing groups, the larger community will be defended by its resident apes against incursions by males from other communities. Females, on the other hand, are welcomed because they replace those that have departed at puberty to other communities. The only apes with a stable group structure are gibbons and siamangs that form monogamous relationships between males and females; in contrast, all other apes reveal a fluidity to group structures that form and disperse, only to form again in a new foraging party that may last for a few days and, at times, for months. In these fluid groups, the only strong ties are between mothers and their immature offspring – a pattern common to all mammals. And, except for gibbons/siamangs that are monogamous, apes are promiscuous, with the result that paternity cannot be known and does not lead to strong ties. All other ties are weak, although a few can be moderately strong. For example, a female gorilla may attach herself for a time to the lead silverback male (primarily for babysitting services); a male chimpanzee may form strong bonds to his brother and, indeed, help him fight for dominance; and a male chimpanzee will generally have moderate to strong ties with his mother that can last a lifetime. Adult females have very weak to non-existent ties to each other in all ape groups and communities. And, in the case of orangutans, which are virtually solitary except for a mother and her offspring and for males and females when they are mating, all social ties among adults are weak and, indeed, mostly non-existent.

Table 2.1 summarizes the ties among species of apes with respect to tie strength, whereas Table 2.2 summarizes ties among representative species of monkeys (Maryanski and Turner, 1992; Turner, 1996a, b, 2000a). A cursory glance at the strong ties, (marked with a + sign) compared to weak ties (marked with an "o" sign) in tables 2.1 and 2.2 does not appear to show dramatic differences in the relative quantity of strong and weak ties. But, the critical difference is *which* age and sex classes have strong ties. And, most importantly, can these ties be used to build more permanent social structures? Most strong ties for apes are those between mothers and their offspring – again, the typical mammalian pattern – but these ties are broken at puberty as all females (and males as well, except for chimpanzees) leave their mothers and indeed their mother's group and, for all except the gibbon/siamang, the natal community as well. This tie pattern cannot, therefore, serve to build continuity of group structure over time. Among chimpanzees, ties between brothers and male friends, coupled with males' attachments to their mothers, can be used to build some continuity in what are highly fluid groups within the larger regional community. And except for these ties among chimpanzees and the monogamous bond among gibbons/siamangs, all other adult ties are weak among apes. Female-to-female ties are weak because they have all migrated into a community from diverse communities and meet as strangers and, for most of their lives, remain distant from each other. Thus, among our closest relatives, the chimpanzees, there are very few

Table 2.1 Strength of ties among extant ape species

		(Hylobates) gibbon	(Pongo) orangutan	(Gorilla) gorilla	(Pan) chimpanzee	Last common ancestor
Adult-to-adult ties	male–male	o	o	o	o/+	*o
	female–female	o	o	o	o	*o
	male–female	+	o	o/+	o	*o
Adult-to-child procreation ties	mother–daughter	+	+	+	+	*+
	mother–son	+	+	+	+	*+
	father–daughter	+	o	o	o	*o
	father–son	+	o	o	o	*o
Adult-to-adult procreation ties	mother–daughter	o	o	o	o	*o
	mother–son	o	o	o	+	*o
	father–daughter	o	o	o	o	*o
	father–son	o	o	o	o	*o

Key

o = weak or absent ties

+ = strong ties

o/+ = weak or moderate ties

Note

*All primates have preferential relationships within and between age and sex classes (see Cheney *et al.*, 1986; Hinde, 1983). For primates, the strength of social bonds is assessed on the basis of social grooming, food sharing, aiding and protecting, continual close proximity, embracing (excluding sexual contact), alliances and the length and intensity of a social relation. This table is focused on the structural regularities in the patterning of relations among conspecifics and the emergent properties that characterize these relationships.

Table 2.2 Strength of ties among some well-studied terrestrial species of monkeys⋆

		Gelada	Patas	Macaque (most species)	Baboon (most species)
Adult-to-adult ties	male–male	o	o	o	o
	female–female	+	+	+	+
	male–female	o	o	o/+	o/+
Adult-to-child procreation ties	mother–daughter	+	+	+	+
	mother–son	+	+	+	+
	father–daughter	o	o	o	o
	father–son	o	o	o	o
Adult-to-adult procreation ties	mother–daughter	+	+	+	+
	mother–son	o	o	o	o
	father–daughter	o	o	o	o
	father–son	o	o	o	o

Key
o = weak or null ties
+ = strong ties
o/+ = weak to moderate ties

Note
⋆ The absolute number of ties shown here is not of great significance. What is significant is whether a tie can serve as a building block for extended networks. The mother–daughter bond is the focal center in monkeys for generating both large and tight-knit kinship cliques and for providing continuity through intergenerational time.

strong ties, and none are sufficiently strong to build local group continuity over time.

The result is that apes and monkeys are organized in very different kinds of social structures. For monkeys it is the local troop or group built around male dominance hierarchies and female matrilines. For apes (with the exception of the distantly related gibbon/siamang) it is the regional population with a considerable amount of fluidity in foraging groups that form and disperse.

In search of the last common ancestor

In cladistic analysis, these kinds of data on tie strength are used to reconstruct the likely nature of ties and social structures among the last common ancestor. The last column in Table 2.1 represents Maryanski's reconstruction (as per convention, denoted by an asterisk). The reconstruction begins by asking: What tie patterns are common to all extant species of apes? That is, what do all four sets of species (gibbons/siamangs, gorillas, chimpanzees, and orangutans) have *in common* (four out of all four sets of species, or 4/4)? All adult female ties are weak or non-existent. All mother–daughter ties are initially strong but are forever broken when daughters reach puberty and leave the natal group (if not community). All father–adult daughter ties are, except for the gibbon/siamang, unknown (because of great ape promiscuity), and once daughters leave the community at puberty there is no chance for father–daughter ties to develop in all species of apes. Now, let us examine those ties where three of the four extant species reveal a common tie pattern (3/4). Except for chimpanzees, adult male-to-adult male ties are weak or non-existent in species of apes. Father–daughter ties and father–son ties are non-existent for all apes, except the gibbon/siamang. All mother–adult son ties are broken, except for a moderate tie between chimpanzee mothers and their sons. Turning to those tie patterns among two of the four species, or 2/2, gibbons and gorillas have moderate or strong ties between adult males and females, orangutan and chimpanzee males have very weak ties to adult females.

These patterns can tell us a great deal about the common ancestor to all present-day apes and, of course, humans. The conclusion is inescapable: virtually all adult ties among the last common ancestor were probably weak; only the basic mammalian attachment of mothers to offspring was strong in the last common ancestor. To avoid the conclusion above would force us to assume that the common tie patterns evolved independently in the four species after their split with the last common ancestor – not a likely scenario. Moreover, our control group of tie patterns among old-world monkeys shows that the tie pattern among apes *is unique to apes* and not evident in other sister super-families. True, we must be careful not to over-infer, but we can have some confidence that the last common ancestor to present-day apes and humans lived alone or in very fluid groups, with virtually no strong ties except those between mother and young offspring, with individuals moving about alone or in very temporary foraging parties revealing no permanent structure, except perhaps some tendencies for male dominance.

As evolved apes, then, humans may not be as "group oriented" or "social" as is often inferred by sociologists and philosophers. Of course, there has been at least six million and perhaps as many as eight million years of evolution since our hominid ancestors split off from the last common ancestor to present-day apes. Natural selection could have worked to produce more propensities for sociality than was evident for this last common ancestor, and, indeed, this is what probably occurred but not in any direct way with "genes" for high sociality. As I will argue, natural selection worked indirectly by heightening hominids' and then humans' emotional capacities that could then be activated to forge strong bonds. In this way, the lack of bioprogrammers for group, pod, pride, herding, and pack structures so typical of most mammals could be overcome – given selection pressures for more cohesive group structures.

If I had to guess, the orangutan represents the best image of what our last common ancestor was like. The fact that chimpanzees deviate from the orangutan in terms of male-to-male attachments and son-to-mother ties argues for the possibility that such basic propensities could have evolved among last common ancestor to chimpanzees and humans – perhaps some five or six million years ago. But these propensities would not be fitness-enhancing if selection favored tighter-knit group structures, as was certainly the case when many now extinct species of apes were forced to survive in open-country savanna conditions in Africa. Present-day apes, with their loose group structures, can survive because they live in or at the edges of forests which provide refuge. Out on the savanna, they would all be dead, as was eventually the case for all species of apes except humans – the only extant ape capable of living full time on the savanna. To survive in the predator-ridden African savanna requires organization – much like that evident among monkeys – and all species of apes could not recreate a monkey pattern because selection requires some propensity for matrilines on which to select, and this propensity had been selected out of apes for thirty million years.

Why do apes have weak ties and low sociality?

There is a longer and more scholarly answer to the above question (see Maryanski and Turner, 1992; Turner and Maryanski, 2005), but let me recapitulate this longer argument and move to the bottom line. Many of the physical differences between apes and monkeys and, most certainly, the organizational differences are the outcome of what occurred when apes and monkeys all lived in the arboreal habitat of Africa. In essence, monkeys gained an advantage in the trees, perhaps related to the ability to digest unripe fruit. Whatever the exact cause, we know that species of apes were forced to the terminal feeding areas of the trees; monkeys took over the larger and more verdant spaces at the core of trees. In competition with monkeys, species of apes were successively pushed to the tops of the trees and to the undersides of branches high in the forest canopy. As a result, monkeys could sustain much larger groupings in the core areas of trees, whereas apes could not do so because of the limited resources, including enough space to support more permanent groups. To limit the size of ape groupings in the forest canopy, natural selection hit upon a solution to this potential problem by wiring apes for the female transfer pattern that, in essence, breaks the group apart at puberty and by weakening ties among all adults so that they could move alone or in temporary and small foraging parties in the forest canopy. Weak ties, mobility, individualism, and fluid groups were fitness-enhancing in the marginal niches of the arboreal habitat, whereas among monkeys that were, in essence, kings of the arboreal habitat, the larger groups built around female matrilines could not only be supported but, coupled with dominance hierarchies and tight-knit group structures, could be used to push apes to the extremities of the forest habitat. It may seem less than noble, if not embarrassing, to realize that humans are descendants of species that lost out in competition with monkeys, but such appears to have been the case.

Comparing other features of apes and monkeys

As strong-tie propensities, particularly ties among related females, were selected out of apes, other important features of apes' anatomy emerged in order to enhance fitness in the extreme reaches of the canopy. Apes have stronger and more dexterous hands, fingers, wrists, arms, and shoulder joints than monkeys that are better suited for hanging and traveling about the tops of trees where one false move means death by gravity. Apes also have a unique capacity to brachiate, or swing arm-over-arm from branch to branch (much like children on the bars of a "jungle gym"). In contrast, monkeys scamper about on all fours on the tops of branches and would break their shoulder joint if they tried to brachiate. Apes also have larger brains than monkeys because intelligence would enhance fitness in a precarious niche where knowledge of branch strength and routes to sparse food supplies would increase survival and reproduction. For millions of years, when all apes and monkeys lived in the trees, natural selection differentiated apes from monkeys not only in their bodies, including their neuroanatomy, but, as I have emphasized, in their patterns of tie-strength and social structure.

There is another feature of apes that distinguishes them from monkeys. Great apes have the ability to recognize themselves when looking into a mirror (Anderson and Gallup, Jr., 1999; Gallup, Jr., 1970, 1979, 1982; Heyes, 1995), although there remains some controversy about whether or not all apes can recognize themselves (Hyatt and Hopkins, 1994; Lin *et al.*, 1992). If a great ape is presented with its reflection in a mirror, it will generally recognize itself, whereas a monkey and most other mammals will look behind the mirror to see who is there, apparently not recognizing its own reflection. There has been some debate about what these "mirror studies" mean, but they do suggest an important cognitive capacity: to see self as an object in an environment. This is a capacity that could be subject to selection if self-awareness increased fitness; and such would certainly be the case if hominids were to become moral creatures, seeing and evaluating themselves in the "looking glass" of others' responses (Cooley, 1902) or from the perspective of culture or the "generalized other" of the group (Mead, 1934).

There remain, of course, common features among apes and monkeys. The most important are five fingers and an opposed thumb as well as high levels of dexterity and sensitivity for the hand and fingers, although apes have more sensitivity and dexterity than monkeys. Apes and monkeys have a generalized skeletal structure with a large trunk and four appendages that can be used to walk upright if need be and to grasp objects. Apes and monkeys are visually dominant and can see objects in color with very high resolution (a useful adaptation in the forest, but very deviant for a mammal, most of which are olfactory dominant).

In this shift to visual dominance, the brain of primates was rewired, creating new association cortices to integrate as well as subordinate haptic (touch) and auditory (sound) sensory impulses to vision (for example, you will immediately look when you feel or hear something). These association cortices are found where the temporal (auditory), parietal (haptic), and occipital (visual) lobes meet, and they work to eliminate sensory conflict by subordinating haptic and auditory sense impulses under vision (olfactory is less directly connected because the bulb for this sense modality is sub-cortical). As we will see, these new association cortices became the preadaptation, providing the essential wiring among more intelligent apes, and for language (Geschwind, 1965a, b, 1970; Geschwind and Damasio, 1984).

Human bodies are, therefore, those of a primate, as this primate legacy was changed over the last six to eight million years. The features of the great apes give us a distant mirror by which we can see our ancestors and their bodies, including the neuroanatomy of the brain, that were subject to selection when apes were forced to live in a new habitat: the African savanna. The story explaining the characteristics of humans, including their emotionality, revolves around an account of how natural selection grabbed various features of primate anatomy to create an animal that became bipedal, smarter, and emotional.

Despite differences in patterns of tie-formation, apes and monkeys share some behavioral propensities. Both apes and monkeys appear to have a built-in sense of reciprocity and justice. Capucin monkeys, for example, will learn to perform behaviors if they are rewarded, as will any mammal, but they will immediately stop performing if they see that another monkey is getting more reward for the same behaviors. The monkey will resume the behavior when the reward is ratcheted up to the level enjoyed by the other monkey

(Bronson and de Waal, 2003). There are some very critical cognitive and emotional capacities in this kind of behavior. First, monkeys as well as apes probably have a sense of reciprocity: I do this trick for you, and you will reciprocate by giving me a reward. Second, there is a comparison process that may be wired into their respective neuroanatomies because the pay-offs for one individual are compared to those of another. Third, there appears to be some calculation of justice, which is adjusted through a comparison process: my rewards should be proportionate to those of others performing the same behaviors. Fourth, there is clearly an emotional response to perceived injustice: when an individual does not get the same reward as another, it will become agitated, if not angry, and will cease performing behaviors. Fifth, there is an implicit sense of self in these comparison processes in which the individual perceives self as distinct from other, so much so that calculations of justice for who gets how much for what behavior can be made. Sixth, there may be an implicit attribution dynamic involved in these calculations of justice: outcomes are attributed to trainers who are seen as the cause of the under-reward as well as the potential cause of a more just reward. Also involved in the above may be a gestalt-like propensity for cognitive consistency in which rewards, effort, and payoffs for self and other must be congruent. All of these neurologically generated cognitive and behavioral capacities in apes and monkeys could be subject to further selection, if enhancement of these propensities increased fitness. As I will argue, the cognitive-emotional structure of the basic ape brain was indeed enhanced as natural selection worked on hominid neuroantaomy to overcome weak-tie propensities of apes to forge stronger and more enduring social ties and groups with higher levels of solidarity.

Another trait common to apes and monkeys, and many other mammals as well, is the practice of ritual greetings. Apes are weak-tie animals, but there are greeting rituals that at least acknowledge the existence of others. Monkeys have more elaborate rituals because they are stronger-tie animals, but apes have the rudiments of rituals, using hands, pats on the back, and mutual grooming – all of which could be subject to further selection if they could enhance hominid sociality and group solidarity.

Apes and monkeys both have a sense of territory, but among apes this sense is for the home range or larger community. At the level of the group, apes are not highly organized, but at the level of community, they have a keen sense of who belongs and who does not; and should a party of males from another community "invade" a territory, males will mobilize intense emotions and fight to sustain the boundaries of their home range. A sense of community is, therefore, hard-wired into apes; and the willingness to mobilize anger and aggression to defend community is also hard-wired. Such a strong emotional and behavioral propensity could be subject to further selection, if such selection would enhance group solidarity and hence fitness in new habitats.

The shrinking forests and the expanding savanna

Somewhere around sixteen to eighteen millions years ago, the forests began to recede and, in their place, open-country savanna in Africa began to expand. Some species of apes and monkeys were forced out onto the savanna. At first, these species may have lived where the forest meets the savanna, but in the end, some had to go out to the grasslands to find food. The savanna is, obviously, a very different habitat than the forests, and it presents new challenges. The most important is that predators abound in the savanna, and animals that are not well organized or that do not naturally form herds are highly vulnerable to being picked off by meat-eaters. Apes are particularly vulnerable to the savanna, along many fronts. First, they are slow compared to most herding animals; they will always have trouble running away from danger in the open country where swinging into the non-existent trees is no longer a viable strategy. Second, apes are visually dominant and cannot easily smell potential predators (or prey); they must see or hear a predator or prey to be responsive. Moreover, the high grasses would have made it difficult for ancestral apes to even see sources of danger, and coupled with little speed, apes would be very vulnerable. Apes can stand upright for short periods, and they can even walk upright; and so, selection could, and clearly did, work on this ability to overcome, at least partially, the handicap of being quadrapedal without the ability to smell predators or run fast. Seeing above the grasses would be fitness enhancing, and it is evident that this was one of the first adaptations for savanna-dwelling apes. Apes are also very emotional and loud; and when danger is present, they become noisy and agitated, calling attention to themselves. Such behaviors are not maladaptive when life is lived in the trees but are a disaster when a slow primate calls attention to itself with uncontrolled emotional displays and without the ability to run away from the danger causing these emotional outbursts. And, finally, all of these vulnerabilities could be mitigated if apes were well organized and could coordinate the search for food or the defense of the troop. This is the great advantage of monkeys on the savanna; they are very well organized, marching across the savanna in military-like formation, with smaller females and offspring in the center of the troop flanked by larger males. These males will coordinate defense of the troop, making predators think twice about an all-out assault on the troop. In contrast, chimpanzees get emotional and start screeching as they run around as individuals; only when they defend the boundaries of their home range do they coordinate aggression, although the propensity to defend territory could have been subject to selection to get apes to defend the troop in danger on the savanna. But still, with millions of years of evolution for fluid groups, individualism, mobility and weak ties, apes in general are not well suited to the savanna habitat.

And, it is for this reason that most apes went extinct, except for the small handful that now exist in the forests. At one time there were probably hundreds of species of apes; now there are only a few. Selection may have taken savanna-dwelling apes on a number of paths. One may have been to enhance dominance hierarchies, but such a strategy would be a dead end without the female matrilines to sustain group continuity. We can only imagine a dominant male trying to herd together unrelated and unresponsive females into matrilines to recognize that this strategy could not work. Apes had long ago lost the behavioral propensity for forming matrilines. Another strategy was for large size, with some inhabitants of the savanna becoming truly huge for a primate (up to ten feet tall), but the problems of cooling and feeding such large bodies on the hot savanna eventually made this strategy a dead end about two million years ago. Thus, as natural selection reached dead ends for successive species, the apes died off; and we can conclude that, except for humans (on whom the verdict is still out), apes appear to be doomed for extinction (unless humans keep them alive in zoos, which seems only fair because it is human behavior and organization that are taking away the last arboreal habitats of present-day apes).

Selection on emotions and survival on the African savanna

For the hominid ancestors of humans, natural selection hit upon, I believe, another strategy: enhancing emotions along with the cognitive capacities listed earlier. A more emotional animal could become more fit, if this emotionality and accompanying cognitive enhancements could increase strong ties and higher levels of solidarity among apes. There may have been many variants of this basic strategy, but neurology is complex, and it may be that natural selection crossed wires on many species as it worked on the primate neuroanatomy to increase the range, intensity, variety, and complexity of emotions that could be used to forge stronger bonds of attunement and commitments to the group.

The sociology of emotions must be viewed in this context. What we study represents *an adaptation* to a difficult habitat – at least for an ape – and we cannot understand the dynamics of emotions and their relationship to social bonds, social structures, and culture without some appreciation for how natural selection worked on specific regions of the brain to produce a new kind of ape: one who used emotions to sustain the group and, thereby, survive on the African savanna.

Emotionality as an adapative strategy

William Wentworth on "deep sociality"

William Wentworth and various coauthors were probably the first to recognize the significance of emotions as an adaptive strategy for what they termed "deep sociality" (Wentworth and Ryan, 1992, 1994; Wentworth and Yardly, 1994). For Wentworth, the innate palate of emotions is small, revolving around, as they put it: "flight, fight, fuck, feed, and startle." This colorful phrasing aside, Wentworth argued that anger, disgust, fear, hatred, and sadness were perhaps the primal emotions that, subsequently, were elaborated to produce deep sociality. Wentworth also anticipated an argument that I made (Turner, 2000a) that emotions were the first medium of communication among humans' hominid or hominin ancestors for two basic reasons. First, emotions are biologically potent in that they alert and orient animals very quickly, and second, they arouse the same or reciprocal emotions in others in a manner that promotes social bonding. Let me detail Wentworth's argument.

For Wentworth, the more a species relies upon learning, the greater is the need for speed in the acquisition of information and for rapid as well as relevant "information retrieval." Rapid and relevant information retrieval is facilitated when information comes in gestalts or schemas that can be processed quickly, and in Wentworth's view, emotions become critical in this kind of processing. Emotions are "regulators" of attention, immediately alerting an individual to attend to some aspect of the environment; they also determine how long and with what level of intensity attention must be sustained. Emotions dramatically increase the storage of memories because they tag cognitions with affective significance; conversely, emotions allow individuals to recall memories rapidly and bring information to bear on assessments of the environment.

Emotions also make for better role-taking as individuals read the emotional cues of the face and anticipate others' dispositions and likely courses of action. Emotions energize individuals, providing motivation to perform certain tasks and, equally important, to take cognizance of cultural directives because such directives are given power when embellished with emotions. Indeed, morality cannot exist unless moral codes have "teeth" and the capacity to activate intense negative emotions if they are not followed. For Wentworth, emotions like fear of, and anxiety over, isolation or detachment from the group are essential for social control, as individuals monitor self, others, and situation to be sure that the social fabric is being sustained.

I was not aware of Wentworth and his colleagues' argument when I made a very similar argument in my *On the Origins of Human Emotions* (2000a), but clearly we were all thinking along the same lines. What I brought to the table was Maryanski's cladistic analysis, coupled with more detail on the likely nature of the hominids or hominins which evolved into humans. Emotions not only represented a viable strategy but, in fact, they were *the only strategy* for survival of a low-sociality ape on the African savanna. As Maryanski's analysis documents, apes possess a preponderance of weak ties, with very few ties offering the possibility for enduring and stable social structures at the level of the group (as opposed to larger community). I will not trace the specifics of hominid evolution, only the details relevant to understanding how emotions became a viable strategy. Figure 2.2 summarizes the long-term evolution of monkeys, apes, and hominids.

A quick review of hominid evolution

About four million years ago, the genus homo emerged, with *australopithecus afarensis* and *Kenyanthropus platyops* being the currently favored candidates for the ancestors of homo. Long before homo emerged, hominids had been walking upright, foraging in bands and apparently living off seeds and tubers (teeth structure gives us these clues; see Turner and Maryanski, 2005:129–30 for more details). With *Homo habilis* and *Homo rudolfensis*, the brain of hominids shows its first big jump in size, with the cranial capacity of *habilis* in the range of 509 to 674 cc and the size of *rudolfensis* in the range of 752 to 810 cc (the modern human range is 1,200 to 1,600 cc). Thus, for several million years, natural selection had not significantly enlarged the brain, indicating that early hominids did not possess culture beyond what we might see among apes. *Homo erectus* is the next species on the human line, coming in with a brain in the range of 700 to 1,100 cc – close to the lower level of the human range. *Homo erectus* was also much larger than previous hominids, with some fossils indicating that *erectus* could stand as tall as six feet.

Unfortunately, behaviors and social structures do not fossilize; and so, we cannot know for sure just what these early representatives of the genus, homo, were doing and how they were organizing. The tool kits of *Homo erectus* (or *ergaster*, as some prefer to denote *erectus* and similar fossils) became more sophisticated, and *erectus* apparently used fire for cooking and, no doubt, for keeping warm. The fact that *Homo erectus* migrated to most parts of the world also suggests that they were better organized, moving in foraging groups that could adapt to very diverse ecologies and, in the process, find food and defend themselves. What was the basis for this increased degree of social organization? And, how did hominids overcome the liabilities of weak-tie apes and become more organized so that they could first survive on the savanna and then move out across the globe?

Emotions and increased sociality

The emergence of the horde

Recently, Alexandra Maryanski and I have revived an old notion that appears in the work of early sociologists, such as Durkheim, and some anthropologists: the horde (Turner and Maryanski, 2005). Using Maryanski's cladistic analysis of ape social relations, we asked the question: What would the social structure of hominids look like before the family evolved? Our answer is developed by listing the social ties among chimpanzees, our closest relative, that could be used to build strong group structures if selection favored strong ties and increased group solidarity (as it certainly did for apes on the savanna). Below is a list of the core ties of chimpanzees, our best looking glass into our ancestors' past (Turner and Maryanski, 2005:134):

1   *Mother–prepuberty male* offspring ties are strong
2   *Mother–prepuberty female* offspring ties are strong
3   *Mother–adult daughter* ties are broken forever at puberty
4   *Mother–adult son* ties can remain moderate to strong for a lifetime
5   *Adult female–adult female* ties are weak or non-existent
6   *Adult male–adult male* ties can be weak to strong
7   *Adult male–adult female* ties are weak.

Now, we can ask the simple question: Which of these seven sets of ties could create more permanent groupings? Only the moderate to strong ties between mothers and their adult sons and the weak to strong ties among adult males (often brothers) could initially serve as a basis for increased social solidarity. The horde, therefore, was constructed from ties among mother and her son(s), brothers, and perhaps male friends coupled with incoming females from other communities (recall that females always leave their natal community and transfer to a new community).

These would be biologically based propensities on which natural selection could "select." But this form of social structure presents problems: adult males and females remain promiscuous, like all apes (except gibbons/siamangs) today, and hence the "family" as a reproductive unit probably did not exist. As the brain became larger and, hence, as infants had to exit the womb earlier, the vulnerability of a mother and her infant would increase, and especially so in open-country savanna conditions. Thus, as the brain of *Homo erectus* grew, selection pressures for a more stable reproductive unit would escalate because neurologically immature infants would pose problems for what is already a long period of infant dependency among apes; in the open country, these pressures would be that much greater.

For several million years, I believe, the brain had been undergoing rewiring for enhanced emotionality for many of the reasons cited by Wentworth and his colleagues. Since these changes would be subcortical, they might not be fully revealed by endocasts of fossilized skulls, but the initial increases

---

Notes to Figure 2.2

Fossils are dated with a variety of methods. Absolute dates rely upon radiometric techniques, such as radiocarbon dating (14C), potassium-argon dating (K/Ar), and fission track dating, that date within a probability range. Relative dates (or dates by association with something else) rely upon such methods as faunal correlations and paleomagnetism.

* All fossils attributed to a taxa fall between the ranges indicated.

** *H. erectus* fossils are found throughout the Pleistocene and as late as 50,000 years ago in Indonesia. The newly discovered *H. floresiensis*, who died some 18,000 years ago, may be a descendent of *H. erectus* (see Gibbons, 2004).

*** This provisional listing of hominids after the split from the last common ancestor of present-day chimpanzees and humans is constantly being revised. Our listing summarizes the data as they stood in early 2005.

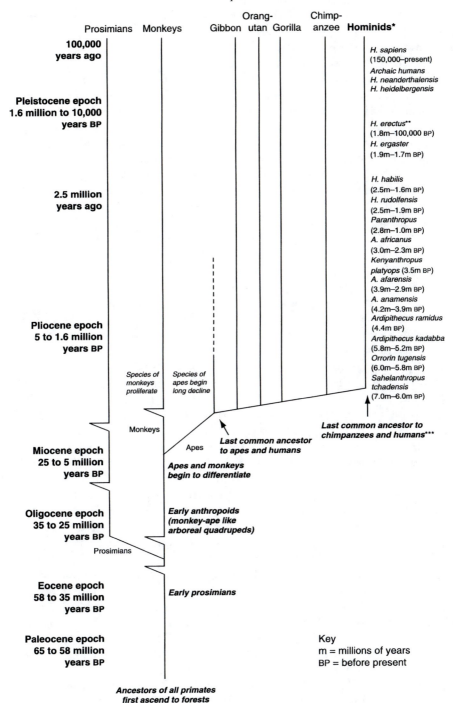

Figure 2.2 The hominid (hominin) line through time.

in brain size before *Homo habilis* were, I argue, mostly subcortical in the emotion centers of the brain; and this enhanced emotionality led to the formation of the horde, described above. Once in place and operating as a successful strategy for survival, the emotions could be subject to further selection to create even stronger social bonds, eventually between males and females so that nuclear family in the foraging band became the basic structure of homo – including modern humans – organizing social life.

A thought experiment might be a good way to get a better purchase on the points emphasized by Wentworth and colleagues. We can ask: What increases positive emotional arousal and solidarity among humans today? By outlining the basic process enhancing emotions and social solidarity among present-day humans, we can get a sense for how natural selection was rewiring the brain of hominid ancestors. What, then, are the ingredients of strong social ties and social solidarity?

Ingredients of strong ties and solidarity

The first ingredient for using emotions to enhance solidarity is increasing the arousal of positive emotions. This is an obvious ingredient but there is an obstacle to positive emotional arousal: three of the four primary emotions are negative (see Table 1.2). Selection would need to find a way to mitigate the power of negative emotional arousal, while at the same time increasing the propensity for hominids to experience positive emotional arousal.

A second ingredient is interpersonal attunement in which the dispositions and likely courses of actions of others can be read through facial expressions and body language. Attunement comes primarily from reading emotions, and so natural selection would need to enhance primates' visual dominance to be particularly attentive to emotions. Since contemporary apes appear to be able to read each other's emotions (Menzel, 1971), there were existing neurological capacities on which selection could work to increase interpersonal attunement or, in George Herbert Mead's (1934) terms, role-taking. Moreover, there are clear areas of the brain that light up among humans when they empathize with others, indicating that there has been selection for greater degrees of interpersonal attunement through emotions (Singer *et al.*, 2004).

A third feature of interactions generating positive emotions is emotional entrainment and rhythmic synchronization (Collins, 2004). As interactions become synchronized, positive emotions emerge and increase the intermingling of emotions so that individuals become entrained. Thus, natural selection would have had to work on the hominid brain to increase mutual responsiveness, rhythmic flow of gestures, and emotional entrainment. Since chimpanzees can engage in what is described as collective "carnaval," there may have already been a biological capacity for rhythmic synchronization on which selection could work.

A fourth ingredient of high solidarity is exchange of valued resources.

Emotions, per se, attach value to objects; and so, at one level, exchange is not possible unless individuals can attach emotional valences along a positive to negative continuum (Collins, 1993). Thus, natural selection would need to increase the propensity to tag objects, gestures, and other features of the world with reward value. Exchange, per se, also generates positive emotions, as Marcel Mauss (1925) emphasized a long time ago and as recent experiments by Edward Lawler and colleagues (Lawler and Yoon, 1993, 1996, 1998) have demonstrated in controlled experiments. Since chimpanzees reveal propensities for exchanges and reciprocity, natural selection already had a propensity on which to go to work.

A fifth ingredient of solidarity is sanctioning, in which conformity to expectations is rewarded with positive emotional responses, while failure to meet expectations is punished with negative emotions. Since three of the four primary emotions – anger, fear, sadness – are negative, the key for natural selection was to increase the proportion of positive to negative sanctions in order to build stronger social bonds.

Finally, social solidarity depends upon moral coding whereby individuals symbolize relationships in values and norms, while representing the group with totems. Symbols must be seen as moral which, in turn, requires that they have emotional valences attached to them. Not only must social relations take on this moral character, individuals must be disposed to engage in rituals directed at the symbols, thereby activating the emotions contained in the symbols.

This list of ingredients corresponds roughly to Émile Durkheim's analysis in *Elementary Forms of the Religious Life* (1965 [1912]) and, more recently, to the elements in Randall Collins's (2004) interaction ritual theory. Natural selection needed to rewire the neuroanatomy of low-sociality apes in several ways to install in hominids and, then, in humans these capacities. First, to survive on the African savanna, cortical control of emotional responses would be necessary so that emotional displays drawing the attention of predators or scaring prey away could be managed. Second, the range of emotions that could be used to symbolize the group, to tag alternatives, to sanction, and to communicate would need to be expanded beyond variants of primary emotions. Otherwise, emotional communication would not be nuanced; and, as a result, subtle forms of attunement would not be possible. Third, emotions would need to become "linguistic" because without emotional phonemes and syntax, emotions as a basis of solidarity in pre-verbal species could not be used to sustain longer-term relations among ape-like animals that do not have herding or packing behavioral propensities. The key was for emotions to become the basis for increasing social bonds and solidarities in local groups or foraging troops so that they could coordinate food collection and defense. We should see, therefore, some evidence in the anatomy of the brain of natural selection's handiwork, if my speculations have any merit.

The neurology of strong ties and solidarity

In the appendix to this chapter, I summarize in more detail the neurology of emotions. For the purposes of my argument, I will only focus on a general comparison of the brain structures among apes and humans. As noted earlier, emotions are generated in subcortical areas of the brain, below the neocortex. These emotion centers are sometimes referred to as the "limbic system" (MacLean, 1990) or more recently as "modules" by evolutionary psychologists. To the extent that sociologists pay any attention to the brain, they tend to focus on the neocortex because this is where culture is generated and stored. But, as is now well documented, for culture to have meaning and morality, it must be emotionally valenced (Damasio, 1994), and so culture is ultimately dependent upon those subcortical areas of the brain that tag cognitions with emotional valences. And the more complex the available valences that can be generated, the more complex can culture become.

Thus, the dramatic increase in the size of the neocortex depends upon enhanced emotional capacities in the older, more primal part of the brain below the neocortex. As the brain began to grow some 2.5 million years ago and, eventually, increase hominids' capacity for culture, the emotion centers of the brain also had to grow. And, if a sense of self were to become important for evaluation from the perspective of others and the morality of the group, then the capacity to not only see self as an object in the environment but also to evaluate self through emotions would also be crucial for social (self) control and enhanced solidarity. As I argue, the emotion centers had probably already grown and, indeed, represented a pre-adaptation for a more complex symbolic representation of self and the world.

Table 2.3 records measurements of key areas of the brain in apes and humans, controlling for body size which is correlated with brain size (for a

Table 2.3 Relative size of brain components of apes and humans, compared to *Tenrecinae*

Brain component	Apes (Pongids)	Humans (Homo)
Neocortex	61.88	196.41
Diencephalon thalamus hypothalamus	8.57	14.76
Amygdala	1.85	4.48
centromedial	1.06	2.52
basolateral	2.45	6.02
Septum	2.16	5.45
Hippocampus	2.99	4.87
Transition cortices	2.38	4.43

Sources: data from Stephan, 1983; Stephan and Andy, 1969, 1977; Eccles, 1989.

Note
Numbers represent how many times larger than *Tenrecinae* each area of the brain is, with *Tenrecinae* representing a base of 1.

figure depicting areas of the brain, see Figure 2.3 in the appendix). The methodology for producing the numbers in Table 2.3 involves using a very simple mammal, *Tenrecinae*, that is similar to the rodent-like animal that climbed into the forest canopy to originate the primate line. All numbers in Table 2.3 involve comparison to *Tenrecinae*, which represents a value of "1," with the numbers for apes and humans denoting how many times greater than "1" various structures of the brain are for apes and humans. This procedure allows for comparison of ape and human brains in terms of a common measuring stick (the "1" of *Tenrecinae*). Thus, the neocortex of an ape is almost sixty-two times larger than that of *Tenrecinae*, while for humans, the neocortex is 196 times the size of *Tenrecinae*'s. The human neocortex is thus three times the size of that in the great apes, controlling for body size. What intrigued me about these figures, however, was the differences in subcortical areas of the brain responsible for emotions. On average, human subcortical areas are a little less than twice the size of those among the great apes. Why should this be so?

These are, of course, gross measurements and cannot tell us much about the details of brain structure and processes (but size does matter and, by reading the appendix, it becomes clear that these are some of the critical structures in the production of emotions). Since humans and the great apes as a whole share about 97 percent of their genes (with humans sharing 99 percent of their genes with common chimpanzees), these differences in the size of delicate structures like the brain mean that they were subject to intense selection. Indeed, recent techniques for measuring how much selection particular brain structures have been under indicate that the centers for spoken language *have only recently* been under intense selection for the last 200,000 to 120,000 years, which corresponds to the emergence of humans (summarized in Balter and Gibbons, 2002; see also Enard *et al.*, 2002a, b). Thus, full-blown speech may be very recent, and we can ask: What was the basis of communication *before* spoken language emerged among humans and, perhaps, their immediate hominid ancestors?

Other evidence indicates that the brain first expanded on the right side, away from the main speech areas which are arrayed on the left side of the brain; and, as is well known, the right side of the brain is more responsible for the "prosodic features of speech" such as rhythm, tone, and emotional content (Falk, 2002). Thus, natural selection was first operating on emotional elements or ingredients, listed above, that would increase solidarity. Natural selection seems to have worked, first, on increasing hominid emotions; and then, only after millions of years of increasing the size of subcortical areas of the brain, in conjunction with the right side of the neocortex, did selection turn to enhancing humans' auditory capacities for spoken language.

To some extent this sequence makes sense because apes are clearly already wired for language because they can learn to use a vocabulary of about 1,000 words and put these words into a syntax via sign language or pictograms on a computer (Savage-Rumbaugh *et al.*, 1993). But apes cannot "speak" because they do not have the physical equipment to do so; natural selection had to change a great deal – tongue, facial and jaw muscles, throat and associated structures – to make articulated speech possible. If selection was punctuated, then a much faster route was to take existing capacities for phonemes and syntax, and then create an emotional language revolving around increased emotional capacities and the already strong visual acuity that all primates have. The first language, then, was visually based but it was not the language of hand signals so often hypothesized (e.g. Hewes, 1973) but, rather, *the language of emotions.* I think that the footprints on the brain make a much stronger case for the first language being that of emotions than speech, especially because apes do not have the physical equipment for auditory language, but they do have the ability to read emotions visually and the capacity to use language as long as they have a non-verbal means for expressing themselves.

If natural selection was working quickly, grabbing structures on which it could select to increase affective bonds and social solidarity, it is far more important to enhance emotions than speech abilities because the visual reading of gestures marking emotions is *still* how humans generate solidarity. Thus, in my view, speech was piggy-backed onto the original and more primal language: the facial and body language of emotions that allowed weak-tie apes to gain some degree of solidarity under the intense selection pressures presented by the African savanna.

Cognitive and emotional interactions

With an enhanced capacity to arouse and control a wider array of emotions, cognitive development was also enhanced, once the neocortex began to grow. Initially, the anterior cingulated cortex grew and, then, ever more neocortical layers were created to form the large neocortex – some three times larger than that in apes (see also Figure 2.3 in appendix). One of the principle outcomes of the interaction between expanded emotional and cognitive abilities is increased rationality. As Damasio (1994) and colleagues have documented, rational thought – that is, choosing among potential alternatives so as to increase gratifications – requires that potential lines of conduct be emotionally valenced. When damage to the neurons connecting the prefrontal cortex (see Figure 2.3) to subcortical emotion centers is severed, individuals have difficulty making any decisions, and they usually make suboptimal decisions (Damasio *et al.*, 2003; Damasio, 2003). I would add the corollary to this finding that the more complex the emotional valences that can tag lines of conduct, the more complex will be calculations. The concept of "mind" in George Herbert Mead's (1934) terms is not possible without the arousal of emotions that determine which lines of conduct will be (emotionally) gratifying and which will not. Thus, as natural selection expanded the neocortex on top of an already enhanced capacity for emotional arousal, this expansion accelerated the capacity for rationality.

A related capacity is memory. For experiences to be remembered, they must be emotionally valenced; and if they are then stored in the hippo-campus and retrieved in thought, the emotions aroused at the time of the original experience will be "replayed," although in somewhat diluted form and, if repeated, will eventually be shipped up to the prefrontal cortex. The more emotions homo could arouse and use to tag experiences, the more complex memories could become, and the greater would be the facility to retrieve them when needed. Without a prior expansion in the range of emotions, growth of the neocortex would not have had the same effect on memory and, hence, would not have been as fitness enhancing. Indeed, it could be argued that there would have been little fitness-enhancing value of a larger neocortex, per se, without the prior expansion of emotional capaci-ties that could make increased rationality and memory possible. In my view, it is the *interaction between cognitive and emotional capacities* that makes rational-ity and memory possible on a human scale. An animal whose neocortex grew in size would not be smarter unless its emotional range had also increased. Thus, as selection expanded the emotional capacities of hominids over several million years, it set the stage for intelligence on a human scale, once the interactions between cognition and emotion could be maximized, and this interaction effect would depend upon the language of emotions.

One of the most important interactions among cognitions, memories, and emotions is the ability to see self as an object. This capacity would increase with a larger neocortex and with a wider array of emotions with which to tag cognitions. Given that apes already have a limited capacity to see self as an object, it was probably not a dramatic step to select on this capacity, giving homo the ability to define self in emotionally laden as well as purely cognitive terms. As the neocortex grew, individuals could store emotionally tagged cognitions and memories about self from past inter-actions, and, over time, these would develop into a more general or global self-conception that could supplement more immediate role-identities in situations. With self and identity, social control becomes a more powerful force because individuals seek to sustain and verify themselves in the eyes of others and the group's moral codes. Much sanctioning could now become self-sanctioning, thereby eliminating the need to have moment-by-moment monitoring and sanctioning by others. Indeed, as I will argue in later chap-ters, the dominant transactional need of homo is for verification of self, and a good many of the dynamics of emotional arousal revolve around these self-verification processes.

A related dynamic also emerges with an expanded sense of self, a large palate of emotions, and an enhanced cognitive facility: repression and defense mechanisms. If individuals become oriented to verifying self, complex nega-tive emotions like shame and guilt arise when self is not confirmed. Since these are combinations of the three negative emotions (see Table 1.4), they are powerful forces of social control, but they are something else: they are painful when used to evaluate self. As a consequence, the increased cognitive capacity to control emotions also generates the ability to engage in a defense of self by pushing emotions below the level of conscious awareness. Once repressed, emotional dynamics become more complex and powerful because, as I will argue, repression intensifies emotions and, often, transmutes them into new emotions. A sociological theory of human emotions must, therefore, take into account the dynamics revolving around cognitive control of emotional arousal as these lead to repression and other defensive strategies to protect self.

With expanded cognitive facility, gestalt processes become more likely. When emotionally tagged cognitions can be held simultaneously as well as remembered and invoked, assessments of consistency become possible. Indeed, it is not the inconsistency in the actual cognitions, per se, that causes "dissonance" and "incongruity"; rather, it is the conflict among the emotions attached to these cognitions that creates dissonance and, thereby, adds yet another negative emotion to the affect stew. When cognitions are in "the here and now," and when relatively few are invoked at a single moment, inconsistency is not a salient issue. But, the capacity to hold several cognitions in working memory (see appendix), to retrieve them from shorter-term storage from the hippocampus as well as from longer-term memory in the prefrontal cortex, dramatically increases not only the number of cognitions in play at any given moment but also the number of emotions as well. It is emotional dissonance, I believe, that drives gestalt processes that seek to restore congruence and consistency in cognitions.

A related gestalt dynamic is attribution. Smarter animals are, I believe, more likely to assess causality and, moreover, to react emotionally to perceived causes of events. Mammals in general will often act aggressively (be angry) toward perceived sources of punishment, and even B. F. Skinner's pigeons in their famous box sanctioned the bar and box when not receiving expected rewards. Thus, there is plenty in the animal line on which natural selection could work to expand this propensity to assign causes of outcomes. And, when dramatically escalated cognitive capacities, memories, and emotions exist, there is an even greater propensity to assign causes to outcomes. Thus, what is only a tendency among most animals with intelligence becomes a much more powerful force in animals that can see self and other objects in their environments and that can bring to bear cognitive power, memories, and emotions to assess the causal relation between self and other objects. In fact, I think that it is self that increases propensities for making attributions in several ways. First, self-verification is, itself, an attribution process because it orients individuals to see who and what verifies or fails to verify self. Second, self increases the likelihood that individuals will invoke defense mechanisms to protect a self that goes unverified; and, as I will argue, external attributions are one of the most important, if not the most important, defense mechanisms from the perspective of a sociological analysis of emotions. Thus, the more self-aware individuals are about themselves and their relations to objects in the environment, the more they become likely to make assessments about causality for outcomes to self. And since self is always emotionally valenced, as are most objects in the environment, behavioral propensities to make causal attributions become ever more likely as emotions, whether positive or negative, are aroused.

Direct and indirect forces of natural selection

Humans' emotional abilities emerged – like all other features of the humans as biological entities – through the forces of evolution. Sociologists often forget this obvious fact, and then they compound this error by seeing brain size as producing culture that somehow obviates biology. Even in the sociology of emotions, most sociologists are not willing to give biology its due, with many arguing for a socially constructed conceptualization of all emotions. People learn the language of emotions through socialization into an emotion culture, to be sure, but they are also biologically programmed to learn signs attached to emotions in their culture much like they are innately disposed to learn those for spoken language. Infants are predisposed to learn the primal emotional language because it is one of our species' most unique biological characteristics and, in my view, it was the key to our ancestors' survival. Hence, like all biological characteristics it evolved. One way to summarize the argument that I have made is to break the evolution of emotions down into indirect and direct forces of selection on the human anatomy and neuroanatomy (Turner, 2000a).

Indirect selection forces

Much of what we are is, of course, the outcome of selection pressures that worked on those small mammals that clawed their way into the arboreal habitat some sixty million years ago. Some of the most important character-istics of humans, as an evolved primate, come from what natural selection did to the mammalian body of our very distant ancestors who looked something like a rat or mouse (this is also, by the way, why clinical trials and studies on mice and rats can tell us a lot about ourselves, since evolution is a conservative process, keeping what works and only changing what is essential for survival). The biggest change to mammals that must live in the trees is the shifting of sensory dominance from olfactory to visual, and this change involves rewiring of the brain to convert our ancestors from animals that relied mostly upon smell to one that was visually dominant, with bin-ocular color vision. This alteration in the basic way that primates perceive the world has enormous effects on human emotionality. Humans seek to read emotions in the face and body not only because they are expressed this way but, more importantly, because this is our dominant way of gathering information. Thus, the sociology of emotions requires that we attend to the visual dimensions of emotions because this is how we role-take and get a sense for others' emotional states. True, voice inflections can add additional nuances but, fundamentally, we search for visual confirmation of all other emotional cues. We do this because we are primates.

A related effect of the transformation to visual dominance was the creation of new association cortices to subordinate the other sense modalities to vision (see Figure 2.3 in appendix). One outcome of this rewiring of the brain to increase the number of association cortices was to pre-wire the human brain for language, as I noted earlier. Chimpanzees can learn the basics of language because they have large brains for a mammal and because they have the association cortices, in and around the inferior parietal lobe, that make language possible, as Norman Geschwind (1965a, b, 1970) along with Antonio Damasio (Geschwind and Damasio, 1984), have argued. The neurological structures allowing for language evolved for reasons very different than present-day language production; rather, they evolved to subordinate other senses – primarily auditory and haptic – to vision.

If we think about how language could have emerged, it is clear that there must have been pre-adaptations already in place on which natural selection could go to work over a long period of time. The capacity for language is a complex process and could not have suddenly emerged as a mutation since most large mutations are harmful and would not enhance fitness. More importantly, assume that one animal somehow gained the capacity for language: How would it enhance fitness if no one else had this mutation? Indeed, language facility would have no fitness-enhancing effect, or perhaps a negative effect; and in either case it would be selected out. Thus, the neurological capacity for language is a pre-adaptation that came with the complex rewiring of the brain for visual dominance (which had fitness-enhancing consequences) but, once in place, it could be selected upon *if* language further increased chances of survival.

My view is that this capacity or pre-adaptation did not just "sit there" in the primate neuroanatomy until a couple of hundred thousand years ago when humans developed auditory speech. Rather, it was selected upon much earlier in the form of an emotional language, revolving around emotion phonemes (mostly of the face but also of the body) strung together by a syntax to communicate emotional states. Thus, when studying emotions, we should not be showing subjects still photographs of faces (*à la* Ekman, 1973a, b), but instead we should use video technologies showing the emission of gestures over time as emotional phonemes are strung together by the emotional syntax of a culture. This is how we read emotions in others; and we are able to do so because we have learned the emotional language of our culture.

There are more anatomical features of primates that also influence how humans interact and emote. We have very generalized skeletons, with four limbs and very dexterous and sensitive hands – all adaptations to the arboreal habitat. These allowed us to stand upright, if needed, and to expose full body and face to others, thereby making ourselves visually present to others who can better read our emotions. Our hands and fingers becomes another mode of communicating emotions; and the fact that we have such sensitive haptic senses on our fingers and hands adds, if wanted, another route for communicating emotion – as a gentle touch or handshake will inevitably do. Thus, when we read emotions in others, we seek to observe the face and then supplement this information with attention to body movement, countenance and, if possible, touch.

Direct forces of selection

The ingredients of social bonds and solidarity that I delineated earlier can be viewed in a somewhat different light as selection pressures. If we ask how would a low-sociality, weak-tie primate with no bioprogrammers for tight-knit groups get organized, the answer is, of course, that most could not – as the mass extinction of apes over the last sixteen million years clearly attests. If emotions were to become the key to survival, then selection worked in a particular direction and sequence. First, mobilizing and channeling emotional energy toward bonds would be essential, and so there was selection on our ancestors' primate neuroanatomy for this capacity. More than being emotional was involved, however, since all primates can be very emotional; rather, selection worked on the hominid neuroanatomy to increase control over emotions. With control came selection to increase the diversity of emotions that could be mobilized, and once this capacity began to emerge from natural selection, it increased interpersonal attunement which, in turn, increased the fitness-enhancing effects of emotions in a cycle that could rapidly expand the use of emotions for interpersonal attunement and social solidarity. As emotional capacities expanded, then the emotions themselves became reinforcers and valuable in exchanges of reciprocal affect, and then once emotions became the coinage of reciprocity, they would serve as even more effective sanctions; and these processes, once initiated, would all feed off each other as long as they increased solidarity and fitness. With a greater array of emotions, the expansion of the neocortex would have dramatic fitness-enhancing effects through new capacities to remember, to retrieve memories, to evaluate self, to engage in self-control, and to code with moral content social relations and group solidarity.

This package of direct selection pressures fed off each other, with changes in one causing changes in the others, and vice versa. This set of events was a very punctuated process during which hominid emotional capacities rapidly expanded as they forged fitness-enhancing social bonds and group solidarity. This is how our ancestors survived, and I should emphasize that culture came late to these dynamics; indeed, cultural codes of any sophistication require a wide range of emotional tags and prompts, which evolved before the neocortex grew to the point of enabling our ancestors to use culture as yet one more fitness-enhancing capacity. It is emotions – once controlled, channeled, and expanded – that allowed our ancestors to survive, even with small brains that could not produce any more culture than the limited cultural repertoire of present-day chimpanzees.

Only later did the neocortex grow to the point of generating the complex cultural systems evident among humans, but this capacity to produce culture depends upon humans' abilities to mix cognitions and emotions together. Social constructionists tend to underemphasize the biological substrate that allows for culture; for it is not simply enlargement of the neocortex; instead, it is the complex interconnections between the neocortex and subcortical areas of the brain that allow elements of culture to be emotionally labeled, and hence useful in human affairs. Social constructionists usually argue that it is emotions that are culturally labeled, producing an emotion culture, but if we look at the matter from an evolutionary perspective, we would reach the opposite conclusion: it is culture that is emotionally tagged. And so, if anything, culture is emotionally constructed by humans' neurological capacities to produce complex arrays of emotional states.

A sociological theory of human emotions cannot forget this fundamental fact of life: humans are an animal that evolved like all other life forms. One of our most unique biological features is our capacity to generate and use a wide variety of emotions to build social relations or to breach them, and to build social structures or to tear them down. This is not a constructed capacity; it is part of our biology, to a far greater extent than most sociologists are willing to admit. Culture and social structure cannot exist without humans' emotional capacities, and these capacities are not neocortical. They are subcortical and evolved long before humans' unique cognitive abilities.

Conclusion

Many sociologists will be less enthusiastic than I am in introducing biology to the sociological analysis of emotions, and especially for an analysis of the selection pressures that worked on hominid and human neuroanatomy to make humans so emotional. Recognizing this bias in sociology, I have written this chapter so that it can be skipped. Yet, if you are still reading these words, perhaps I have made some progress. Sociologists have come – somewhat late – to recognize the importance of emotions in understanding interaction and social organization, but they must go further and see the importance of biology to an informed sociological analysis of emotions.

Commitments to, anger at, or alienation from social structures and culture are generated under specifiable conditions, and they have effects on social structures and culture. The goal of this book is to develop a theory of this two-way relationship – what sociocultural conditions generate what emotions that, reciprocally, have what effect on what sociocultural conditions? This question, when viewed in evolutionary terms, emphasizes that from the very beginning of hominid evolution, enhancing emotional capacities was the key to increasing the degree of social organization among weak-tie primates that were forced to survive on the open-country African savanna. Because emotions were the key to our ancestors' survival, it should not be surprising that they are still one of the essential forces behind the complex sociocultural arrangements that humans have created in the contemporary world. We do not survive as a species by culture and social structure alone; people have to be emotionally committed to culture or social structures, and these commitments or their converse are made possible by our unique neuroanatomy. Without humans' capacity to arouse a wide variety of emotions and to use these emotions to infuse affect into culture and social structure, our ancestors would have gone the way of most apes over the last sixteen million years.

While my evolutionary tale may seem interesting (or perhaps not), it is more than an academic story. Understanding the neurology of emotions and how natural selection works on the primate neuroanatomy to produce humans' special emotional abilities is necessary to address the problems that are of most interest to sociologists. We cannot simply acknowledge that humans have emotional capacities and then simply explain how they operate to forge social bonds; we can do this, of course, as most sociologists do, but we miss an important set of dynamics when we ignore the biological underpinnings of emotions.

When we ignore biology, we begin to make mistakes in analysis, as is the case with those who argue that all emotions are culturally constructed. This fundamental error is easily compounded, and analysis moves away from understanding just how emotions really work in human affairs. To take one example that is central to my argument: sociologists tend to ignore repression of emotions, and the neurology that makes repression possible and, indeed, likely. The result is sociological theories that are far too cognitive, seeing emotions as an indicator of cognitive incongruence. This kind of gestalt analysis is not wholly wrong; it is just woefully incomplete. How can we understand violent revolutions, terrorism, fanatical conformity, war, collective behavior, and many other processes where the emotional intensity is very high with only a cognitive view of emotions? The answer is that we cannot; we need to see emotions in their most robust terms, as a force in human action that evolved and that continually operates to increase or decrease the viability of culture and social structures.

APPENDIX: THE NEUROLOGY OF EMOTIONS [1]

Sociological theories of emotions do not adequately conceptualize the biology of emotions, in two senses: (1) the evolutionary forces that created the

---

1 Adapted from J. H. Turner (1999a), "The Neurology of Emotion: Implications for Sociological Theories of Interpersonal Behavior." In D. D. Franks and T. S. Smith, Eds. *Mind, Brain, and Society: Towards a Neurosociology of Emotion.* Social Perspectives on Emotion Vol. 5. Stanford, CT: JAI Press, pp. 81–108, with permission from Elsevier. See also Turner (1999b) and (2000a), especially chapter 4.

neurological wiring in the human brain for the production and use of such a wide variety and array of emotions; and (2) the operation of these brain mechanisms during the course of interaction. Some serious work by sociologists has focused on the operation of brain mechanisms (e.g. Kemper, 1990; Smith and Stevens, 1997a, b; TenHouten, 1989, 1997), but these approaches have not been sufficiently global nor have they addressed broader evolutionary questions, such as selection forces that produced the neurological wiring for emotions in the first place.

There is no reason, of course, to study the biology of emotions *unless it makes a difference* for the kinds of processes studied by sociologists. We could simply assume that neurology is a black box for our purposes and, then, proceed to study emotions in their purely social contexts. The argument in this appendix is that we need to know something of the evolution and neurology of human emotions if we are to conceptualize more adequately emotions in their social contexts. My goal is not to develop a complete theory, but to suggest important biological processes that sociologists should consider. Indeed, my own thinking in this area is still evolving; and what I present here is more of a preliminary statement than a firm conclusion. Yet, by introducing the biology of emotions into sociological analysis, I hope to reconceptualize emotions in more robust terms and in ways that can augment the creative work in sociology over the last thirty years.

I became interested in the biology of emotions because of the fact that humans are very emotional animals in two senses. (1) Humans can become emotionally aroused in ways that other animals cannot; for example, we can produce emotions like rage, terror, ecstasy, shame, guilt, and other very powerful but complex emotions. (2) Humans can generate a very large variety of emotions and interpret them effortlessly and, in fact, unconsciously. These two issues led me to ponder how innate, primary emotions become elaborated into variations and combinations, an issue that many have explored (e.g. Kemper, 1987; Plutchik, 1980; Izard, 1992a, b; Ekman, 1992a; and as I examined in Chapter 1). I wanted to know how variations in emotions were created by the neurochemistry of the human brain and body, and how they became combined to generate subtle and often complex mixes of emotions. While "mixing" of primary emotions is probably a bad metaphor, it is useful to describe how primary emotions are "elaborated," as I explored in Chapter 1.

There are many neurological systems involved in producing emotions; and assuming all emotional potentials in these systems were activated and then "mixed" into every combination and permutation, many thousands of emotional variants and combinations could be generated. But this is not what happens, of course; and, in fact, humans signal and interpret around one hundred emotional states during the course of interaction, as can be seen by a cursory review of tables 1.1., 1.2, 1.3, and 1.4. If something like the mixing of emotions is the proper way to visualize what is going on, then humans do not utilize the full range of their neurological capacity to generate variants and elaborations of emotions. This might be expected because people can interact in very subtle and highly complex ways utilizing just a few dozen emotions; and to add more shades of emotional texture to the process would make interaction too complex and, probably, exhausting.

A feature of human neurology that gives me pause about the metaphor of mixing is that emotions come from not just discrete nuclei or modules in the brain, but also from *systems* of nuclei located in various regions of the brain. This systemic quality of the structures producing emotions – what is sometimes loosely termed the "limbic system" (MacLean, 1990) – is not one system but a series of systems involving neocortical, subcortical, and brain stem structures (Le Doux, 1991, 1993a, 1996). Each of these systems can, to a degree, generate a large range of emotions, but they do not operate separately; they are interconnected to each other; and they are involved in relations with body systems that make their effects on each other and, hence, on humans' emotional states that much more complex.

To have "a feeling" is only a special case of being cognizant of how your body or that of another person has been mobilized, but conscious feelings are only those emotions that penetrate neocortical functioning from the much greater number of emotions that we send and receive subcortically, or subconsciously. Indeed, the flow of interaction on an emotional level is typically a subcortical process involving the mobilization of body systems by participants to an interaction; and subcortical responses to the emotions revealed by the body circumscribe the flow of interaction.

Humans possess an emotional memory system residing outside of the neocortex; and while this system can be attached to memories stored in the neocortex, such need not be the case (Le Doux, 1996). Hence, human responses to each other's emotions may not only be conducted subcortically, they may also involve stocks of emotional memories that are not, or cannot, be retrieved consciously. In fact, a good portion of humans' emotional responses to each other may involve invoking subcortical emotional memories about which we remain unaware.

These kinds of initial insights come from a simple review of the literature on the neurology of emotions, and they indicate to me that sociologists need to learn something about emotion systems in order to develop more accurate and robust theories of emotion. Where, then, do we begin to learn about the biology of these emotion systems? My answer to this question is to start with evolutionary scenarios on why humans had to become emotional in the first place (as I just explored in the body of this chapter) and on what changes in the structure of the brain were involved in transforming hominids (primates on the human line) into such emotional creatures.

If one compares the human brain to our closest living relatives – i.e. the great apes (gorillas, chimpanzees, and orangutans) – several dramatic differences are evident. First, humans reveal asymmetries in significant portions of the neocortex, indicating that the left and right sides of the brain have somewhat differentiated functions (Bradshaw and Nettleton, 1983;

Needham, 1982; Sperry, 1982). Associated with this "split" of certain brain functions is the greatly expanded connectivity through the corpus callosum between the right and left sides (Bogen and Bogen, 1969; Eccles, 1989). Asymmetry allowed portions of the neocortex to have increased cognitive capacities without increasing the size of the neocortex to the point that it would exceed the female's capacity to pass the newborn through her cervix. Much of the specialization involved dedicating areas to language production (Broca's area) and comprehension (Wernicke's area) on the left side of the brain and to pattern recognition (right side) integrated with temporal recognition (left side).

Second, much of the increase in size of the human brain is in the frontal lobe where thought, long-term memories, and other cognitive functions are carried out. Yet, more recent data suggest that across the apes and humans there has not been as dramatic an increase in the relative size of the frontal lobe as once thought, although the issue remains unsolved (Semendeferi *et al.*, 1997; see also Ruff *et al.*, 1997). At a minimum, it is clear that humans' prefrontal cortex (lower anterior portion of the frontal lobe) is developed considerably beyond that in any other primate; and it is this structure that is particularly important to emotional responses, thinking, planning, and decision-making (Damasio, 1994).

Third, and most relevant to the argument presented in this chapter, there was significant growth in ancient limbic systems in the symmetrical sub-cortical regions of the brain. As Table 2.3 documented, the septum, amygdala, hippocampus, and diencephalon (thalamus and hypothalamus) are all significantly larger than their counterparts in apes (controlling for body size). Thus, humans' capacity to emit emotions increased, and dramatically so, during the course of hominid evolution, as I have argued in this chapter.

In Figure 2.3(b) and (c), I have drawn a medial cross-section of the brain so as to expose the subcortical systems, plus the cingulate gyrus which appears to be a special kind of neocortical system and the forebrain which is clearly neocortical (Vogt, 1993). I have not, it should be emphasized, drawn all structures of the brain, but only those that appear most crucial to the production of emotions. In looking at this medial view, it is important to recognize that the diencephalon portrayed on the right penetrates into the core of the subcortical regions of the brain and is therefore encapsulated by both the remaining subcortical systems and the neocortex. Similarly, the midbrain portion of the brain stem penetrates into the core of the neocortex. The diagram can give the impression of these areas being stacked on top of each other which, in terms of their successive evolution (MacLean, 1990) may be an appropriate metaphor, but they are also enveloped by newer centers of the brain, and, indeed, they penetrate into the middle of the brain. Figure 2.3(a) represents the neocortex, as one would look at it from the outside. Along this left hemisphere are language centers (Broca's and Wernicke's areas), the sensory lobes (Parietal for haptic, Occipital for vision, and Temporal for auditory) which receive inputs from the specialized

(a) Left hemisphere of neocortex

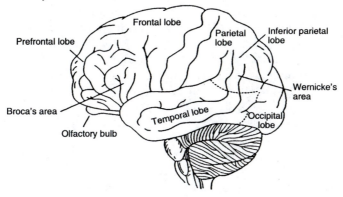

(b) Cross-sectional outline of paleomammalian complex (and components of limbic system)

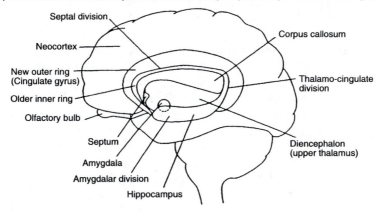

(c) Cross-sectional outline of reptilian complex (diencephalon)

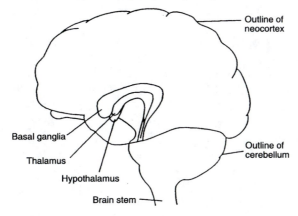

Figure 2.3 Key structures and regions of the human brain

sensory areas of the Thalamus, the Olfactory bulb which projects directly
into subcortical areas, and the frontal and prefrontal lobes.

Figure 2.3(c) highlights the top of the brain stem and diencephalon, as
well as the pituitary gland that is activated by the thalamus and hypothalamus. The production of neurotransmitters is also affected by these
structures around the diencephalon (Kandel *et al.*, 1995). The diencephalon
composed of the thalamus and hypothalamus, along with the pituitary gland,
are mediators of emotionally charged sensory inputs (Le Doux, 1996), while
being critical to the production of hormones and peptides involved in
emotional responses (Shepherd, 1994:603).

Figure 2.3(b) represents those limbic systems surrounding the diencephalon. The amygdala is the center for fear (Le Doux, 1996), anger
(MacLean, 1990), and, in its basolateral portions, apparently for pleasure as
well (Eccles, 1989), while being a major center for integrating emotional
responses between subcortical and cortical areas (Le Doux, 1996). The septum is the center for instinctual sex drives (MacLean, 1990); and in humans
additional nuclei generate pleasure and satisfaction (Eccles, 1989). The
hippocampus and related transition cortices are involved in integrating
emotional memories, both those that become part of long-term memory
and, perhaps, those that remain subcortical (Le Doux, 1996). The basal
forebrain or prefrontal cortex is involved in integrating emotional responses
to thought, planning, and calculation by receiving inputs from all other
limbic systems – hippocampal, transition cortices, diencephalon, amygdala,
and septum – and using these to construct lines and courses of action for self
(Damasio, 1994). In particular, layer four of the prefrontal cortex – often
termed the granulofrontal cortex – is especially critical to (1) anticipation
and planning, (2) empathic and altruistic feelings, (3) concern for welfare of
self and others, (4) visual reading of gestures (via connections to vision
cortices), (5) touch as these reveal emotional content (via connections to
motor areas), and (6) crying and laughing (via connections to cingulate
gyrus). The cingulate gyrus, particularly the anterior portion, is also involved
in integrating other emotion systems and the forebrain (Le Doux, 1996;
Devinski and Luciano, 1993; Vogt, 1993; MacLean, 1993), while being the
locus of unique mammalian behaviors like mother–infant bonding,
audio-vocal communication, such as the "separation cry," and playfulness
(MacLean, 1990).

These areas of the brain are critical to most of the theoretical questions
that micro sociologists pursue: the nature of self, the dynamics of decision-
making and choice, the processes involved in consciousness and feelings, the
use of memory and stocks of knowledge, and the dynamics of role-making
and role-taking. While language and related features of linguistic abilities
like pacing and intonation are important, these processes are not as fundamental to micro-level interactions as non-verbal emotional dynamics. How,
then, do we begin to get a handle on these emotional brain systems? I do not
have a complete answer to this question, only some tentative suggestions for

what to examine. Let me begin with what I will term, in deference to Damasio's (1994) "somatic marker hypothesis," the nature of emotional body systems.

Gross neuroanatomy of emotional body systems

I will label Body system 1 the autonomic nervous system (ANS) which is composed of the smooth muscles that control visceral responses accompanying emotional arousal. These responses include respiration, heartbeat, muscle tension, dryness of mouth, sweating, and tenseness of stomach (Shepherd, 1994:395). Figure 2.4 presents a very rough diagram of some of the important brain systems involved in ANS responses. By far the most important is the hypothalamus which receives inputs from other areas of the brain and converts neural information into hormonal information by targeting areas of the pituitary gland that secretes hormones into the bloodstream. Once activated, the ANS operates as a feedback system, working primarily through the thalamus which takes inputs and projects them to other emotion systems and to the cerebral cortex (Le Doux, 1996). As Damasio (1994) and Le Doux (1996) have argued, these kinds of feedback processes are crucial in emotional arousal; initial arousal in response to some stimulus mobilizes a body system in ways that feedback to sustain, change, or enhance the original arousal, while activating other emotional body systems. And, as I argue, it is the mobilization of these body systems that is so important in presentations of self (including unconscious emission of gestures) or role-making (R. H. Turner, 1962) and in the responses of others to these

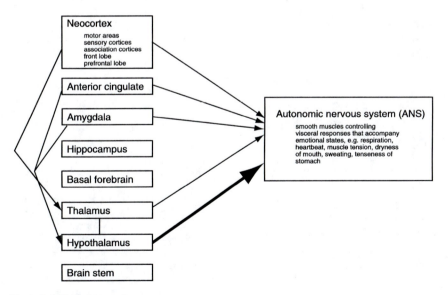

Figure 2.4 Body system 1.

presentations, or role-taking (Mead, 1934). Moreover, individuals are often unaware of their body mobilization until they role-take with others and see the responses of these others to their unconscious emission of gestures. Thus, the feedback from the arousal of an emotion system is not only internal to the individual; it often depends upon role-taking with others who are responding to the visible signs of body system mobilization. What is true of the ANS system is, as we will see, true of the other three body systems as well.

Body system 2 revolves around the release of neurotransmitters; the most important are listed in Table 2.4 and Figure 2.5. Most of the neurotransmitters involved in emotional states are released by the midbrain portions of the brain stem, usually under stimulation from other emotion systems and, as work by Drevets *et al.* (1997) underscores, under the influence of the subgenual prefrontal cortex. The basal forebrain also appears to release one neurotransmitter, acetylcholine (ACh); and it may be that the thalamus is also directly involved (Bentivoglio *et al.*, 1993). Indeed, emerging research

Table 2.4 Effects of neurotransmitters and neuroactive peptides

	Effects on brain
Neurotransmitters	
Acetylcholine (ACh)	Cortical arousal, learning, and memory as these stimulate body systems; some evidence that ACh is related to mild satisfaction
Monoamines	
dopamine	Regulates motor and hypothalamic functions and stimulates most limbic systems
noradrenaline (norepinephrine)	Enhances ability of neurons to respond to inputs and stimulates arousal
adrenaline (epinephrine)	Same as noradrenaline
serotonin	Regulates sleep–wake cycles and generates relaxation and pleasure
histamine	Not completely understood, but appears to be involved in autonomic neuroendocrine functions
Amino acids	
y-aminobutyric acid (GABA)	Inhibitory action controls outputs of neurons
glycine	Unclear, but may modulate effects of glutamate
glutamate	Causes excitatory action in neurons, including those in the limbic system
Neuroactive peptides	Of the several dozen known peptides, many are produced in the brain and act like neurotransmitters because of their small size and ability to travel in the brain's vascular system. These appear to affect a wide range of emotions stimulated by various limbic systems. The opioids appear to be particularly important in emotional responses. Larger peptides are more likely to work through the endocrine system and more inclusive circulatory system of the body. Recent data indicate that Substance *P* may be critically important in emotional responses (Wahlestedt, 1998; Kramer *et al.*, 1998), especially in relation to monoamines.

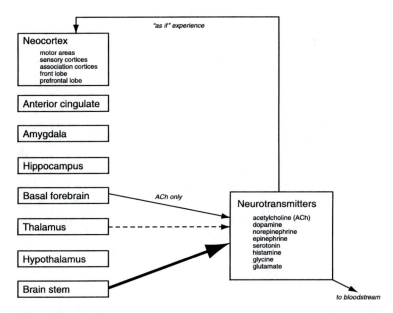

Figure 2.5 Body system 2.

appears to indicate that neurotransmitters are released in more areas outside the brain stem than was once thought to be the case. It is tempting in discussing neurotransmitters to list the mood-enhancing effects of each, as is implied in Table 2.4. For example, we might view serotonin as involved in creating a sense of well-being, relaxation, and sleep, or we might see dopamine as a stimulus to attention, arousal, and feeding. Yet, the effects of these and other neurotransmitters probably vary for each individual, and their interaction effects are not well understood. As Kety (1972:120) noted long ago: "it seems quite futile to attempt to account for a particular emotional state in terms of the activity of one or more biogenic amines. It seems more likely that these amines may function separately or in concert as crucial nodes of the complex neuronal networks . . . (but these) are probably derived from the . . . experience of the individual." Yet, because of the potential profits in pharmaceutical research on neurotransmitters, a considerable amount has been learned about their effects; and so, in the future, sociologists will be able to use this growing literature on neurotransmitters to better understand how they influence emotions.

There are two properties of neurotransmitters that are interesting to note. First, they can work very rapidly to generate an "as if" effect – as if, in the sense that the release of the neurotransmitter within the brain fools the individual into sensing that other body systems have been fully mobilized. This is why, I suspect, that individuals on antidepressant drugs that activate neurotransmitters without also mobilizing the full body system will sometimes experience emotions in a very "shallow" way, or at least individuals who role-take with them perceive the emotion to be less than real because other body systems are not mobilized in ways corresponding to the emotional mood described by an individual. Second, portions of the endocrine system operate as neuro-modulators. These are termed neuroactive peptides in Figure 2.6, and they modulate the connections between axons and dendrites. These neuroactive peptides are produced in the cell body, packaged in secretory granules, and transported from the cell body to terminals. They are released by the hypothalamus, pituitary, and closely associated areas (Heimer, 1995:388–93; Kandel *et al.*, 1995:298–301); and as they travel to target areas, they modulate the connections among neurons. In so doing, they act very much like neurotransmitters, except that they are hormones. Peptides are released all over the body, and it is becoming clear that there are many more than previously believed. There are at least fifty clearly identified, but there may well be several hundred peptides. It is only recently that their effects on the brain have become fully recognized; and further research will, no doubt, reveal their involvement in neurotransmission. They may also be generated by structures less directly involved in hypothalamic activity.

Neuroactive peptides are seen as part of the neurotransmitter body system because they are produced in and operate within the brain's vascular system. Other hormones and peptides operate through the more general endocrine system, at times coming back to the brain to exert their effects. Peptides generally work with less speed than neurotransmitters, which can be activated very rapidly (especially those, like ACh, involved in modulating muscle movements). And so, the effect of neuroactive peptides on emotions will, in general, take longer to be evident to the individual and others in his

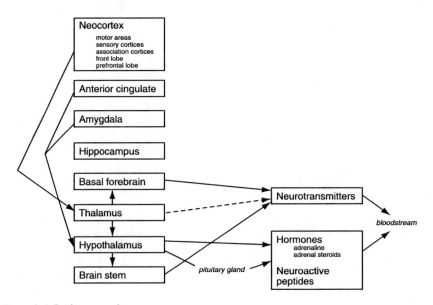

Figure 2.6 Body system 3.

or her environment; and, moreover, the effects on mood will tend to be longer lasting than those of other body systems. Much of the current research on peptides has focused on their role in various addiction problems, but they are clearly an important system in the production of emotions. For example, the opioids are much involved in creating emotions on the pleasurable side of the scale and in suppressing activation of other body systems (Smith and Stevens, 1997a, b). Yet, a great deal needs to be learned about how they operate; and for the present we can only recognize that they have important, though not fully understood, effects on human emotions.

Body system 3 involves the endocrine system and the flow of neuroactive peptides through the blood stream of the brain as well as the more inclusive vascular system of the body. The hypothalamus receives inputs from other limbic systems, and either directly or, more typically, through the pituitary gland and closely related areas, causes the release of hormones and peptides into the blood stream. As these circulate they activate the body and, as they work through and come back to the blood system of the brain, they have important feedforward and feedback effects on other limbic systems (Le Doux, 1996). These effects take time, of course, because hormones must often circulate through the body.

Body system 4 is the musculoskeletal system which involves stimulation of the striated muscles controlling skeletal structures that dictate body movements. The basic processes operating in this system are roughly outlined in Figure 2.7. Again, the hypothalamus is crucial in channeling inputs from other limbic systems into contractions of striated muscles; and because striated muscles react more rapidly than the smooth muscles of the ANS, the

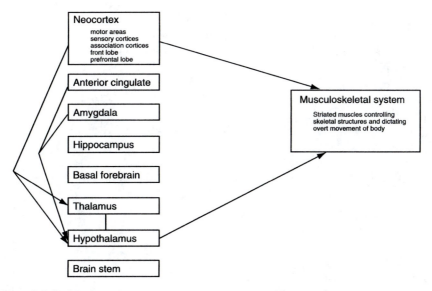

Figure 2.7 Body system 4.

emotional arousal associated with their stimulation and the feedbacks from their contraction are rapid (Le Doux, 1996). In fact, it could be hypothesized that the initial role-taking of individuals (and role-making, whether inadvertent or intentional) relies upon cues from the musculoskeletal system, especially the muscles of the face. As Ekman and various associates have clearly documented (1982, 1992b), primary emotional responses of the face do not vary dramatically cross culturally because humans all have the same muscular set up on their face, and the stimulation of the striated muscles works so rapidly (in milliseconds). Moreover, since neurotransmitters are involved in muscle contractions, reading of facial gestures will reflect both musculoskeletal and neurotransmitter body systems.

The body feedback system

Figures 2.4 through 2.7 imply that these four body systems are discrete, which in a way they are, but these systems are also very much interconnected. For example, musculoskeletal and ANS responses are facilitated by neurotransmitters; neurotransmitters are augmented by neuroactive peptides; endocrine processes are activated by the other body systems, and vice versa. Thus, the systems involved in mobilizing the body emotionally play off each other in complex ways that are not fully understood. Moreover, as *systems*, they are also involved in iterations of responses; and thus their interconnections are further complicated by the way they play off each other over time during the course of successive waves of activation and deactivation. This interconnectedness points to the importance of feedback processes in these body systems, which are so important to human emotions.

As is emphasized in Figure 2.8, these four systems feed back to the rest of the limbic system, primarily via the thalamus which, in turn, can stimulate other limbic structures and make emotional responses available to the neocortex (Le Doux, 1996). Short-term or working memory, lasting just a few seconds, can also pick up body mobilizations but these do not become full-blown feelings unless other limbic systems are activated, particularly the hippocampus. But it should be emphasized that this feedback system can remain unconscious; and individuals can literally be unaware of the emotions being aroused by their four interconnected body systems (Le Doux, 1996). Others will usually be aware of the operation of these body systems and, in fact, they will use the signals that these body systems provide as their primary bases for role-taking. Indeed, conscious awareness of emotional body systems is more a special case of the much older and primary (in an evolutionary sense) subcortical feedbacks from all four body systems.

As Le Doux (1993a, b, 1996) has emphasized for the amygdala and as is probably the case for other limbic systems, animals have an emotional memory system that is often unconscious. Just how and where such emotional responses to various stimuli are stored is unclear, but it appears that humans can maintain repertories of emotional memories and responses outside of

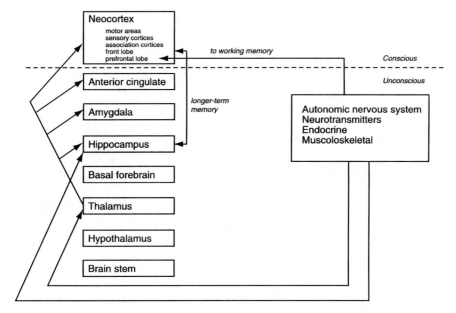

Figure 2.8 Body feedback system.

the neocortex. Figure 2.9 offers a rough approximation of the processes involved. The existence of an emotional memory system assures that many of the emotional signals emitted by a person, and read by others, will remain removed from the person's conscious thought. They will be emotions but not feelings; and, again, it can be hypothesized that these unconscious emotional memories are, in many respects, more fundamental to role-taking than conscious ones. Indeed, if others communicate to a person that they are picking up certain emotional responses or if bodily feedbacks are strong enough to penetrate consciousness as emotional feelings, the person can still be surprised that they are giving off or experiencing certain emotions and, not only surprised, but also unsure as to the source of their emotional responses. A further implication of this unconscious memory system is that it may prove difficult to disentangle repression of emotional responses from simple unawareness of emotional responses that are stored subcortically.

Consciousness and feelings

There is considerable debate over whether or not other animals possess consciousness in the human measure: awareness of internal and external stimuli, seeing self as an object, and reflection on self and sources of stimulation in an environment (e.g. Heyes, 1998). We need not enter this debate for my purposes in this appendix, although I suspect that apes and perhaps other higher mammals possess the rudiments of these cognitive capacities

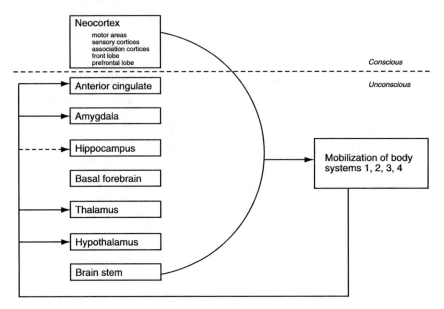

Figure 2.9 Unconscious emotional memory system.

(Savage-Rumbaugh *et al.*, 1993). The key brain structure in consciousness is the prefrontal cortex which has connections to virtually all parts of the brain: the neocortex, the limbic systems, and other subcortical systems as well (MacLean, 1990; Damasio, 1994). Consciousness of a stimulus involves receipt of an input via the sense modalities – vision, auditory, olfaction, and haptic – which then goes to a specialized sensory area of the thalamus; and from there the sensory input travels to both subcortical limbic systems and the appropriate lobe of the neocortex (Le Doux, 1996): occipital for vision, temporal for auditory, parietal for haptic, and olfactory bulb for smell (the latter, it should be noted, projects directly into subcortical areas housing the various limbic systems, especially the amygdala; and for this reason, smells can often excite emotions very rapidly). The association cortices, which comprise a good part of the neocortex and which are involved in integrating sensory inputs, generate an image that is temporarily stored in buffers (Geschwind, 1965a, b). The transition cortices consisting of the parahippocampal, perirhinal, and entorhinal cortices then pool the images and send them to the hippocampus which, in turn, creates a representation that is sent to the transition cortices for intermediate storage as a memory (Le Doux, 1996; Heimer, 1995; Gloor, 1997). After a few years, if the images are reactivated through experience or thought, the assembled images will be shipped to the neocortex, most particularly the frontal lobe, for storage as long-term memory (Damasio, 1994; Eichenbaum, 1997; Vargha-Khadem *et al.*, 1997).

The subcortical memory system is very much involved in this process, sending via the thalamus, hypothalamus, amygdala, and anterior cingulate information to the hippocampus and to the prefrontal cortex which then places this information into temporary buffers to be pooled by the transition cortices and represented by the hippocampus. Thus, consciousness almost always involves inputs from the limbic systems, either directly from limbic memories or indirectly via intermediate and long-term memories that have been previously tagged by the hippocampus with emotional inputs from the limbic body systems. Figure 2.10 delineates some of the key processes.

Feelings of emotion are simply an extension of these processes, as is outlined in Figure 2.11. What makes consciousness emotional is the arousal provided by the four body systems outlined earlier (Damasio, 1994; Le Doux, 1996). The prefrontal cortex is the central structure because it receives inputs from the four body systems, the limbic structures, the hippocampus, the sensory cortices, the association cortices, and the motor areas (Damasio, 1994). Without inputs from one or more of the emotional body systems outlined in figures 2.4 through 2.7, however, consciousness will reveal little real feeling, only abstracted and emotionally flat cognitions about feelings.

Memories involve pulling from the transition cortices and frontal lobe, via the hippocampus, coded instructions which then fire off the relevant sensory cortices. Thus, to remember does not involve pulling ready-made and fully developed pictures or images stored in the neocortex, but rather to remember involves activation of short-hand, coded instructions stored in the neocortex, or more intermediately in the transition cortices, that

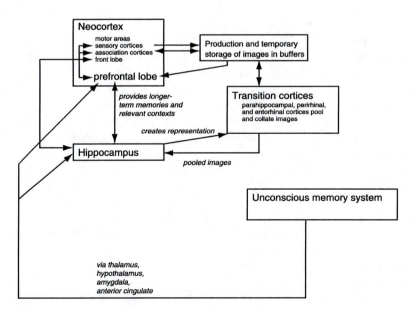

Figure 2.10 Conscious memory system.

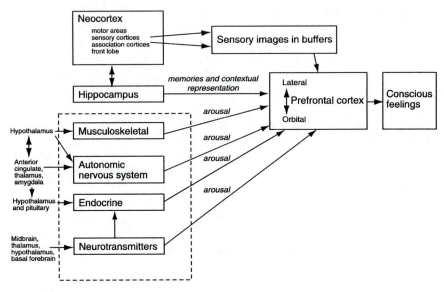

Figure 2.11 The neurology of consciousness.

reactivate the sensory cortices and the relevant body systems in order to reproduce in rough form the experience that was coded in memory (Damasio, 1994). If this experience had heavy emotional content, then reproduction of this memory will set into motion the four body systems which then give the memory much of the same emotional flavor as the original experience.

Why should sociologists care about these dynamics producing feelings? My answer is because it makes a big difference in how we conceptualize feelings in analyzing social interaction. When a person feels shame, guilt, happiness, anger, or any emotion, these feelings involve mobilization of the four body systems – from direct stimulation of the thalamus in the present and from re-firing of sensory cortices so as to re-stimulate the relevant body systems that were activated in the past. The character of the feeling is thus a complex mixture of present stimulation of limbic systems via the thalamus at subcortical and cortical levels, coupled with re-stimulation of memories that have been tagged and represented in the past by the hippocampus as coded sets of instructions which reactivate the relevant sensory cortices and body systems. But long before a person recognizes self as feeling an emotion, others in this person's environment can usually see the underlying emotions that are expressed subcortically through the body systems and that only sometimes penetrate consciousness as a feeling. Thus, a sociology of feelings is only a special case, and perhaps the less important case, of a more general and, in evolutionary terms, more primal mobilization of emotional body systems.

Thought and thinking

Sociologists and cognitive scientists tend to have, I believe, a poor model of humans as organic calculators, in which we (a) weigh options in light of the present situation and past memories, (b) assess alternatives, and (c) select lines of conduct to maximize utilities. This process is, of course, an important part of thinking; and like so much in the brain, the prefrontal cortex is critical. Damasio's (1994) review of cases reveals that damage to the prefrontal cortex appears to disrupt the capacity to plan and make rational decisions. As Damasio has also emphasized, the reason for this failing of subjects to think and behave rationally is because the prefrontal cortex is linked to both the neocortex and subcortical regions of the brain; and it is only because emotional valences are brought to bear on alternatives from various limbic systems that individuals can make "rational" decisions. Collins's (1993) emphasis on emotion as the "common denominator of rational choice" is well supported by the neurology of the brain, and this neurology revolves around the connection between cortical and subcortical emotion systems.

Another problem with sociological conceptions of thought and thinking is their verbal bias. The view that thought is internalized conversation is widespread, but a moment of reflection would reveal this to be impossible. If thinking were merely covert talk, we would seem very dimwitted because talk is a sequential modality and, hence, very slow. Moreover, we have Broca's and Wernicke's areas on the left hemisphere of the neocortex to translate auditory signals back and forth into the "brain's way of thinking," which is in patterns and gestalts. Thinking occurs in a "brain language" that, I would argue, relies heavily on the right hemisphere to produce patterns among images that can be manipulated with incredible speed and, when needed, can be converted into auditory or written speech. Moreover, we can often slow the process of thinking down by "talking to ourselves" but this kind of thinking is the exception rather than the rule of thinking.

A further speculation on why thinking occurs in patterns and configurations stems from the fact that, unlike most mammals that are olfactory dominant, humans are a primate and, hence, are visually dominant (Forbes and King, 1982); and, as I noted earlier, the association cortices at the point where the temporal, occipital, and parietal lobes meet – areas such as the inferior parietal lobe – involve integration of sensory information under vision (Geschwind, 1965a, b). This subordination of other sensory inputs under vision shapes, I believe, the way humans think: as blurs of images, many of which do not penetrate our consciousness.

Emotions are very much a part of these images, above and beyond the values that they may give various options that might be considered when individuals try to make decisions. Whether from the transition cortices and hippocampus or pulled up from the subcortical emotional memory system, thought involves a constant tagging of images with emotional valences. But these emotional tags are not always accessed by consciousness; indeed, I would guess that the vast majority of thought does not occur in ways about which we are conscious, and to the extent that emotions are part of "the brain's way of thinking," we do not have easy access to the emotions that are indeed structuring in unknown ways human thinking. Only when we become consciously aware of feelings which we represent to ourselves in words do we become self-aware of how emotions are implicated in thinking. But it may well be that others can "read our thoughts" in ways that we cannot, because if the emotional valences are high, mobilization of body systems can tip others off as to what emotions are behind our thinking, long before we become aware of our own emotional responses.

Thus, to the extent that sociologists are concerned with thinking as it influences the flow of interpersonal behavior and, ultimately, the kinds of cultural and social systems that are built from interactions, it is essential to know something about how the process occurs at a more neurological level. If the above speculations seem plausible, then the way we study interaction would shift away from a talk and general verbal bias to a non-verbal, emotional emphasis which, as I have argued in this chapter, was the first language system among hominids and, later, humans.

The self

Let me illustrate this conclusion with an argument about how to reconceptualize self. We see ourselves as objects in situations primarily via the right brain which generates pattern recognition in space; and our image of ourselves in situations is heavily biased toward spatial representations of where we are. As to *who* we are in a situation, this involves role-taking with others and bringing forth more enduring concepts of self. Like any cognition that comes from memory, self cognitions have been tagged with emotions, and, at the same time, they may re-stimulate sensory cortices, especially the visual, and re-mobilize limbically stimulated body systems. Thus, humans see themselves not only in Cooley's looking glass and thereby derive a "self-feeling," they also invoke their memory and emotion systems to enhance this self-feeling. Much of the emotion invoked, however, may not be a feeling at all, in the sense that it remains subcortical and can, therefore, only be read by others who tune into the mobilization of others' body systems in their role-taking.

The difficulty in measuring self is related to our verbally biased measuring instruments, which are too crude given the complexity of the processes involved. Moreover, the problem of measurement also resides in the unavailability of measuring instruments for gaining access to subcortical emotional states and to the emotionally laden thoughts of individuals as they think in the visually biased "brain's way of thinking." Others can often do a better job of assessing our self because they can see mobilization of our emotional body systems; sometimes an individual can gain access to these by having an emotional feeling of self as an object in a field of objects, but these feelings are frequently difficult to interpret because they come from subcortical, limbic memories. Indeed people are often surprised by their conscious feelings, wondering where they came from. Thus, self is not so much a cognitive construct as an activation of the emotion systems implicated in storing memories in the frontal lobe, in thought processes couched in the brain's way of thinking, in subcortical emotional memory system, and in the reactivation of the emotional body systems. Given the complexity of these dynamics, it is not surprising that people oftentimes do not know who they are or where they stand; or to state the matter less dramatically, they have difficulty giving verbal expression to cortical and subcortical processes that are occurring outside of their working memory.

Implications for studying interpersonal processes

Role-making and role-taking are, on the one hand, conscious processes of responding to situational cues and bodily signals through the use of working and longer-term memory systems. On the other hand, role-making and role-taking are subcortical and unconscious processes of responding to cues and signals through activation of the emotional body systems outlined in figures 2.4 through 2.7. The dimensions of role-taking and role-making are not opposed and, in fact, they often become intermingled as limbic processes penetrate the working memory as feelings, or as limbic processes are given conscious interpretations through vocabularies of motives and emotions during self talk. Understanding something of the neurology of the brain and bodily systems adds, I believe, some useful insights to theorizing about interpersonal processes. Let me enumerate a few.

Much of what occurs during the course of interaction is subcortical, revolving around mutual emissions of signals via the body systems and, reciprocally, responding to these signals limbically. I would go so far as to argue that most of the emotional dynamics of interaction operate subcortically, and only under relatively high degrees of emotional mobilization do limbic processes become part of conscious feelings. Moreover, in terms of sustaining a sense of interpersonal contact, focus, tracking, and rhythm, I suggest that role-taking and role-making subcortically are more important than talk, rhythmic conversational turn-taking, and conscious reflection. Even if this extreme conclusion is not accepted, sociology needs a more neurologically informed conceptualization of non-verbal, "body language" processes.

At a neurological level, our most hard-wired and ancient emotion system is the amygdala, especially those older portions activating fear responses. A species that does not possess fear would soon be selected out by predators; and since aggression is also part of the amygdala and, indeed, part of the fear response as defensive aggression, fear and aggression are humans' most fundamental emotions (Le Doux, 1996). Indeed, separate nuclei in the amygdala appear to be involved in different types of fear conditioning (Killcross *et al.*, 1997). One implication of this fact is that humans are especially attuned both cortically and subcortically to signals of fear and aggression. Among hominids, these amygdala-generated emotions were, no doubt, used to overcome weak-tie propensities and, thereby, to build social structure on the basis of fears about receiving negative sanctions (with such sanctions being expressions of anger by those doing the sanctioning). Thus, individuals are particularly attuned to negative sanctions, and these sanctions have the most power to affect us emotionally; and this is so because they are ancient and hard-wired. If a low-sociality primate had to build conformity to moral codes, keep individuals in line, force them to stay alert to others and the rules of the situation, and pay attention to breaches of codes and interpersonal cues, then negative sanctions as they activate fear responses would be an effective means to build some degree of structure in hominids that were biologically disposed to individualism and loose-group structures.

Yet, activation of fear and use of negative sanctions are very costly, in several senses: these emotions can consume physical and emotional energy as body systems are mobilized; they can ratchet up anger-aggression to heightened levels as those who receive negative sanctions become angry, while those seeking to sanction become even more angry over the aggression from those they have attempted to sanction; they can eventually activate depression, whether through use of defense mechanisms or alterations in the release of neurotransmitters and neuroactive peptides; and they can cause maladaptive and anti-social behaviors. Thus, solidarity and cohesion cannot be built on fear and aggression alone.

Once it is recognized that selection worked to create more associative or positive emotions to build sociality and solidarity, some of the rewiring of the amygdala for pleasure, and the septum as well, makes sense. Moreover, the expansion of the anterior cingulate gyrus, as the center for playfulness and mother–infant bonding, may also have been rewired to produce a more generalized source for happiness and propensities for bonding, altruism, and reciprocity. Add to these the possible reconfiguration neurotransmitter, hormones, and neuroactive peptides to generate more pleasurable emotional responses, and we can see that much of the rewiring of the human brain is the result of selection creating centers for associative emotions. Such emotions are the backbone of positive sanctions which are much more likely to produce solidarity than negative sanctions because the former activate pleasure, satisfaction, happiness, and other variants and combinations of the satisfaction-happiness emotions listed in tables 1.2 and 1.3. Yet, at the same time, we must recognize that these are a late evolutionary add-on, working around more primal emotions of fear and anger. Thus, more positive emotions are, I argue, always layered over potentially negative ones; and so, positive sanctions always contain the implicit threat that if these do not work more negative ones will follow.

Moreover, to the extent that positive emotions come from neuroactive peptides and hormonal circulation in the blood stream they will tend to work less rapidly, even if only a few seconds slower than fear and anger responses mobilizing musculoskeletal and neurotransmitter responses; and while this may not seem like much time, it is an eternity in neurological time and even in interpersonal real time where individuals read and respond to gestures in milliseconds. Thus, fear and anger are much more likely to emerge rapidly, moods of happiness and its variants will take a bit more time, although neurotransmitter activation can also occur rapidly. Moreover, fear and anger will immediately activate the musculoskeletal body systems long before happiness will have done so. A smile takes a bit longer to form than a frown, and the reasons for this is that the latter is being activated by the amygdala whereas the former is the product of several neurological systems, some of which take more time.

As implied in the above remarks, the four body systems work at different speeds, and this fact has implications for how people role-make and role-take. The musculoskeletal system is the fastest; although neurotransmitters like ACh must be released to contract muscles; in milliseconds, the striated muscles can contract under stimulus, move an organism, and in the case of humans and higher primates become an emotional response and, perhaps in humans alone, a conscious feeling. Thus, the first and fastest signals that individuals mutually send out and receive are musculoskeletal, particularly the muscles of the face. Thus, we first seek, if only subcortically, information about the operation of the musculoskeletal system, and the effects of neuro-transmitters on that system. The other emotion systems take longer, again sometimes less than a second but often several seconds to much longer time spans. Aside from the neurotransmitters facilitating motor responses, they can also have mood-enhancing effects in "as if" feeling, but these must often become involved in iterations of bodily feedback to exert their full effect. The hormone-peptide system can also work fairly rapidly, especially under stimulation for fear by the amygdala, but the opioid hormones producing pleasure appear to take longer to generate their effects. The ANS system is primarily a fear system, working as rapidly as smooth muscles can under stimulation by the amygdala and release of neurotransmitters affecting stimulation of muscles, although more pleasurable states of the ANS take longer, especially when other body systems must also be activated. More-over, ANS activation for more associative emotions often involves conscious interpretation of what is occurring and, as a consequence, this process takes a considerable amount of time, again neurologically speaking. Thus, outside of "as if" neurotransmitter effects, contentment and happiness require longer to form in humans; and we all implicitly recognize this in our role-taking where we initially scan, usually subcortically, for aggression-anger, while waiting a bit for more associative responses to form (if the situation dictates that they should). Augmenting Collins's (1975, 1988, 2004) theory, I would also venture the speculation that rituals are often necessary to kick-start positive emotional energy because the human emotion system is still trying to work around the more ancient fear–aggression systems.

Sadness is the last of the primary emotions listed in Table 1.2. And, in many ways, it is the most complicated because no clear center for this emotion exists in the human brain, although recent evidence indicates the amygdala in its integration functions and the subgenual area of the pre-frontal cortex appear to bring on clinical depression when damaged (Drevets *et al.*, 1997; Damasio, 1997). Yet, even with recent findings of hard-wired centers, sadness may still be an emotion that comes from con-figurations of neurotransmitters, neuroactive peptides, and other hormones, or, more typically, from a lack of such activity in neurotransmitters like serotonin, dopamine, norepinephrine and from endocrine processes that work through the blood circulation system. It thus takes longer to form, especially if it also involves stress hormones or the suppression of hormones involved in the production of more positive emotional states. Also, defense mechanisms are often implicated as individuals consume emotional and physical energy through repression or otherwise dealing with highly unpleasant emotions such as anger, fear, guilt, and shame (see chapters 3 and 4). Thus, while sudden disappointment may operate very rapidly on the musculoskeletal system, as facilitated by neurotransmitters like ACh responding to stimulation by the amygdala, the "mood" of being sad takes considerably more time to form, anywhere from a few seconds to hours as neurotransmitter release is suppressed and as hormones/peptides operate through the bloodstream to dampen emotional energy.

We might ask a further question: Why would there be selection for sadness beyond mild disappointment? One answer is that sadness is simply a by-product of depression of neurotransmitters, neuroactive peptides, and, as recent imaging studies reveal, underactivation of the subgenual prefrontal cortex as well (Drevets *et al.*, 1997). Another answer is that sadness is a very effective mechanism of social control. For example, guilt and shame are often the outcome when a person senses that they have made others unhappy or sad by not meeting expectations; and so moral codes and con-formity to them are built not just on positive and negative sanctions but also more complex sanctioning practices that avoid the full mobilization of anger. Sadness is a very effective negative sanction because it does not con-tain the volatility of anger-based negative sanctions; and it is effective as a direct sanctioning technique by others, while, at the same time, often evok-ing sadness in the person who feels that they have failed to meet others' or their own expectations (recall from Table 1.4 that sadness is the dominant emotion in guilt, shame, and alienation). Thus, guilt, shame, and other emo-tions like alienation where sadness is a dominant component are probably more than a by-product of suspension of other emotional responses; sadness is a key to social control revolving around negative sanctioning that avoids the volatility of anger and fear, although these latter emotions are part of complex second-order elaborations like shame, guilt, and alienation.

Thus, this provisional list of implications should arouse sociologists' interest in the neurology of emotions. Much remains unknown about emotions, but over the next decade advances in neurology will come very rapidly; and it is important for sociologists to be on the ground floor of future breakthroughs. We cannot simply see the brain as a black box, because to do so limits our understanding of face-to-face interaction. So many concepts in sociology are vague, metaphorical, and perhaps wrong because we operate in ignorance of biology. If micro sociology is not to be left behind, it needs to become more neurologically informed. In the above, I may have certain things wrong, but the critical point is that sociologists studying emotions cannot ignore their biological basis, nor (in my view) the selection forces that wired hominids to be so emotional.

3 Social structure, culture, and emotions

Just as emotional dynamics are embedded in human biology and the selection processes that generated this biology, so emotions are embedded in social structure and culture. We are now on more familiar terrain for sociologists, but surprisingly, sociology in general and the sociology of emotions in particular reveal relatively little consensus over the nature of culture and social structure. Most approaches in the sociology of emotions view structure in relatively narrow terms, typically as status (prestige) and power (authority) within a group or relatively small network. In contrast, the incorporation of culture is somewhat more expansive, focusing upon emotion ideologies and vocabularies, feeling and display rules, expectation states, and norms of justice. Still, even though conceptualizations of culture are more macro, most work in sociology on emotions is decidedly micro in emphasis and pays comparatively little attention to the meso- and macro-level forces and structures that determine the distribution of power and status or the emotion vocabularies, ideologies, and rules that govern encounters in small groups.

Indeed, in a good portion of empirical studies, the groups themselves are virtual, with individuals interacting with computer algorithms rather than real people face to face. This emphasis on the micro is, of course, not entirely misplaced since it is generally at the level of the encounter that emotions are aroused, but if we are to have a more robust sociological theory of emotions, we need to pay attention to the broader context in which encounters are embedded. Moreover, if we are to fully understand the effects of emotional arousal at the micro level on meso and macrostructures, we need a broader vision of the conduits by which emotions affect meso and macrostructures (and their respective cultures), and vice versa. Thus, emotions are systematically generated under sociocultural conditions and, once aroused, they have effects on these conditions. We require, therefore, a conceptual scheme on which we can hang a theory.

A simplified conceptual model of social structure and culture

In recent years, I have been working with the model portrayed in Figure 3.1. This model reflects two general assumptions with which I begin most analyses of social processes. Let me briefly enumerate these assumptions.

Levels of social reality

In my view, social reality unfolds at three levels: (1) the micro level of the encounter, (2) the meso level of corporate and categoric units, and (3) the macro level of institutional domains, stratification systems, whole societies, and systems of societies. This tri–part division of reality is an ana–lytical distinction, to be sure, but it is also the way that social *reality itself* unfolds.

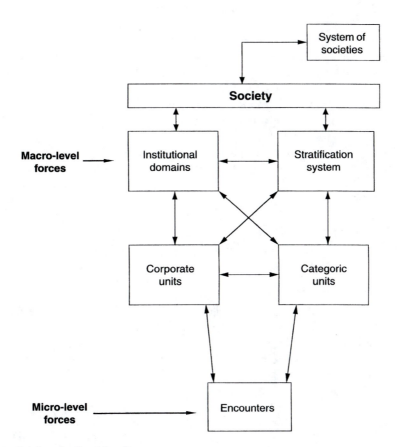

Figure 3.1 Levels of social reality.

Micro-level social reality

I follow Erving Goffman's (1959, 1961, 1963, 1967, 1971, 1983) view of encounters as episodes of face-to-face interaction; and I also accept his division of encounters as being of two basic types: focused and unfocused. The properties of focused encounters are a single visual and cognitive focus of attention, mutual and preferential openness to verbal communication, heightened mutual relevance of acts, eye-to-eye ecological huddle coupled with mutual perception and monitoring of behaviors, ritual and ceremonial punctuation of openings, closings, entrances, and exits, an emergent "we" feeling, emotional arousal, and procedures for corrective compensation of deviant acts (Goffman, 1961, 1967). In contrast, unfocused encounters revolve around mutual monitoring and the avoidance of eye-to-eye contact as individuals move about in public space (Goffman, 1963, 1971).

Meso-level social reality

At the meso level of social organization are two basic types of structures: corporate and categoric units. This distinction is one that I borrow from Amos Hawley (1986). A corporate unit is a structure revealing a division of labor organized to pursue goals, no matter how ephemeral the goals may be. There are only three basic types of meso-level corporate units: organizations, communities, and groups. A categoric unit is a social distinction that affects how individuals are evaluated and treated by others. The only universal categoric units are age and sex/gender, but as societies become more complex and differentiated, new kinds of categoric units emerge – social classes and ethnicity, for example. This conception of categoric units is much the same as Peter Blau's (1977, 1994) view of graduated (income, age, education) and nominal (gender, ethnicity) "parameters" and compatible with Miller McPherson's conception of "Blau-space" in which social structures are conceptualized by the number of parameters defining ecological niches, the distribution of people across these parameters, and the networks among individuals in Blau-space (McPherson and Ranger-Moore, 1991).

The macro level of social reality

The macro level of social reality is composed of institutional domains and stratification systems, societies, and inter-societal systems. Institutional domains are those society-wide structures – economy, polity, kinship, religion, law, science, medicine, education, and the like – that have evolved as adaptations to external and internal environmental contingencies. Stratification systems revolve around the unequal distribution of resources among members of a population, the formation of subpopulations or classes on the basis of individuals' respective shares of resources, and the differential evaluation of individuals by virtue of their respective shares of resources.

Societies are geo-political units composed of institutional domains and stratification systems, while inter-societal systems are relations between societies, generally through interactions between key institutional domains such as economy and polity and, at times, through the stratification systems of interconnected societies.

Social forces

A second assumption that I make is that there are forces systematically generating social structures and their cultures. These forces are summarized in Table 3.1. At the macro level, these forces drive the formation and operation of institutional domains and stratification systems, as well as the societies and inter-societal systems that house them. The key forces at the macro level are population, production, distribution, regulation, and reproduction (see Turner, 1995, 2002, 2003 for a review and theory of these forces). At first, it may seem odd to conceptualize the social world in terms of forces, but if we are concerned with how social structures at the macro level are generated, there must be forces that push individual and collective actors to create particular kinds of structures. Actors are always responding to selection pressures, or needs to adapt to contingencies, and these selection pressures come from forces. For example, population growth generates selection pressures to find new modes of production or new forms of political governance; and as actors respond to these pressures they create or change institutional domains and stratification systems. My view of forces is very similar to how they are conceptualized in biology (e.g. the forces of evolution) or physics (e.g. gravity, electromagnetism); these are properties of the social universe that push actors to organize in particular ways, or face the disintegrative consequences.

As actors seek to respond to selection pressures, they generally build meso-level structures, or corporate and categoric units. To respond to particular problems or contingencies generally requires a new kind of structure to organize collective action. Thus, at one time in hominid or human evolution, selection pressures for production and reproduction prompted hunter-gatherers to create (1) bands composed of (2) nuclear families – two types of corporate units – to replace what I visualized as the pre-kinship horde in the last chapter. In so doing, distinctions between gender and age – as the first two categoric units – were organized by the division of labor in family and band. In more complex societies, the same basic processes are at work. For example, population growth generated selection pressures for new forms of community, new patterns of regulation through the consolidation of power, new productive units beyond kinship, new forms of distribution, and eventually, new reproductive units outside of kinship; at each step along the way, additional corporate and categoric units have emerged – thereby increasing the overall level of differentiation in human societies. Today, in the post-industrial world, corporate units and many kinds of categoric units are

Table 3.1 Forces driving the formation and operation of the social universe

Macro–level forces

Population	The number, rate of growth, composition, and distribution of people in a society.
Production	The gathering of resources from the environment, their conversion into commodities, and the creation of services to facilitate gathering and conversion in a society.
Distribution	The construction of infrastructures to move resources, information, and people in space as well as the use of exchange systems to distribute resources, information, and people with and between societies.
Regulation	The consolidation and centralization of power to coordinate and control among members and the units organizing members' activities in a society.
Reproduction	The procreation of new members of a population and the transmission of culture to these members as well as the creation and maintenance of sociocultural systems that sustain life and social order in a society.

Micro–level forces

Emotions	The arousal of variants and combinations of satisfaction-happiness, aversion-fear, assertion-anger, and disappointment-sadness in individuals.
Transactional needs	The activation of needs to verify self and identities, to receive positive exchange payoffs, to sense group inclusion (in the ongoing interpersonal flow), to achieve a sense of trust (predictability, respect, and sincerity) from others, and to achieve a sense of facticity (intersubjectivity and sense that things are as they appear).
Normatizing	The application of culture so as to categorize others and the situation, develop frames delimiting and specifying what is to transpire in the situation, use rituals (open, close, form, and repair interactions) to regulate the flow of interaction, establish forms of communication (talk and body language) in the situation, calculate and assess just shares of resources in a situation, and establish feelings to be experienced and displayed by persons in a situation.
Roles	The presentation of sequences of gestures marking a predictable course of action (role-making) by an individual as well as the reading and interpreting of the gestures emitted by others to understand the course of action of others in a situation (role-taking).
Status	The placement and differential evaluation of individuals in positions vis-à-vis other positions occupied by others in a situation.
Demographic	The number of people co-present, their characteristics, density, and movements in a situation as well as the meanings associated with number, characteristics, density, and movement.
Ecological	The boundaries, partitions, and props organizing the space among individuals in a situation as well as the meanings of these boundaries, partitions, and props.

systematically generated as actors respond to the selection pressures imposed by the macro-dynamic forces listed in Table 3.1.

At the micro level are the forces of emotional arousal, transactional needs, symbols, status, roles, demography, and ecology; and these forces drive the formation and operation of encounters. They can also shape the formation and operation of meso-level corporate and categoric units. On the one hand, these micro-level forces shape the flow of interpersonal behavior in encounters; and in so doing they reproduce or, potentially, change the division of labor of corporate units or the distinctions and evaluations of categoric units. As people interact face to face, they arouse emotions as they build up cultural symbols, create positions and develop roles to be played in these positions, organize actions in space using various props (ecology), and create new categoric distinctions (demography); and as these micro-level forces are played out, encounters create, sustain, or change corporate and categoric units. On the other hand, as I will emphasize in a moment, the dynamic forces of encounters are constrained by existing corporate and categoric units.

Thus, the macro and micro levels of reality have their own unique sets of forces that drive the formation and change of the structures unique to these two levels. At one time, I posited meso-level forces (Turner, 2002, 2003), but I have come to view the structures of the meso level – that is, corporate and categoric units – as standing at the intersection between macro and micro forces. They are the place where macro and micro forces meet, and their structure and operation will be a joint outcome of the forces operating at the macro and micro levels. For example, a class categoric unit is generated by all of the forces at the macro level of social organization, while being sustained or potentially changed as individuals respond to members of categoric units (or to "diffuse status" characteristic in expectation-states theory) in face-to-face encounters. Similarly, a corporate unit, such as a company in the economy, is driven by at least the macro-dynamic forces of production and distribution, while the division of labor is sustained or changed by micro-level forces – say, patterns of emotional arousal or failure to meet fundamental transactional needs.

Embedding of social structures

A third assumption that follows from the above is that structures are embedded inside of each other. Encounters are embedded in corporate and categoric units which are embedded in institutional domains and stratification systems that are, in turn, embedded in whole societies and systems of societies. Embedding imposes constraints from the larger to smaller structure. Thus, institutional domains and stratification systems are constrained by the structure and culture of whole societies or systems of societies; corporate units are constrained by institutional domains and, at times, by the stratification system in which they are lodged; categoric units are constrained by the stratification systems and, often, by institutional domains as these generate categoric distinctions; and encounters are constrained by the culture and structure of the corporate and categoric units in which they are embedded. Thus, the dynamics of any structural unit will revolve around: (1) the macro- and micro-dynamic forces that drive a unit's formation and operation; and (2) the constraints imposed by the structure and culture of the units within which a smaller unit is embedded. For example, an episode of face-to-face interaction will be driven by micro-level forces listed in Table 3.1 and by the division of labor of the corporate unit *and* the properties of the categoric units in which this episode of face-to-face interaction is embedded.

As we will see in later chapters, a theory of emotions needs to take account of the specific properties of corporate and categoric units in which emotion-arousing encounters are embedded. The emotions aroused are constrained by the structure and culture of these meso-level units; and it is through these meso units that the structure and culture of macro-level social reality − that is, institutional domains, stratification systems, societies, and systems of societies − impinge on people in face-to-face interaction. The structures of the meso level are, in essence, conduits for the culture and structure of the macro realm as it filters down and constrains the forces driving micro-level encounters.

The constitution of reality

A fourth assumption is that meso-level units are ultimately built from the bottom up by encounters, while at the macro level, institutional domains are constructed from networks of corporate units and stratification systems are assembled from categoric units. This constitutive aspect of social reality operates much like embedding because forces of the micro realm, as they affect the formation, reproduction, or change of corporate and categoric units, can have more distal effects on the macro-level structures that are built from corporate and categoric units. For example, high levels of emotional arousal at the micro level in iterated encounters over "racism" (the negative evaluation and treatment of members of a categoric unit) can cause the formation of a social movement organization (a corporate unit) that exerts pressure on the political, legal, and economic institutional domains to change their culture and structure which, in turn, places pressures for change on the stratification created by institutions as they distribute resources unequally. If successful, this movement may change the structure and culture of a whole society and, potentially, a system of societies. Indeed, as we will see, emotional arousal is the most powerful force in these kinds of bottom-up dynamics by which the micro alters the meso and macrostructures of a society.

Most of the time, however, embedding imposes powerful constraints on micro-level processes. As a result, the dynamics of encounters work to reproduce corporate and categoric units and, hence, the macro-level structures built from meso-level structures. But at times, under conditions that a theory should be able to specify, emotional arousal at the level of iterated encounters spreads through networks of meso structures, changing key corporate and categoric units or perhaps creating new meso-level structures, that change macro-level structures. If this kind of process did not occur, societies would be stagnant, which obviously they are not.

Culture and social structure

A fifth assumption, which perhaps does not need to be mentioned because it is so obviously true, is that all social structures evidence culture. From a top-down vantage point, culture flows down from macro to meso, and then from meso to micro. Thus, the process of "normatization" at the level of the encounter will be constrained by the ideologies, norms, symbolic media, and technologies of corporate units and the ideologies used to make evaluations of categoric units. Similarly, the culture of a corporate unit will generally represent an adaptation to a particular environment of the institutional domain in which it is embedded and, at times, by the culture of the social classes and class factions of the stratification system from which the personnel of a corporate unit are drawn. In the same vein, a categoric unit will be defined and evaluated by the culture of key institutional domains (ideologies, symbolic media, and norms) that influence resource distribution in a society and by the culture of the stratification system as a whole as well as by the culture of classes and class factions within the stratification system.

Figure 3.2 outlines my general view of the levels of culture that correspond to the levels of social structure. From a top-down perspective, general values, technologies, and texts are adapted to institutional spheres in the form of ideologies (evaluative standards about what should and ought to occur in a domain), institutional norms about how individuals are to behave when acting in a domain (e.g. norms for mother, father, worker, politician, scientist, teacher, and the like), generalized symbolic media of exchange and discourse (e.g. power, money, love, knowledge) within a domain. Similarly, ideologies, norms, and generalized media also direct behaviors of individuals at different class or class-faction locations in the stratification system. In turn, these ideologies, norms, and media are used to structure the division of labor of corporate units and the definitions, relative evaluations, and expectations for individuals who are members of categoric units. And, all of these become the cultural resources that are used to normatize encounters.

Reciprocally, from a bottom-up perspective, encounters can challenge, reinforce, and, potentially, change the culture of corporate and categoric units; and if sufficient change occurs at the meso level, then the culture of institutional domains, stratification systems, and the society as a whole can be also altered. As we will see, it is the emotions aroused at the level of the encounter that ultimately are the fuel driving these bottom-up forces of change in the culture of meso and macrostructures. For most encounters,

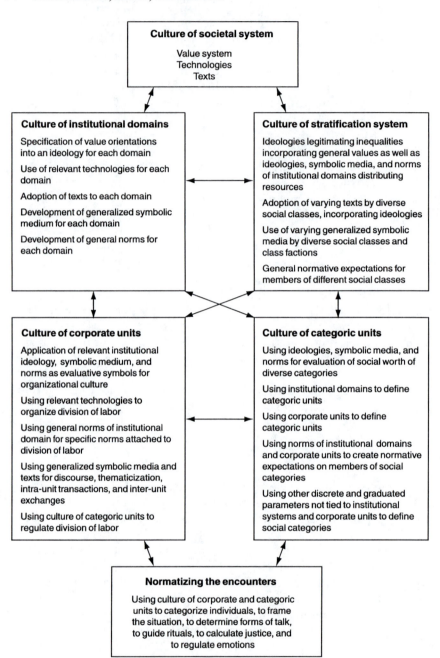

Figure 3.2 Culture and levels of social reality.

however, the culture of mesostructures is reinforced and reproduced which, in turn, sustains culture at the macro level of social organization.

Keeping conceptual schemes simple

The conceptual schemes in figures 3.1 and 3.2 are obviously very simple. It is important, I believe, to keep the conceptual scheme this simple and, then, introduce complexity in the form of propositions or principles describing key dynamics. When schemes become too complex, theorizing becomes excessively concerned with sustaining the architecture of the scheme, as was the case for Talcott Parsons's (1968 [1937], 1951, 1978) ever-evolving action theory. Moreover, when the conceptual scheme is complex, it becomes necessary to make commitments to the vision of the world denoted by the scheme – something that people may not be willing to do. The scheme that I have offered in figures 3.1 and 3.2 only commits the reader to a view of the universe as unfolding at three levels, with levels embedded in each other while, at the same time, providing the building blocks for each successive level of reality. In fact, no commitments to the scheme are essential because the theory will be stated as propositions and use much of the vocabulary of existing theories, rather than the distinctions marked by the conceptual scheme in figures 3.1 and 3.2.

I am not out to vindicate my scheme; it is only a device for getting started. The power of the theory will reside in propositions and principles rather than in analytical distinctions made by a conceptual framework. The goal of my theory is to explain how specific properties of corporate and categoric units, as they constrain encounters, influence the arousal of specific emotions that have effects on meso and macrostructures and culture.

The importance of a comprehensive conceptual scheme

As I noted earlier, the sociology of emotions reveals a clear micro bias which, from one perspective, is appropriate because, as outlined in Table 3.1, I see emotions as one of the micro-dynamic forces shaping the flow of inter- action in encounters. Moreover, most theories of emotions examine the effects of status, roles, transactional needs (like the need to verify self and identities), and expectations on emotional arousal – again an appropriate emphasis. For, as Table 3.1 documents, the forces driving the formation and operation of encounters correspond to many of the points of emphasis in various theories – status, roles, self, norms, expectations, diffuse status charac- teristics. But, if we are to understand the sociology of emotions, we must recognize that encounters and the forces driving them are embedded within meso-level corporate and categoric units that, in turn, are embedded in institutional domains and stratification systems within whole societies and perhaps even systems of societies. The distribution of power and prestige in status, the culture that is brought to bear, the emotion ideologies, the rules and vocabularies, the ecology of space, and the demography of the situation are all constrained by *specific properties* of corporate and categoric units. The structure of the division of labor within corporate units (e.g. size, hierarchy, boundedness, formality) and the properties of categoric units (e.g. discreteness, differential evaluation) load the values for the forces driving encounters; and so, if we are to develop a sociological theory of emotions, we must understand how embedding has these effects.

Conversely, the emotions aroused within encounters can target a relatively small range of potential objects: self, other(s), encounter, corporate unit, categoric unit, institutional domain, stratification system, society, and system of society. A sociological theory needs to be able to explain not only the kinds of emotions aroused under specific sociocultural conditions, but it also must explain *which* emotions with *what* level of intensity and with *what* degree of persistence will be directed at *what* potential targets. Some emotions stay local, circulating in self-appraisals, reactions to others, or feelings about the encounter; other emotions target the structure and culture of corporate and categoric units and even beyond to the institutional domains, stratification system, society, and, potentially, system of societies. A sociological theory should be able to explain such diverse processes as self-loathing and depression, anger at others, vengeance on institutional structures, anger over the injustices in the distribution of resources with the stratification system, social movements fueled by anger and injustice, or acts of terrorism driven by righteous anger; and, conversely, a theory should explain commitments to meso and macrostructures.

The simple conceptual scheme in Figure 3.1 gives us a roadmap as to the immediate structures that constrain the arousal of emotions in encounters and the range of potential targets of emotions, once aroused. This is, of course, a tall order and a large terrain to cover, but the goal of theory is to simplify matters by presenting very abstract principles that are not tied to specific empirical cases. Thus, in the pages to follow, I will use the conceptual roadmap outlined in this chapter to chart my course, but the power of the theory will inhere in many specific propositions and hypotheses consolidated into a relatively small set of very abstract principles. If the theory is useful, it should not have too many propositions, but it should have enough to cover the terrain that the conceptual scheme covers.

Causal effects within and across levels of sociocultural reality

The theory to be developed will specify in greater detail the connections among the forces and the structures that they generate at each level of reality. Before moving into the theory itself, let me pause for a moment to summarize in somewhat more detail causal connections denoted by the arrows connecting the boxes in the conceptual schemes presented in figures 3.1 and 3.2.

Societal and inter-societal systems

Societies are composed of their institutional domains and stratification systems that are built, respectively, from corporate and categoric units which in turn are built and sustained by encounters. A society will evidence a cultural system, composed of texts (traditions, modes of discourse, language), technologies (knowledge about how to manipulate the environment), values (moral codes of good and bad). These elements of culture are, in turn, translated into the cultures of institutional domains and stratification systems and the corporate and categoric units from which these domains and stratification systems are built (and, of course, ultimately into the norms of the encounter). More specifically, macro-level cultural values become ideologies of particular institutional domains (e.g. economy, polity, kinship, religion, law, science, medicine, education, etc.) that specify what should and ought to occur in each domain. Similarly, the ideologies legitimating the unequal distribution of resources and overall stratification system (e.g. income and wealth should come "from hard work," or to those who "make contributions" to society) as well as specific classes or class factions in this system are typically drawn from the value premises of the society and the ideologies of institutional domains that distribute resources. When whole societies are part of a system of societies, it is typically corporate units within institutional domains that become the conduit for moving information, people, and resources across the borders of one society into another. Thus, conquest and political subjugation of one population by another are primarily the result of coercive mobilization of power within the corporate units comprising the institution of polity; or trade is most typically conducted by the corporate units of each nation's economy. Migration patterns across borders of nation states are often families moving from one society to the location of extended kin in another society. Stratification systems also can be involved in inter-societal relations as when, for example, lower class migrants leave one nation for opportunities in another. As relations among societies are developed, their respective cultures are often exported or, as is often the case, a more general set of inter-societal values and ideologies is created that feeds back and affects the institutional domains and stratification systems of each society.

It may be difficult to see how causal effects at these most macro levels have consequences for emotional arousal at the micro level of the encounter. Yet, a moment's reflection signals that many emotions aroused in encounters are indeed related to these macro-level processes. For instance, anger over outsourcing, needs to vent righteous anger by terrorists on the people and institutions of another society, fears about the consequences of migration patterns, and many other emotional states are ultimately connected to societal and inter-society dynamics. Social movements, riots, terrorist attacks, and other volatile processes are thus often fueled by emotions that have been generated in iterated encounters lodged in macro structures.

Institutional domains and stratification systems

The arrows connecting these two macro-level structures indicate that the same forces drive the formation of each – that is, population size and composition, production, distribution, regulation and power, and reproduction. For instance, power involves not only the formation of polity, but once polity exists it has large effects on the distribution of valued resources such as power, money, and prestige. Or, production as it generates a division of labor at the level of corporate units determines how much income and wealth individuals and families can accumulate. The same is true of distribution as a force. Reproductive structures determine the credentials that can be marketed in labor markets and in the corporate units of the economy; and in capitalist economies, reproductive institutions like education also determine people's access to jobs, income, and prestige. Thus, as the forces of the macro realm generate and sustain the operation of institutional domains, these domains determine the nature of the stratification systems and the categoric units from which such systems are ultimately constructed.

The converse is also true. The distribution of income and wealth, the formation of classes, and the distribution of categoric units across classes (ethnicity and gender, for example) have effects on the operation of each institutional domain. For example, a large low-wage, lower-class pool of ethnic labor changes the labor market (and hence distributive dynamics) as well as the division of labor in corporate units within the economy, or it may pose a threat to the legitimacy of the political system that leads to centralization of coercive power in the polity.

This dynamic interplay between institutional domains and stratification systems occurs at the level of corporate and categoric units, and hence, it will affect the arousal of emotions in encounters within these units. Thus, even though this interplay operates at a macro level, embedding insures that it will also play itself out at the meso and micro levels of social reality.

Institutional domains and corporate units

An institutional domain is the set of corporate units that deals with fundamental problems facing populations as these problems generate selection pressures. The culture of a domain is tailored to the specific goals and division of labor of corporate units, and if this culture proves viable at the level of the corporate unit, then the ideologies, symbolic media, and institutional norms of the macro-level domain are reinforced. If this culture proves less viable, it will generally arouse negative emotions at the level of the encounter within the corporate unit, and if these negative emotions lead to collective mobilization, then both the division of labor and culture of the corporate unit will be changed, and ultimately, if key corporate units in a domain change their structure and culture, these changes will alter the culture and structure of the institutional domain.

Stratification systems and corporate units

The distribution of resources across a population and the formation of categoric units around this distribution have large effects on corporate units in various institutional domains. The incumbents of corporate units are ultimately drawn from diverse social classes and categoric units (e.g. gender, age, ethnicity) as these intersect with class. For example, if an ethnic minority is disproportionately lower class, this intersection of class and ethnicity as categoric units will have effects on such diverse structures as neighborhoods in communities, labor pools used by corporate units in the economy, adherents to specific churches, parties in the political domain, or school systems in the educational domain. In one sense, as is emphasized by organizational ecology, the distribution of people across categoric units and their various patterns of intersection create resource niches for corporate units (McPherson and Ranger-Moore, 1991) and, as a consequence, determine the culture and structure of these corporate units. In turn, this line of causality from stratification system to corporate units to encounters has effects on emotional arousal in encounters, and vice versa.

Corporate units and categoric units

Some categoric units are determined in part by the division of labor and culture of corporate units. Thus, at times positions in the division of labor become a categoric unit that is evaluated. For example, the category of student, worker, mother, or slave can serve as categoric units generated from the division of labor in corporate units. The converse is also true, categoric units can have effects on the division of labor in corporate units, as I noted above. A corporate unit that is disproportionately composed of one ethnic or class category will be different than one composed of another ethnic or class category. An organization that is mostly female will have a different culture and structure than one that is composed of males. As we will see, when the division of labor in corporate units is correlated with categoric unit membership, both the division of labor and the differential evaluations across categoric distinctions have more power over what occurs at the level of encounters.

Corporate units and encounters

The forces of the micro level of social reality are affected by the culture and structure of corporate units. The kinds of emotions that can be aroused, the way in which transactional needs are to be met, the normative expectations that apply, the distribution of status and the roles associated with status, the demography, and the props and ecology of the encounter are almost always determined, to a high degree, by the culture and structure of the corporate unit within which an encounter is embedded. As a result, the nature and intensity of emotional arousal in encounters is highly constrained by the structure and culture of corporate units. A theory of emotions must link specific kinds of emotions to specific properties of the division of labor in corporate units and the culture of this unit, and conversely, we will need to specify the likely effects of emotional arousal on corporate unit structure and culture (and, potentially, on a macro-level institutional domain).

Categoric units and encounters

At first, it may be difficult to visualize encounters as being embedded in categoric units, but the long research tradition within expectation-states theorizing should help confirm this view of encounters (Berger, 1988; Berger *et al.*, 1977, 1980; Webster and Foschi, 1988). Diffuse status characteristics, such as gender, ethnicity, and age, are what I term categoric units; and there is ample literature documenting that how people interact at the level of the encounter, how they evaluate each other, and how they react emotionally are very much influenced by the differential evaluations of categoric units or diffuse status characteristics (e.g. Wagner and Berger, 1997). An encounter composed of all women or men, members of only one ethnic population, or incumbents in one social class will reveal dynamics that are very different than those involving both women and men, diverse ethnics, and several social classes. What occurs in the encounter is thus determined by the configuration of categoric units in which it is embedded. Conversely, the dynamics of what transpires in the encounter – and for our purposes, the emotional dynamics that occur – will have an affect on the salience of categoric units and potentially on the macro-level stratification system in which many categoric units are embedded (e.g. Ridgeway, 2000, 2006; Ridgeway and Correll, 2004; Ridgeway and Erikson, 2000; Ridgeway *et al.*, 1998). Thus, we need to know what properties of categoric units have what effects on emotional arousal, and vice versa.

Conclusion

The scheme that I have outlined in this chapter can be used to study much more than emotions; and, indeed, I have sought to do so (Turner, 1985, 1995, and 2002) and will continue to pursue these more general theoretical interests in the future. Perhaps I have presented more detail than necessary, but I think that it will become clear that some sense for the connections among the structural units at each level of social reality is necessary in developing general sociological theory. At the level of the encounter, where emotions are an important force, the structure and culture of corporate and categoric units is immediate and generally relevant, loading the values for the forces that shape the flow of interaction. Because corporate and categoric units are the building blocks of all macro-level structures, while serving as the conduits of these macrostructures and their cultures down to the level of the encounter, it is critical to understand how the diversity of emotions outlined in Chapter 1 is influenced by mesostructures and macrostructures in which they are embedded. A sociological theory must always emphasize social structure and culture – this is, after all, the defining characteristic of our field – as these affect interpersonal behavior. This focus assures that we will seek to determine how corporate and categoric units constrain emotional arousal and, conversely, how emotions reproduce or change the structure and culture of corporate and categoric units and, potentially, the macrostructures and cultures in which these meso-level social units are embedded. This is the promise of a sociological approach; now, let us see how well I realize this promise.

4 Emotional arousal

Basic principles

Human emotions constitute a primal language system in which emotional phonemes are strung together into sequences by implicit rules of syntax that communicate affect. If only by watching a soap opera with the sound turned off, the emotional language of a culture becomes immediately evident. It may be, as Ekman and associates have long argued (Ekman, 1973a, b, 1982, 1984; Ekman and Friesen, 1971; Ekman *et al.*, 1972), that the syntax of the most primary emotions is universal, with perhaps certain refinements added by the emotion culture of society. But the key point is that individuals learn the emotional language of their culture, and they do so almost immediately out of the womb and long before they begin to learn the auditory language of their culture. This capacity for language, as Chomsky (1965, 1980) has argued for all these years, is innate; the human brain is pre-wired and receptive to learn language, at least until about the age of 11. After this point, language acquisition becomes much more difficult.

It has always seemed remarkable to me that most scholars see "body language" as an adjunct to spoken language when, in fact, just the opposite is the case: the language of emotions is more primal and primary because it evolved earlier than auditory language (Turner, 2000a). Evolutionary sequences are often repeated as developmental stages in organisms; and such is certainly the case for emotions because the capacity to use the language of the face and body emerges earlier than the ability to use auditory languages. Indeed, if we simply observe how adults interact with newborn babies, we can see the imprinting of the emotional language through smiles, acts of touching, and verbal cooing that communicate emotions. In fact, adults generally make a special point of aligning their faces to those of infants to communicate their positive affect, and it is very clear that infants are highly receptive to these facial gestures and verbal fillers communicating affect. Thus, long before an infant's left temporal lobe is activated to a significant degree, the right side of the brain in conjunction with subcortical emotion centers is very active in infants.

For a process that is so essential to humans, we should be able to enumerate a few simple principles on emotional arousal. Later, we can add to these principles and refine them in order to account for the fact that emotions are

aroused in *embedded social contexts.* Encounters are lodged in corporate
and categoric units that, in turn, are the conduits for the structure and
culture of macrostructures as they impinge on the face-to-face dynamics of
encounters. I see two basic processes responsible for emotional arousal in
humans: (1) expectations and (2) sanctions. Thus, we need to begin by
enumerating elementary principles on these two processes.

Expectation states and emotional arousal

There is, of course, a large literature on expectation states in sociology
(Berger, 1958, 1988; Berger and Conner, 1969; Berger and Zelditch, 1985,
1998; Berger *et al.*, 1972, 1977; Webster and Whitmeyer, 1999; Webster and
Foschi, 1988; Ridgeway, 1978, 1982, 1994; Ridgeway and Walker, 1995).
Most of the research in this area is conducted in small task groups, with
special emphasis on the expectation states that are associated with status
(prestige) and power (authority). At times, the prestige and power structure
is a given to members of task groups (as a proxy for the fact that many real-
world task groups are embedded in corporate and categoric units); and at
other times, research examines the emergence and change of expectation
states during the course of interaction. This entire theoretical research tradition has produced incremental and cumulative knowledge, but I want to
expand considerably the range of such theories by emphasizing that expectation states exist for much more than status and power. Although expectations from status and power are crucial to the flow of interaction, they are
not the only source of expectations. And, in some contexts, they are not
even the most important.

Individuals almost always enter encounters with expectation states. Indeed,
it is rare for a person to go into a situation with no knowledge of what to
expect. And, if a person is not sure of what to expect when entering an
encounter, this person will generally experience mild negative emotions
such as anxiety, shyness, or hesitancy. As soon as expectation states emerge,
however, individuals will feel much more comfortable, as long as these
expectations are confirmed by the actions of others. There is, then, a
very basic process at work here. Expectation states exist for virtually all
encounters and, as the research literature documents for prestige and power,
emerge rather quickly if expectations do not already exist. The expectations
come from a variety of sources, as I will document later, but they typically
revolve around characteristics of self, others, and situation. They are often
codified into what Affect Control Theory calls "fundamental sentiments"
(Heise, 1979; Smith-Lovin and Heise, 1988) or what some researchers (e.g.
Ridgeway, 2001) term "status beliefs"; and individuals are motivated by
gestalt propensities to see congruence between their expectations for the
actions of self and others as well as their expectations for the properties
of the situation. When individuals' expectations for self, other, and situation
are realized, they will experience mild positive emotions (see Table 1.2),

and if they had experienced some fear about whether or not expectations would be realized, they will experience more intense variants of positive emotions when expectations are met (see middle and right side of Table 1.2, and first-order elaborations like pride under emotions arising from combinations of satisfaction–happiness and other primary emotions portrayed in Table 1.3).

The converse of this generalization is that when the actions of self and others, or situation in general, do not measure up to expectations, individuals will experience negative emotional arousal. There are, however, more options for negative emotional arousal because three out of the four primary emotions are negative (and if we add other emotions to the list of primary emotions (see Table 1.1), most of these are also negative – e.g. disgust). Persons can experience fear, anger, or sadness; and a theory will need to address which of these emotions in what combinations will arise.

There are several general conditions that have large effects on expectations. One is the *clarity of expectations*. If expectations are clear and unambiguous, then individuals have realistic understandings about what is likely to occur; and, as a result, they are more likely to meet these expectations and experience positive emotions. If expectations are unknown, ambiguous, or contradictory, then individuals will enter interaction with negative emotional arousal, revolving around mild variants of fear; and depending upon what transpires in the situation, they will experience a variety of potential emotions on either the positive or negative side. If expectations become clear, removing ambiguity and contradictions, individuals will experience a first round of positive emotional arousal which will be augmented by a second round of positive arousal when self, other, and situation all continue to act or operate in ways that meet expectations. If expectations remain unclear or if they go unmet, then individuals will feel negative emotions, mostly variants of fear or anger (although sadness is also a possibility).

Another condition affecting expectations is the degree to which individuals in a situation employ the same emotional language. There are cultural variations in the phonemes and syntax of emotional languages – by class, ethnicity, gender, age, or subculture. When interactions are conducted with the same emotional language, expectations are much more likely to be clear; and if expectation states do not exist at the beginning of the interaction or if they are ambiguous or contradictory, a common emotional language increases the probability (though, not the certainty) that they will be clarified and, when clarified, met.

The next question follows from the above considerations: What increases the chances that expectations will be clear and unambiguous and that individuals will "speak" or signal with a common emotional language? In general, embedding, per se, will increase clarity of expectations but, as we will see in chapters 6 and 7, the specific properties of corporate and categoric units and their respective cultures also have large effects on clarity. Thus, embedding in general increases clarity but the structure and culture of meso units in which encounters are embedded have further effects on clarity. Moreover, the degree to which mesostructures are embedded in the structure and culture of institutional domains and stratification systems at the macro level of social organization is also critical to the clarity of expect-ations. The more an encounter is embedded in successive layers of social structure and culture, then, the more likely are expectations in encounters to be understood by all participants in the encounter.

Another force influencing expectations is what I term transactional needs. As is summarized in Table 3.1, I see certain need-states as universal among humans in interaction. These need-states also establish expectations, and they will generate emotions of varying types and levels of intensity when these expectations are realized. The most powerful need-state is for verifica-tion of self; the next most powerful is receipt of profits in exchanges of resources, followed in order of their relative power by needs for group inclusion, trust, and facticity. Individuals are motivated to meet these needs, and they almost always have a set of expectations for: (1) what aspects of self can be verified (need for self-verification); (2) what exchange payoffs will yield (needs for exchange payoffs); (3) what level of involvement in the interpersonal flow is possible (needs for group inclusion); (4) how predict-able, how sincere, how much respect, and how in synchronization others will be vis-à-vis self (trust); and (5) what degree of reality is obdurate and common to self and others (facticity). When these need-states are realized, individuals will experience positive emotions; and when they are not, they will experience one or all of the negative emotions in various elaborations (see tables 1.2, 1.3, and 1.4). Moreover, as we will see in Chapter 5, the specific need-states that are met, or go unmet, determine the specific emotions aroused.

Need-states are often ambiguous to the person, thereby increasing the ambiguity of expectation states. For example, a person may not know which identity will be salient in a situation, what resources are relevant, or what signs would mark group inclusion, trust, and facticity. With this kind of ambiguity over fundamental needs, a situation will be approached with some degree of negative emotional arousal. And, if needs go unmet for whatever reason, negative emotional arousal will continue and indeed inten-sify. Conversely, when needs become clear and are realized, initial levels of negative emotional arousal will give way to more intense forms of positive emotional arousal.

All of these forces – common emotional language, embedding of social structures and their cultures, and transactional need-states – influence the nature and clarity of expectation states. They will thus be part of my theory of emotional arousal. In later chapters, I will work to sort out the complex interplay of these forces because each affects expectations and emotional arousal in somewhat different ways, once we move beyond simple portrayals of emotions as either positive or negative. For the present, let us keep matters simple with the following basic principles:

1   *When expectations for self, other, and situation are met in an encounter, individuals will experience mild positive emotional arousal and will be more likely to give off positive sanctions to others (see principle 4 later in this chapter); and if they had some fear about expectations being met, they will experience more intense variants and elaborations of positive emotions.*

2   *The likelihood that expectations will be met in an encounter is a positive function of the degree of clarity in expectations, which, in turn, is a positive and multiplicative function of:*

    A   *The degree to which participants to an encounter use the same emotional phonemes and syntax.*

    B   *The degree to which an encounter is embedded in corporate and categoric units.*

    C   *The degree to which the meso-level corporate and categoric units are embedded in macro-level institutional domains and stratification systems.*

    D   *The degree to which the cultural symbols of meso- and macro-level structural units are explicit and consistent.*

    E   *The degree to which transactional needs generate expectation states that are consistent with A–D above.*

3   *When expectations for self, other, and situation are not met in an encounter, individuals will experience one or more negative emotions. The likelihood that expectations will not be met in an encounter is a positive and multiplicative function of:*

    A   *The degree to which participants to an encounter do not use the same emotional phonemes and syntax.*

    B   *The degree to which an encounter is not embedded in corporate and categoric units.*

    C   *The degree to which an encounter is not clearly embedded in an institutional domain or a location in the stratification system.*

    D   *The degree to which divergent or ambiguous cultural symbols are invoked by participants to an encounter.*

    E   *The degree to which transactional needs are unclear, ambiguous, or unattainable in an encounter.*

These simple principles leave all of the interesting sociological questions unanswered. For instance, what properties of corporate and categoric units, what elements of their cultures, and what aspects of transactional needs influence the clarity of expectations? These and other questions will need to be addressed if we are to have a robust sociological theory of emotions. But, for the present, we can simply state that individuals' emotional reaction to a situation is related to whether or not they realize expectations that, in turn, is partly a function of the clarity of expectations. The key to a sociological theory is to explain the psychological, social structural, and cultural conditions that increase or decrease clarity of expectations. In later chapters, we will explore all of these forces.

Sanctions and emotional arousal

The flow of interaction in encounters is also a process of mutual sanctioning. Individuals provide varying degrees of support (or lack of support) for what others are doing and saying. To some degree, sanctions are in the eye of the beholder because what another does can be perceived differently, as either a negative or positive sanction. Moreover, when individuals meet, or fail to meet, expectations, they may perceive either outcome as a sanction. Yet, for all the potential complexity, the basic relationship between emotions and sanctions is straightforward. When individuals see others as supporting their actions, they will perceive that they are being sanctioned positively and will, as a result, generally feel positive emotions. Conversely, when they believe that others are not supporting their actions, they will see this lack of support as a negative sanction and, as a consequence, experience one or some combination of negative emotions.

There is a clear relationship between expectations and sanctions. When expectations are unambiguous, individuals are more likely to act in ways that allow them to realize expectations. When they meet expectations, others are likely to give off positive sanctions. When expectations are not clear, however, individuals are less likely to know how to behave and, as a likely outcome, will emit behaviors that bring negative sanctions, thereby arousing negative emotions. The same conditions that increase the clarity of expectations thus operate to increase the chances that individuals will be positively sanctioned.

If individuals use the same emotional phonemes and syntax, they can role-take more effectively and calibrate their responses so as to receive positive sanctions from others. If they interact in embedded encounters with consistent cultural symbols and with explicit structures defining their place in the division of labor or their membership in categoric units, they are more likely to know how to behave in a manner engendering positive responses from others. Similarly, the more embedded corporate and categoric units are in an institutional domain or in a class position in the stratification systems and the more the culture of these macro-level structures constrains the culture and structure of meso-level corporate units and categoric units, the more likely are individuals to know how to behave in encounters and, hence, the more likely will they be positively sanctioned. Finally, if individuals are able to understand how transactional needs can be met in encounters, their efforts at meeting these needs can be orchestrated so as to bring positive sanctions from others. The obverse of these conditions will increase the likelihood that individuals will not fully understand how to respond in an encounter, with the result that they may breach the interpersonal flow and bring forth negative sanctions.

When individuals experience positive sanctions, they will generally continue a given course of action vis-à-vis others in a situation and, equally significant, they will typically give off positive emotions that serve as positive

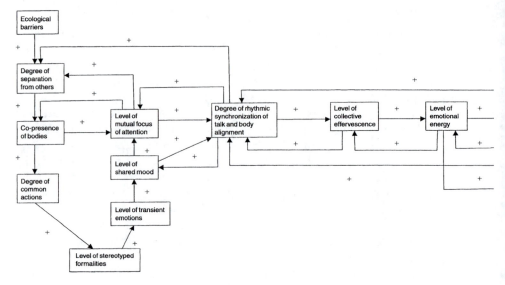

Figure 4.1 Collins's elaborated model of interaction rituals.

sanctions to others. As Randall Collins (2004) has emphasized, a process of "effervescence" can begin to cascade as positive sanctions and emotions feed off of one another – as Durkheim (1965 [1912]) emphasized long ago. For Collins, positive emotional arousal leads to an entrainment of emotional responses that operate as a positive sanction, leading to escalated positive emotional arousal, rhythmic synchronization of talk and body gestures, heightened flow of positive sanctions, increased sense of social solidarity, symbolization of this sense of solidarity, ritual enactments (as overt behaviors and/or covert thoughts) toward these symbols, and emerging particularized cultural capital that enhances the sense of shared symbols and solidarity. Collins's model is outlined in Figure 4.1.

Collins conceptualizes interaction rituals at two levels: (1) the "stereo-typed formalities" that arouse transient emotions at the beginning of the encounter, and (2) the more inclusive ritual sequence of the entire encounter (outlined in Figure 4.1). The former are rituals with a small "r", while the latter or the whole sequence of events in Figure 4.1 is the more inclusive ritual with a big "R." Co-presence, common actions, and ecological bar-riers all contribute to a mutual focus of attention, which is furthered by greeting rituals that create transient emotions leading to a shared mood that helps sustain the focus of attention. As individuals interact with a shared mood and mutual focus of attention, their emotions become entrained and rhythmic synchronization of talk and body occurs, creating the collective effervescence described in Durkheim's rendering of Australian aborigines in *The Elementary Forms of the Religious Life* (1965 [1912]). These processes, as they feed off each other, work to raise the level of emotional energy

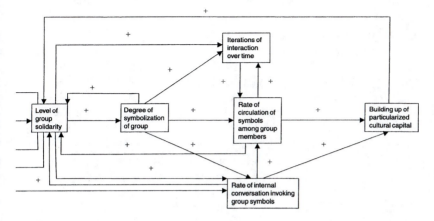

which, in turn, increases group solidarity. And, like Durkheim's portrayal of how a sense of "mana" leads to creation of totems toward which emotion-arousing rites are directed, Collins argues that solidarity generates a tendency for individuals to symbolize the group. This symbolization is more likely when rituals (with a big "R") are iterated, increasing the flow of positive emotions and the circulation of symbols in thought and actions. The result is the emergence of particularized cultural capital (symbols unique to the group and its members' experiences in the encounter). Thus, once positive emotions are aroused, they tend to circulate in terms of the dynamics originally outlined by Durkheim and, more recently, elaborated upon by Goffman (1963, 1967) and Collins (1975, 2004).

Thus, as we will come to see, the flow of positive sanctions in an encounter tends to circulate among the participants to the encounter, with individuals mutually sanctioning each other in ways that build up local solidarities, although at times this flow of mutual positive sanctioning can work its way up to mesostructures and macrostructures. A sociological theory of emotional arousal will need to explain the conditions under which positive sanctioning and the ritual dynamics that it unleashes stay local in the face-to-face encounter and, alternatively, when these positive emotions are transferred to mesostructures and macrostructures.

In contrast to positive sanctioning, negative sanctions stall an interaction and work against solidarity. As I noted in Chapter 2, one of the great obstacles to building social solidarity among humans' hominid ancestors was the fact that three of the four primary emotions are negative. Although the use of negative sanctions may lead individuals to adjust their behaviors and conform to expectations, negative sanctions also arouse negative emotions – fear, anger, sadness, or some combination of these – that work against solidarity. When individuals are angry, fearful, or sad and when these negative emotions are combined to form second-order elaborations (see Table 1.4) like shame, guilt, or alienation, social bonds are disrupted, and solidarity declines. Even if second-order elaborations do not emerge, sanction will often generate first-order elaborations of emotions that do not promote solidarity – emotions such as revulsion, dislike, antagonism, righteousness, melancholy, misery, aggrieved, and other emotions listed in tables 1.2 and 1.3.

One way to visualize this flow of negative emotions is to examine Collins's model presented in Figure 4.1, where I have drawn out in more elaborate form the elements in his theory and signed the arrows connecting these elements. If negative emotions enter this model at any point, these positively signed arrows become conductors of negative emotions. For example, if the initial stereotyped formalities (rituals with a small "r") go poorly and arouse negative emotions, this negative charge will travel down the model, disrupting mood, focus, rhythmic synchronization, collective effervescence, positive emotional arousal, group solidarity, and its symbolization. Or, if rhythmic synchronization breaks down, even after a good beginning, collective effervescence, positive emotional arousal, and other elements of the interaction ritual (with a big "R") turn negative as the positively signed arrows in Figure 4.1 conduct the negative emotions aroused.

Equally important, negative sanctions dramatically increase the likelihood that individuals will employ defensive strategies, and defense mechanisms, all of which revolve around varying levels of repression of the negative emotions aroused by sanctions. When needs for self-verification are intense, it becomes even more likely that a person will experience intense second-order emotions like shame or guilt from negative sanctions; and, as a result, this person will be more likely to invoke defense mechanisms. Once negative emotions are repressed, they become more intense, often erupting in sudden spikes of the negative emotions that have been repressed, leading to more negative sanctions from others, as well as self-sanctioning by a person for their inappropriate behavior, which may then be repressed in a cycle that can perpetuate itself over a lifetime.

Another effect of repression is that the negative emotions are often transmuted into new kinds of mostly negative emotions. For example, shame can become overt anger directed at others (Lewis, 1971); guilt causes people to experience anxiety and fear; or alienation is often filled with anger at the persons or structures from which a person has withdrawn. At times, defense mechanisms like reaction-formation can transmute negative emotions – say, hatred of father – into a positive emotion in which the person professes great love for (the hated) father. Or, sublimation may occur in which repressed negative self-feelings are transformed into positive energies in socially acceptable, if not worthy, activities. Yet, intensifying and/or transmuting negative emotions into new and/or more intense negative or, in some cases, into positive emotions does not operate to build secure bonds of solidarity. Thus, negative sanctioning unleashes a whole set of psychodynamics that affect the emotional experiences of individuals and the targets – self, others, social structures – of their emotions. Indeed, defense of self is a powerful dynamic that, save for a few scholars (e.g. Scheff, 1988; Scheff and Retzinger, 1991), sociologists have tended to underemphasize.

Sanctioning can thus be a potentially volatile force in human interaction when it turns negative, while being the primary force by which positive emotions are built up to create the conditions that promote social solidarity, as outlined in Figure 4.1. Sanctioning itself is a simple process but it generates new complexities that a sociological theory must explain. For the present, let me simply get the basic principle down, with an understanding that we will need to extend and amplify on the dynamics of sanctioning in later chapters.

4   *When individuals perceive that they have received positive sanctions from others, they will experience positive emotions and be more likely to give off positive sanctions to others in an escalating cycle that increases rhythmic synchronization of talk and body language, heightened mutual flow of positive sanctioning, increased sense of social solidarity, representation of this solidarity with symbols, and overt as well as covert ritual enactments toward these symbols. The likelihood that positive sanctions and these interaction rituals will occur is a positive function of the conditions listed under 2A–E above.*

5   *When individuals perceive that they have received negative sanctions from others, they will experience negative emotions; and the more negative these emotions, the more likely are defensive strategies and defense mechanisms revolving around repression, intensification, and transmutation to be unleashed, and the less will be the degree of solidarity in the encounter and, potentially, the less will be the commitments to the meso and macrostructures (and their respective cultures) in which the encounter is embedded. The likelihood that negative sanctions will have these effects is a positive function of the conditions listed under 3A–E and the intensity of transactional needs for self-verification.*

The activation of defensive strategies and mechanisms

The cybernetic control system and emotions

With a few exceptions (e.g. Scheff, 1979, 1988, 1990a, b, 1997; Turner, 1999b, 2002, 2006), sociological theories of emotions reveal a gestalt bias. Persons are conceptualized as a kind of cybernetic control system that when cognitions are inconsistent operates to bring them back into congruity (Powers, 1973). For example, Identity Control Theory (Burke, 1980, 1991, 1996; Burke and Stets, 1999) argues that individuals orchestrate behavioral outputs in accordance with an identity standard; they then engage in "reflective appraisal" of the responses of others to these self-presentations, and when the responses of others confirm the identity standard, behaviors continue along the same lines that brought verification of self. Conversely, when the responses of others indicate in reflected appraisals that behavioral outputs have not met the identity standard, individuals will experience distress and other negative emotions that lead them to adjust behavioral outputs, identity standards, or identities in order to bring identities, identity standards, behavioral outputs, and reflected appraisals into congruence. Similarly, Affect Control Theory argues that individuals make comparisons between their fundamental sentiments or beliefs about actor, behavior, other(s), and situation with their transient impressions. When sentiments about these elements – that is actor, behavior, other, and situation – are not consistent with their transient impressions, they will experience negative emotions that motivate them to engage in behaviors or cognitive manipulations to bring them into line (see Heise, 1979; Smith-Lovin and Heise, 1988). These approaches do capture a very important cognitive propensity in humans, as I emphasized in Chapter 2; humans are, I believe, hard-wired to search for consistency among cognitions (or, in my view, the consistency among the emotions accompanying cognitions). There is a great deal of empirical support for the theories in these two traditions and other gestalt research traditions, and so we must conclude that these dynamics are central to understanding emotions.

Yet, there is a methodological problem in most of these studies: they collect data on relatively low-intensity emotions (indeed, they would not be allowed by federal law to arouse intense emotions in the laboratory experiments). When emotions are of relatively low intensity and where needs for self-verification are also not intense, these cybernetic processes may indeed be the way emotions operate to bring cognitions about self, other, behaviors, and situations into line or congruence. When the emotions are more intense and when needs for self-verification are very high, however, these cybernetic control processes for cognitive consistency may be disrupted by the activation of defensive strategies and mechanisms, revolving around varying degrees and patterns of repression. Congruence is achieved not by reshuffling cognitions, behaviors, and identities, but instead by denying the emotions that signal incongruence, with the result that the cybernetic control system is set off course. Indeed, repression often leads to behaviors that are increasingly out of line with expectations for the situation and for what others demand.

When self is highly salient in an encounter – that is, a person has powerful needs to verify self – negative sanctioning from others and/or failure to meet expectations for self attack the viability of self or identity. Some people may be able to see these negative sanctions and failure to meet expectations for what they are and, as a result, make the necessary cognitive and behavioral adjustments, although the negative emotions that are aroused about such an important cognition as self do not easily dissipate. In fact, even as the person faces up to what has been done and makes the necessary cognitive and behavioral adjustments, these readjustments do not necessarily reduce the anger, fear, sadness, shame, guilt, or other powerful emotions directed at self. If these negative emotions linger, even after the behavioral adjustments have been made and accepted by others, they may be eventually repressed as a way to bring cognitive balance and closure; and so, the smooth operation of the cybernetic control system will, in the end, be disrupted by the lingering sting of negative feelings about self.

Individuals are thus not only motivated to have consistency among cognitions; they are also motivated to protect self. Apes can see themselves as objects in their environment, as the mirror studies mentioned in Chapter 2 document (Anderson and Gallup, Jr., 1999; Gallup, Jr., 1970, 1979, 1982; Hyatt and Hopkins, 1994; Lin *et al.*, 1992), but only humans can attach to these cognitions very intense emotions about who they are and how they should be treated. Since self is one of the most powerful gyroscopes directing human behavior, it should not be surprising that humans also try to insulate self from the pain of the emotions that come from negative sanctions and failures to realize expectations. How, then, are we to get a handle on these dynamics and incorporate them into a sociological theory of emotions?

Repression and the breakdown of the cybernetic control system

We need to begin by recognizing that the psychodynamics of repression are important to sociological theorizing. When emotions are repressed, they intensify and often transmute. And, when the cortical censors break down, and the repressed emotions are expressed, they target varying objects.

If self is the target, then the repressed emotions are generally not transmuted but, instead, come out as more intense forms of the emotions that were repressed. What typically emerges are variants and combinations of emotions like sorrow, depression, and anguish as intense forms of sadness, self-loathing as an intense form of anger at self, high anxiety as a more intense form of fear. Often these emotions seem "to come out of nowhere" because repression has been effective in masking from others and person the intensity of negative self feelings.

When self is protected by repression, the list of potential targets expands to include other(s), encounter, categoric unit, corporate unit, institutional domain, and stratification system, whole society, or even system of societies. Thus, people's hostility toward, anger at, and alienation from social structures and the cultures that they embody are often very much an outcome of repression at the level of the face-to-face encounter. Defensive strategies and mechanisms have, therefore, great relevance for understanding dynamics that are central to the sociological enterprise; and it is for this reason that I emphasize them here.

Defensive strategies

Individuals protect self to varying degrees; and depending upon the *degree* and *persistence* of repression, the emotional dynamics will vary. There are, at the low end of repression, defensive strategies (McCall and Simmons, 1978). One of these defensive strategies is selective perception of the negative sanctions from others and/or the degree to which behaviors have not met expectations; another is selective interpretation of sanctions as positive and behaviors as meeting expectations; still another strategy is to withdraw from a situation where sanctions work against self-verification and/or where expectations cannot be met; and yet another is use of "short-term credit" or a past legacy of positive sanctioning or success in meeting expectations to ride out what is perceived to be a momentary lapse in self-verification. Another set of defensive strategies revolve around disavowal of a performance as a measure of one's true self, thus deflecting negative sanctions or failings as a temporary aberration; and, alternatively, a more intense strategy is to disavow the audience of others who have delivered negative sanctions or indicated to a person that he or she has not met expectations.

These kinds of defensive strategies are often temporary and are invoked during a particular episode of interaction. The person protects self and moves on, although others in the encounter may experience frustration and anger that may lead them to offer additional sanctions, including withdrawing from the interaction. If use of these defensive strategies is chronic, being invoked just about every time a person feels that self is being negatively sanctioned and disconfirmed, then they signal a more intense form of repression. To consistently misperceive, reinterpret, and habitually invoke any of the other defensive strategies becomes a form of repression that intensifies the emotional dynamics. Others become angry at a person, and this person no longer feels the emotions appropriate to the receipt of negative sanctions or the failure to meet expectations. As a result, the repressed emotions intensify and potentially become transmuted into new kinds of emotions that are directed outward toward others and social structures.

Repression of negative emotional arousal

Full repression generally occurs when self is highly salient and negative sanctions and/or failures to meet expectations make a person feel shame. Shame is a particularly powerful emotion because it makes a person feel "small" and "unworthy." It is an emotion that arises when an individual feels incompetent in the eyes of others; and negative sanctions from others are one route to arousing shame, although a person can also self-sanction by imagining the sanctions of others. While shame often emerges from sanctioning, either by others or self, it can also arise when people feel that they have not lived up to expectations, and if these feelings are intense and make self feel small and inadequate, then they operate much like self-sanctions.

Guilt can also be repressed if it is sufficiently intense and chronic. Guilt emerges when persons feel that they have "done a bad thing," but unlike shame which often is repressed, guilt can lead to proactive behaviors as individuals seek to make amends (Tangney and Dearing, 2002). Still, when individuals have long biographies of feeling guilty, especially over powerful moral codes and taboos, this accumulated guilt begins to attack a person's more global sense of self-worth (rather than a particular "bad behavior"); and when guilt becomes more diffuse in this manner, it too can be repressed.

There are many names given to repression in the literature. For example, Helen Lewis's (1971) analysis of transcripts of her own and others' psychotherapy sessions led her to conclude that what was often seen as guilt by therapists is, in reality, shame. She concluded that shame can manifest itself as either "undifferentiated shame" in which the person has painful feelings but hides the shame by words and gestures denoting other emotions or as "bypassed shame" in which the emotion is not allowed to emerge fully because rapid speech and actions keep the person from actually experiencing the shame. Thomas Scheff (1979, 1988) borrowed this distinction and, later, relabeled it as "underdistancing" and "overdistancing" of shame, with the former corresponding to Lewis's undifferentiated shame and the latter to her bypassing of shame. In underdistancing of shame, the person feels emotional pain but does not acknowledge that it is shame, whereas in overdistanced shame the person does not even acknowledge emotional pain, much less the shame.

These kinds of distinctions can be useful, but in my analysis I see repression and denial as the master defense mechanisms. Through a variety of potential routes, individuals do not feel nor do they possess cognitive awareness of painful negative emotions, whether shame, guilt, anger at a loved one, jealousy, or any emotion that will lead to a negative evaluation of self. Negative sanctions in encounters are, of course, a very rapid route to negative evaluation of self, and so, it is not surprising that individuals may repress the shame or any other self-feeling arising from negative sanctions. Similarly, a person may experience shame when they have not realized expectations but, rather than face this self-evaluation, the shame is repressed; and, of course, if others negatively sanction a person for failing to realize expectations, then the likelihood of repression is that much greater because the pain is given focus by the sanctions from others.

Once repression is initiated, a variety of other defense mechanisms can be activated. These are listed in Table 4.1 as displacement, projection, sublimation, reaction-formation, and attribution. What is particularly important about the specific mechanisms used to repress negative emotions is that each leads to different types of transmutation of the repressed emotion and to different targets for the emotions that surface in a person's cognitive assessments and behaviors.

Down the left column of Table 4.1 are the negative emotions that can be aroused with negative sanctioning: anger, sadness, and fear individually or in second-order elaboration of these three emotions like shame and guilt. It is also possible to have first-order emotions arise, but these are not portrayed in Table 4.1. The second column denotes the particular defense mechanism by which repression works, while column three summarizes the likely transmutation that will occur. Finally, the last column on the right summarizes the likely targets of the repressed and transmuted emotions when they are expressed and when they guide overt behaviors. I should emphasize again that repression also tends to increase the intensity of the emotions that

Table 4.1 Repression, defense, transmutation, and targeting of emotions

Repressed emotions	Defense mechanism	Transmutation to	Target of
anger, sadness, fear, shame, and guilt	displacement	anger	others, corporate units, and categoric units
anger, sadness, fear, shame, and guilt	projection	little, but some anger	imputation of anger, sadness, fear, shame, or guilt to dispositional states of others
anger, sadness, fear, shame, and guilt	sublimation	positive emotions	tasks in corporate units
anger, sadness, fear, shame, and guilt	reaction-formation	positive emotion	others, corporate units, and categoric units
anger, sadness, fear, shame, and guilt	attribution	anger	others, corporate units, or categoric units

have been pushed below the level of consciousness; and, as a result, the transmuted emotion is often more intense than when repression does not intervene.

I should also note that the dynamics of repression may cycle before transmutation of the repressed emotions occurs. A person may repress any of the negative emotions – fear, anger, sadness – but eventually this repressed emotion will erupt in sudden and intense spikes of anxiety, rage, and depression. When these kinds of eruptions occur, a person may then begin to experience shame and guilt, which will also be repressed, only to erupt in sudden spikes of shame and guilt or in intense eruptions of any of the three emotions that make up these two second-order emotions (see Table 1.4). A person may never repress beyond this point, but I would predict that, over time, repressive censors will become more complete and, as a result, the emotion will increase not only in intensity but also be transmuted into a new emotion, most typically anger which is then directed away from self.

Let me now review each of the defense mechanisms that route repressed emotions. *Displacement* almost always transmutes (whatever the negative emotions repressed) into anger at safe targets that cannot easily fight back: others who are not powerful, corporate and categoric units, and at times, the macro-level institutional domain and stratification system in which corporate and categoric units are embedded. Displacement, then, will generate tensions and conflict because anger is targeted outward, and this anger is often highly intense. *Projection* involves much less transmutation because the emotion about self is simply imputed to another – whether fear, sadness, anger, shame or, guilt. Projection is less volatile but it will generally generate anger in those who are imputed to have emotions that they do not feel. *Sublimation* and *reaction-formation* both reverse the polarity of negative emotions, with sublimation generally converting negative emotions into positive emotional energy toward tasks in corporate units, while reaction-formation converts often very intense emotions, particularly anger, into positive emotional energy directed at others and, potentially, corporate and categoric units. These kinds of emotions are not as disruptive because the negative emotions turn positive, activating the processes reviewed in principle 1 summarized earlier. The last defense mechanism is attribution which, I believe, is the most important sociologically and, thus, requires some extra attention.

Attribution is a process originally highlighted by gestalt psychology; and within psychology proper, this emphasis on the cognitive side is still retained, although the dynamics of attribution and emotions have been explored in great detail by more recent approaches (see, for example, Weiner, 1986, 2006). Within sociology, there is an attribution dynamic in a number of theories (e.g. Kemper and Collins, 1990; Ridgeway, 1994; Ridgeway and Johnson, 1990; Lawler, 2001; Turner, 2002). However, I conceptualize attribution processes somewhat differently than in psychological approaches and more in line with Edward Lawler's (2001) approach. Internal attributions are those causal assessments directed at self; that is, an individual sees self as responsible for particular outcomes. External attribution is an assessment that others or social structures are responsible for outcomes. Thus, when individuals blame self for negative emotions from sanctions or failure to meet expectations, they are making an internal attribution or, as I will use the concept, self-attributions; and when persons blame others, categories of others, the structure of a corporate unit, or a macrostructure for negative emotional arousal, they are making an external attribution.

Attributions are often accurate and, hence, do not involve activation of defense mechanisms. For example, another person may indeed be responsible for some outcome, or the structure of a corporate unit may be accurately blamed. But, and here is the critical point, attributions can also *operate as defense mechanisms* because they are frequently made to protect self from negative feelings.

The reason that I think attributions are so important in sociological analysis is that individuals are constantly making causal attributions as to the sources of various outcomes. This cognitive process is, as I noted in Chapter 2, probably hard-wired into ape and, thus, human neuroanatomy. Moreover, given humans' greatly expanded brains compared to our ape cousins, individuals can construct long chains of causal effects and store memories of past causes of outcomes. There is then an in-place biological propensity to make causal attributions. And so, this capacity can also operate to push below the level of consciousness negative emotions that attack self; and perhaps as part of an effort to restore cognitive consistency, individuals will then blame others, encounters, mesostructures, and macrostructures for negative outcomes, once they have cognitively taken self out of the calculations of causality. Attributions thus become a principal route for attaching emotional reactions to others and social structures, with the consequence that social structures (and the cultures that they embody) are potentially targeted with repressed anger, fear, sadness, shame, or guilt that has been transmuted into negative emotions that are directed outward. With attributions, negative emotional arousal becomes a heat-seeking missile, with a guidance system provided by external attribution dynamics.

Edward Lawler (2001) has noted that the arousal of positive emotions reveals a "proximal bias" in that individuals are likely to see self as responsible for rewarding outcomes and, thereby, to make self-attributions for these outcomes. Thus, positive sanctions or meeting expectations are likely to be seen as the result of the person's own actions, with the result that this individual will direct positive emotional arousal toward self and then give off positive sanctions to others in the encounter which, as principles 1 and 4 above emphasize, set into motion those ritual processes that increase the flow of positive emotions in the local encounter. A person will also see others as helping in the receipt of positive outcomes, especially if others are the ones giving positive sanctions, thereby accelerating the processes outlined in principles (1) and (4) as the individual gives off positive emotions like happiness and gratitude to others who reciprocate in kind.

In contrast to positive outcomes, negative emotional arousal reveals a "distal bias," with individuals making external attributions as to the causes of these outcomes (Lawler, 2001; Turner, 2002). In this manner, self avoids blame for failing to meet expectations, for negative sanctions, and for any negative outcome. Once repression becomes organized around external attributions, the emotions aroused are generally transmuted into more intense forms of anger which is then directed at a limited number of objects: other(s), micro-level encounters, meso-level corporate and categoric units, macro-level institutional domains, stratification system, societies, and even system of societies.

There is a further aspect of this distal bias: external attributions will generally jump over local encounters because to vent anger in the local encounter composed of other(s) invites negative sanctions which further attack self and force renewed repression and activation of defense mechanisms. As a result, it is generally easier to blame meso-level structures because they are still immediate, but cannot so easily strike back and bring self into focus. Since encounters are embedded in these mesostructures and, hence, are immediate to the person, the targeting of mesostructures provides a sense of efficacy and power, without risking direct negative sanctioning from others. Indeed, there are fewer emotional risks in assigning blame to entities that are not persons and that cannot retaliate in very personal ways. Yet, once anger begins to flow outward, there are conditions under which this anger targets ever more macrostructures; and as we move into the details of the theory that I propose, we will have to take account of this outward movement of anger.

Together, the proximal and distal biases generate some interesting dilemmas for the stability of social structures. If positive emotions stay local and circulate in terms of the processes summarized in principle 1, the emotional energy is not directed outward at macrostructures; and if positive emotions are not so directed, then commitments to, and the legitimacy of, meso and macrostructures become more problematic. It is for this reason that legitimacy of macrostructures is often a most tenuous process. For commitments to, and legitimacy of, mesostructures and macrostructures, along with their attendant cultures, are ultimately generated and sustained by positive emotions directed outward; and if positive emotions have a proximal bias, these emotions will have a tendency to stay local at the micro level as individuals make self-attributions and, at best, give off positive emotions to others in the encounter. And so, we can ask: How are macro-level structures ever legitimated? As I will outline in later chapters, the conditions under which attribution dynamics push positive emotional energy outward toward meso and, eventually, to macrostructures can be theorized.

The negative side of emotions leading to external attributions presents the same dilemma. If negative arousal reveals a bias to bypass others in order to avoid breaching the encounter and incurring the risks of negative sanctions toward self, then negative emotions about self will move outward and reduce commitments to, and erode the legitimacy of, mesostructures and macrostructures as well as the cultures of these structures. In social systems where shame and other negative emotions are consistently activated in embedded encounters, we can predict that commitments to and legitimacy of meso and macrostructures become ever more difficult to sustain, given the distal bias of attributions. Of course, other defense mechanisms such as sublimation and reaction-formation can work to overcome this distal bias of negative emotional arousal (reversing the polarity of the emotions and creating their opposite), but, as I will argue, the questions of most interest to sociologists are more likely to be answered by attribution dynamics than by invoking the operation of other defense mechanisms that reverse the polarity of negative emotions. Such is not always the case, of course, but I believe that an emphasis on external attributions is more likely to provide the best answers to sociological questions.

And, it is for this reason that attribution is an important sociological process because social structures and cultures are only viable in the long run when individuals develop positive emotions toward them, while at the same time muting the arousal of negative emotions targeting social structures. The sixth and final of the basic principles in the theory thus concerns the activation of defensive strategies and defense mechanisms:

6 *When individuals experience either positive or negative emotional arousal, they will make attributions about the cause of their emotional experiences to one or more of the following objects: self, others, structure of encounter, structure and culture of corporate unit, members of categoric units, institutional domain, stratification system, society, or system of societies. (a) Positive emotional arousal reveals a proximal bias, with individuals making self-attributions for meeting expectations and receiving positive sanctions, thereby initiating the ritual dynamics that*

sustain the flow of positive emotions (propositions 1 and 4), whereas (b) negative emotional arousal evidences a distal bias, with individuals making external attributions for the failure to meet expectations or for the receipt of negative sanctions, with a propensity to bypass others and the local encounter and target the structure and culture of corporate units and members of categoric units.

Conclusion

These six principles form the core of my theory but, as will become ever more evident, other principles will need to be added to take account of (1) the structural, cultural, and psychodynamic forces that arouse specific emotions in encounters, and (2) the effects of these emotions on reproduction of, or change in, varying levels of social structure and culture. For, in the end, a sociological theory of emotions must specify in some detail *what* conditions generate *what* emotions to *what* effects on *what* levels of culture and social structure. As we will see, the conditions that generate emotions inhere in the structure and culture of corporate and categoric units in which encounters are immediately embedded as well as the institutional domains and stratification systems in which these meso-level structures are embedded. The effects of emotions radiate out from self to others to encounter to mesostructures and, potentially, to macrostructures; and a sociological theory needs to explain *which* emotions target *what* levels of social structure. It is evident, then, that these six very simple principles only get us started, but the basic dynamics that they highlight will remain central to the theory that unfolds in the following chapters.

5 Transactional needs and emotional arousal

The notion of universal human need-states does not enjoy great currency in sociology. Yet, a quick appraisal of existing sociological theories documents that most posit need-states that motivate individuals to behave in certain ways. For symbolic interactionists, it is the need to verify self; for the exchange theorist, it is the need to derive profits in exchange payoffs; for expectation-state theorists, it is the need to meet expectations; for ritual theorists, it is the need to derive positive emotional energy; for ethno-methodologists, it is the need to sustain a sense of a common reality; and so it goes for virtually all micro-level theories. The same can be said for more macro-level theories. For instance, Émile Durkheim (1951 [1897]) posited a human need to feel integrated in the group and to be regulated by cultural norms in order to avoid the pain, respectively, of egoism and anomie; Marx argued that humans have a need to avoid alienation and determine what they produce, how they produce it, and to whom they distribute the results of their labor; and, more recently, Niklas Luhmann (1988) implies a psychological need to reduce complexity, while Anthony Giddens (1984) argues for a need to achieve ontological security. Thus, we do not have to look very hard to see that sociologists theorize need-states for humans and, to some degree, these needs motivate individuals to behave in certain ways and, thereby, channel energies in face-to-face interaction. In turn, this channeling of interpersonal energies can have effects on the formation of culture and social structures, and vice versa.

It is unlikely that a force like need-states so central to humans and their sociocultural creations would not arouse emotions. When needs are realized, people experience variants of satisfaction-happiness; whereas when they are not met, they will experience negative emotions of potentially many varieties – primary, first-order, and second-order (see tables 1.2, 1.3, and 1.4). My goal in this chapter is to lay out what I see as universal human needs in all encounters and, then, to develop some simple principles on how they generate and channel emotional arousal.

Universal human needs

As is outlined in Table 3.1, I conceptualize these universal needs as *transactional needs* because, each and every time individuals interact in face-to-face encounters, these need-states are activated and direct the flow of interaction. When these needs are consummated, positive emotions are aroused and generate the processes summarized in principles 1, 4, and 6a; and, conversely, when they are not realized, the processes summarized in principles 3, 5, and 6b are activated.[1] There are, I believe, at least five fundamental transactional needs: (1) needs for self-verification, (2) needs for profitable exchange payoffs, (3) needs for group inclusion, (4) needs for trust, and (5) needs for facticity. This listing of needs is also intended as a rank-ordering of their relative power, with (1) being the most powerful force on the interpersonal behavior and the others pushing the course of interaction to the degree suggested by their respective numbers. Let me outline in more detail just what each need-state entails (Turner, 1987, 1988, 1994a, b, 1999b, 2002, 2006; Turner and Boyns, 2001).

Needs for self-verification

Like all great apes, humans can see themselves as an object in their environment; and because of their large brain and expanded emotional capacities, self becomes more persistently salient in all interactions with others. Self is both a set of cognitions and emotional valences about a person that is mobilized in face-to-face interaction; and because interaction is so mediated by the give and take of gestures (rather than being driven by "group instincts"), interaction involves a considerable amount of negotiation. During these negotiations, individuals mutually communicate not only who they are but also their willingness to accept the self-presentations of others. With a sense of self on the line during interaction, the emotional states are dramatically raised because individuals want to have their views of themselves verified. Indeed, interaction is dominated by the reciprocal presentation of self and the willingness of audiences to verify this self. There is, of course, a long tradition in psychology (e.g. James, 1884, 1890), philosophy (Mead, 1934), and sociology (Cooley, 1902; Simmel, 1955 [1890]) that argues for the central place of self in human affairs, and this tradition has been carried forward by contemporary symbolic interactionists (e.g. Stryker, 1980, 2004; R. H. Turner, 1962; Burke, 1991; McCall and Simmons, 1978) and by dramaturgical approaches to interaction (e.g. Goffman, 1959).

---

1   For convenient reference, these and other principles are listed in Chapter 9.

Levels of self

Self is, as noted above, a cognitive and emotional force in human interaction. Humans carry cognitions about themselves that are emotionally valenced; and because these cognitions are emotionally charged, they are more salient and more likely to elicit further emotional responses during the course of interaction. No other animal, I am sure, has the propensity to see self as an object in virtually every interaction, to store memories and emotions about self from past interactions, to see self in imaginatively rehearsing future lines of conduct, and to see and evaluate self when thinking about the past, present, or future. Moreover, humans are probably unique in that self operates on at least three levels, as outlined in Figure 5.1.

The first level is the core self-conception that persons have about who they are in all situations. These are cognitions about the characteristics of self, as well as powerful emotions evaluating self, that persons carry from encounter to encounter. Moreover, this core self is typically the basis for thought and reflection about self outside of encounters. This core self is built up through role-taking with others and seeing their responses to self presentations in what Cooley (1902) termed "the looking glass" provided by others' gestures. As individuals gaze into the looking glass, they also derive self-feelings; and for Cooley the central feelings were pride and shame. That is, individuals are always in a state of low-level pride or shame as they record others' responses to self and generate self-evaluations. I do not, however, limit the range of emotions to only pride and shame that can be felt in role-taking with others and in deriving self-feelings, but the key point is that over time a more stable, trans-situational self emerges by adulthood and becomes the principle gyroscope directing an individual's behaviors. The core self is thus relatively stable, and it represents the basic collage of feelings that persons have about who and what they are, and what they deserve from others in encounters.

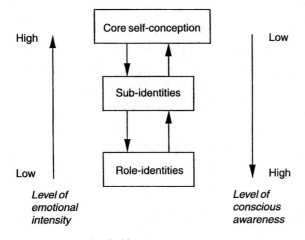

Figure 5.1 Levels of self.

As the arrows in Figure 5.1 denoting emotional intensity and cognitive awareness emphasize, the core self is the most emotionally valenced aspect of self, and yet, people often have difficulty putting into words just what this core self entails. Indeed, I would argue that the dynamics of emotion, memory, and repression often create unconscious emotions about self to which an individual does not have easy access (see appendix to Chapter 2 for a review of the neurology involved in unconscious emotional memories). The core self is, therefore, a mixture of conscious and unconscious feelings that have been built up over a lifetime and, by late adolescence, coalesce into a stable self-conception that resists change over an adult lifetime.

The structure of the core self presents profound methodological problems of how it can ever be measured. Most tests of self in sociology are, ultimately, paper-and-pencil tests that ask people to write down or to check off words describing themselves. My view is that these kinds of tests do not adequately measure the core self because much of this level of self remains unconscious. Moreover, individuals do not always have words to describe the emotional valences of who they are; and given that repressed emotions and/or unconscious emotional memories may also be part of these valences, it is always difficult to get an accurate description of core self. At some point in the future, other measures through brain imaging technologies may give us better access to the core self, but to argue that such a self does not exist because it cannot be easily measured is to define away in terms of sociology's limited research methodologies a crucial force in human interaction.

The next level of self is what I term sub-identities (Turner, 2002). These are emotionally valenced conceptions that individuals have about themselves in institutional domains and stratification systems. For example, a person will have a sense of themselves as a father, mother, son, daughter, worker, religious worshiper, resource-holder; and each person will attach evaluations to conceptions of themselves in the macrostructural domains and class positions that are salient to them. A person might, for instance, see self as a negligent father but a hard worker who brings home resources that assure high rank in the stratification system. Each of these emotionally valenced cognitions — father, worker, place in class systems — constitutes a sub-identity, and together they lead individuals to see and evaluate themselves as a particular kind of person. Individuals have a much clearer conception of their sub-identities than their core self-conceptions; and, indeed, if we ask an individual about how they see themselves as husbands and fathers, we can usually get more precise information than if we ask them about what kind of person they are in general. The more differentiated a society is at the macro level of organization, the greater will be the number of sub-identities possessed by a person.

A role-identity or situational-identity is the conception that a person has of self in a specific role within a particular social structural context. To some degree, role-identities fade into sub-identities, but role-identities are more situational: What kind of student am I in this specific school, or in this specific class? What kind of mother am I when providing affection, or in helping children with homework? Indeed, in almost all sets of iterated encounters in corporate and categoric units, individuals develop relatively clear cognitions and evaluations of themselves in specific roles. As Figure 5.1 emphasizes, individuals have the most cognitive access to role-identities, but these identities are less emotionally valenced than either sub-identities or core self-conceptions.

If, however, a person feels that a particular role is crucial to verification of a sub-identity or the core sense of self, then the emotional stakes will be raised when a person presents this identity to others. Indeed, during the course of interaction in an encounter, we seek to determine implicitly *which level* of identity is wrapped up in a particular role; and if we sense that a core self-conception or sub-identity is salient in a particular role, we will generally try to verify the identity, if we can. To not do so invites powerful emotional reactions that breach the encounter and, hence, are best avoided.

Thus, in most interactions, individuals present a differentiated self and, depending upon which self is being presented, the emotional reactions of persons will vary. In general, the more self-presentations reflect the core self-conception, the more intense will be the emotional reactions of an individual to verification and, in particular, failure to verify this self. At the other end of the continuum, role-identities will generate the least amount of emotion; and sub-identities carry more emotional potential than role-identities but less than a core self-conception. Moreover, some sub-identities and role-identities are of greater salience to a person and, thus, will arouse more intense emotions. For instance, a person may believe that he is an average worker and not attach great emotional significance to this view of self; as a result, confirmation or disconfirmation of this view of self will not have the same power compared to the role-identity of a father. Should this latter identity not be confirmed, the emotional reaction will be much more intense. Generally, those sub-identities and role-identities that are highly salient to a person are also those identities in which a person's more global self-conception is invested; successful verification of these identities is seen as a marker of who and what individuals implicitly feel about themselves as persons. As a result, the emotional potential is increased when either sub-identities or role-identities embody a more general self-conception.

This layering of self presents another kind of methodological problem: most studies measure role- or, at best, sub-identities which will elicit much less emotional arousal than core self-conceptions. As long as research focuses on those layers of self that generate the least amount of emotion, they will end up studying relatively mild emotions – mild satisfaction-happiness or low levels of assertion-anger or any other set of emotions. What will be missed in these studies are the dynamics that are unleashed when deeper and more emotional layers of self are on the line – dynamics such as repression, emotional intensification, transmutation, and targeting of negative emotional energy. The cognitive bias of most studies of identities, especially the view of self as a cybernetic control system, makes a great deal of sense for the level of self and emotions aroused in these studies; role-identities will generate the least emotion and, hence, will be the least likely to become tied up in the dynamics revolving around repression. As a result, individuals can simply make behavioral or cognitive adjustments to bring presentations of self, reactions of others to these presentations, and identity standards into incongruence. When core self is on the line, however, "congruence" is often achieved by defensive strategies or repression, neither of which is likely to sustain cognitive balance over the long run as repressed emotions increase in intensity and become transmuted into new kinds of emotions that often disrupt social relations.

Self, expectations, and sanctions

Whatever level of self is presented to others, it carries expectations that it will be verified. Thus, core self, sub-identities, and role-identities are a major source of expectation states in encounters; and to the degree that they are realized, the more likely are the processes in principles 1, 4, and 6a to be activated,[2] whereas to the extent that these self-related expectations are not met, the dynamics summarized in propositions 3, 5, and 6b will be unleashed.

Individuals constantly scan the gestures of others to see if their self-presentations have been accepted and verified, and the information gleaned is constantly compared to the expectation states that configurations of selves generate in a situation. Again, individuals' access to these expectation states corresponds to the level of self that generates them. Individuals will be most conscious of expectations associated with role-identities, still somewhat aware of the expectations that come from their sub-identities, and only partially cognizant of the expectations that are created by their core self-conception. Indeed, people are often amazed at their emotional reaction in some situations because they were not fully aware of the degree to which very salient expectation states – those revolving around their core self-conception – were operative in an interaction. Moreover, when a role-identity also carries the burden of being the principle conduit by which the core self-conception is verified, the emotional reaction can often seem disproportionate because powerful subcortical emotions about self are setting up expectation states, some of which a person may not fully understand at a conscious level. Only when the expectations are not met do these expectations reveal themselves.

When individuals fail to signal that they verify self, these signals operate much like a negative sanction, even if they did not intend such to be the

---

2 Again, Chapter 9 lists all of the principles in the theory for quick reference.

case. And, when individuals use negative sanctions more consciously and deliberately to inform a person that the self presented will, or will not, be accepted, the emotional reaction will be even greater. Thus, the responses of others to self-presentations can double up, as it were, and signal to a person that expectations about self have (or have not) been met and, moreover, that efforts to meet these expectations will be (or not be) accepted by others as they mete out sanctions. The more the core self is presented, the more emotional potential when expectations associated with this self are met (or go unmet) and when others sanction this presentation of self, either positively or negatively. As the self presented moves through sub-identities to role-identities, the emotional reactions will correspondingly decline.

Self and intensity of emotional arousal

When individuals confirm self by meeting expectations associated with self and when others offer positive sanctions for individuals' self-presentations in an encounter, they will experience variants of satisfaction-happiness; and if they had some fear about meeting these expectations and/or being positively sanctioned, they will experience first-order emotions like pride (happiness + lesser amounts of fear). And, the more self-presentations are guided by core self-conceptions, the more the emotions experienced move to more intense variants of satisfaction-happiness, setting into motion the dynamics summarized in principles 1, 4, and 6a.

If these emotions are experienced across a variety of encounters embedded in diverse corporate units lodged in institutional domains or class positions in the stratification system, these emotions will be more likely to circulate beyond the local encounters in which they are generated and cause individuals to direct positive sentiments toward macrostructures, thereby giving these structures legitimacy while creating commitments to the corporate and categoric units from which these macrostructures, and their culture, are constructed. For example, those individuals who have self verified in a range of encounters within corporate units that distribute resources – say, education, economy, and polity – will generally develop positive emotions for the institutional domains and stratification systems of a society, for the ideologies of these macrostructures, and for the structure and culture of a society as a whole.

Thus, while positive emotions will tend to circulate within the encounter, they will migrate out to mesostructures and macrostructures when individuals *consistently* meet expectations and receive positive sanctions across the encounters in diverse corporate and categoric units embedded in those macrostructures distributing valued resources. This movement of positive emotional energy outward is particularly likely when expectations for core self are met and when sanctions verifying this deeper level of self are received. Under these conditions, positive emotions become even more likely to move outward from the encounter through corporate units to macrostructures. Self-verification is the most powerful transactional need, and when it is consistently confirmed, the positive emotional energy generated becomes sufficiently great to target macrostructures. It is perhaps obvious, but nonetheless fundamental, that successful people in a society are also those most likely to give the macrostructures and culture of these macrostructures legitimacy and to become committed to them; they are willing to do so because all levels of self have received consistent support across diverse encounters embedded in corporate and categoric units that, in turn, are embedded in institutional domains and classes in the stratification system.

The failure to verify self leads to the more interesting outcomes. When individuals perceive that they have not met expectations associated with self and/or have been sanctioned negatively for presenting this self, they will experience any or all three negative primary emotions: anger, fear, sadness. And, if they experience these emotions simultaneously, they will likely feel shame; and if moral codes were salient and part of self-evaluations, they may experience guilt as well. If they experience these emotions consistently in iterated encounters, they will withdraw from the encounter and the corporate unit in which it is embedded, if they can. If they cannot withdraw, the activation of the three negative emotions may transmute to alienation, as the most likely second-order elaboration (listed in Table 1.4).

Attribution processes intervene to affect the emotions experienced and the intensity of the affect aroused. If a person makes a self-attribution, this individual can experience each of the three primary emotions separately. The person can feel sad, be angry at self, or be fearful of the consequences to self. If this individual experiences these emotions simultaneously, he or she will feel shame and, if moral codes were salient, guilt as well. And, over time, this shame and/or guilt may shift to alienation, an emotion that is built from the three negative primary emotions but an emotion that is far less painful to self than either shame or guilt.

When shame is experienced, however, individuals will often repress the shame. In turn, it becomes more likely that individuals will make external attributions. Moreover, the emotions will become more intense and transmute into anger that will target either other(s), encounter, corporate units, members of categoric units, institutional domains, stratification systems, whole societies, or systems of societies. If others in the encounter are powerful, if the encounter is iterated over time, and if a person cannot withdraw from the encounter and the meso-level units in which the iterated encounter is embedded, then it is likely that the anger will be directed at the culture and structure of the corporate unit. If categoric unit memberships are correlated with the division of labor in the corporate unit — that is, positions in the division of labor of the corporate are held disproportionately by members of discrete categoric units — the anger may be directed at these categoric units, with individuals developing negative prejudicial beliefs about the characteristics of people in a categoric unit. Once these prejudices develop, the categoric unit, per se, may become a more generalized target of shame (transmuted into anger) that is aroused in encounters.

When individuals consistently experience shame in a wide variety of encounters embedded in the corporate units of institutional domains that distribute resources, such as economy, education, and polity, and when they have a long biography of shame experiences in these domains, it becomes more likely that the shame, if repressed, will be transmuted into intense anger that will be directed outward beyond the meso level to the culture and structure of institutional domains, stratification systems, societies, and systems of societies. If this shame is experienced collectively, the anger may be codified into ideologies that justify protest and potential violence against meso and macro units of a society or those of another society; and it becomes more likely that individuals will mobilize into corporate units that attack the institutional domains and stratification systems of their own societies or those of another society (see Chapter 8 for an elaboration of this point).

Needs for profitable exchange payoffs

All interactions involve an exchange of resources, in which one person gives up resources in order to receive resources provided by other(s). The nature of the resources available and their value to persons vary enormously, but the critical point is that interaction always revolves around an exchange of resources. Individuals have needs, I argue, for earning a "profit" in the exchange of resources. Profit is, however, a complex cognitive and emotional process but, at its core, individuals are motivated to receive resources that exceed their costs and investments in securing these resources. Costs are the resources forgone to receive a given resource from others as well as the resources that must be "spent" to receive resources; investments are accumulated costs over time that a person has incurred to receive a particular resource. When individuals make a profit in their exchanges with others, they experience positive emotions and initiate the processes described in principles 1, 4, and 6a; and when they do not receive a profit, they experience negative emotions in line with principles 3, 5, and 6b.[3]

The process of resource seeking

When individuals enter an encounter, they typically have expectations for the nature and level of resources they can gain, as well as what it will cost them to secure these resources. Such is not always the case, and when it is unclear what resources exist in a situation, individuals will experience mild forms of aversion–fear. There is, I believe, a sequence to resource seeking

---

3   Again, consult Chapter 9 to review these propositions.

which is more costly when individuals are not sure of what resources are available and when they are uncertain about what resources they will have to give up during the course of the encounter.

The first step is a scan for the available resources. If a person has expectations for what resources are available, then scanning of the situation revolves around affirming these expectation states. When expectations are not clear or do not exist, then this scanning process will be more involved and take more time. The individual will need to assess all aspects of the encounter – the corporate units in which the encounter is embedded and the resulting distribution of power and prestige, the available roles and positions for self and others, the emotional mood, the needs of others and self, the demography and ecology of the encounter, and the relevant cultural symbols – before determining the nature and levels of resources available, as well as what resources will need to be given up to secure these resources. The second step in this scanning process – often entailed in the first step – is to determine which resources in a situation can verify self, and the level of self (core, trans-situational; sub-identity; and role-identity) that is salient. For, just "how much" a person is willing to "spend" securing resources is very much related to the degree that the resources available will allow for verification of self, at any or all three levels. A third step in an encounter involves the resources available for meeting other transactional needs – above and beyond needs for self-verification and profits in exchanges. Individuals will search for the resources marking group inclusion, trust, and facticity; and on the basis of their assessment, they will implicitly determine their possibilities in securing these resources and the costs involved.

Most of the time, individuals perform this scanning operation without actively thinking about the distribution of resources. Past experiences and other processes that have loaded up humans' implicit stocks of knowledge (Schutz, 1967 [1932]) generally contain information about available resources and the costs to be incurred in securing these resources in basic types of situations. The stocks of knowledgeability become part of the expectation states that individuals have for what will occur in an encounter. Expectation states about exchanges revolve around two related forces: (1) the reference points used to determine what a "just share" of resource for a person is and (2) the moral codes specifying what is fair and just, or unfair and unjust. Let me explore these in more detail (Turner, 2007a, b). In general people will experience positive emotions when expectations are met, and negative emotions when they are not realized, but *which* emotions they experience and *how they target* these emotions are influenced by these two related dynamics – that is, reference points and moral standards.

Reference points and expectations

There is a large literature on "justice" in exchange relations. George C. Homans (1961) was the first to bring such considerations back into sociology in his analysis of "distributive justice." For Homans, calculations of distributive justice revolve around assessments of one's own costs and investments relative to rewards received, compared to the cost, investments, and rewards received by others. When individuals perceive that the resources received are proportionate to their costs/investments, they will perceive that distributive justice prevails *if* the resources received by others in the situation are proportionate to their respective costs/investments. In Homans's early approach, then, there is both a comparison process (self's rewards, costs, and investment relative to those of others) and a congruence dynamic (rewards should be proportionate to, and consistent with, investments and costs for self and others). Homans argued that people will experience positive emotions when distributive justices prevails, and when distributive justice is not perceived to be operative, persons will feel angry. There are two routes to this anger because a person may perceive that his or her rewards do not exceed costs/investments or that the rewards of others are too high relative to their costs/investments. Later, Homans (1974) moved to an approval-aggression argument that emphasized expectations: when individuals do not receive rewards that are expected, they become angry; and when they receive expected rewards, they experience positive emotions, although if they perceive that they are over-rewarded (relative to expectations, plus costs and investments), initial pleasure may eventually give way to guilt.

Subsequent sociological theorizing on justice has elaborated upon this early formulation by Homans (Jasso, 1993, 2001, 2006; Markovsky, 1985, 1988). Guillermena Jasso has presented a theory of justice in highly formal terms, arguing that individuals compare their shares of resources to their conception of what a "just share" would be, with justice being the logarithmic function of the ratio between a person's actual shares to just shares and with the further proviso that it takes more of an over-reward than under-reward to generate a sense of injustice. Jasso also introduces the notion of expectations by arguing that individuals assess rewards and punishments relative to expectations for rewards and punishments, with a smaller amount of punishment generating as much injustice as will greater amounts of punishment (even when punishments are expected). A final element in Jasso's formulation is that individuals' calculations of justice also involve comparisons with others; persons will experience positive emotions when their rewards exceed those of others and negative emotions when their rewards are less than others.

Jasso's and others' analyses of justice lead me to view that a person's conception of "just shares" is related to the reference points that they use in developing this conception of just shares and the ideologies and norms about what is fair in a situation (Turner, 2007a). Together these two forces – reference points and ideologies – generate an expectation state for what resources are available and what would constitute a "just share." And, to the degree that actual shares correspond to conceptions of just shares, a person will experience positive emotions; and to the extent that there is incongruence between actual and just shares, negative emotions will be aroused, although it will take much more of an over-reward (above what is considered a just share) to produce a negative emotion like guilt than under-reward to generate emotions like anger. Thus, it is useful to determine what factors go into people's formulation of just share; for, as I will argue, the emotional reaction varies with *which* reference points are part of this formulation and *what* moral codes for justice and fairness generate the general expectations for the resources that a person *should* receive in a situation.

In an encounter, the most immediate reference point is another person or others in the encounter. The characteristics of others are often used to determine what would be a just share for them and for the person making the calculation. There is a large literature within the expectation-states theoretical research program that documents the effects of status character-istics of persons in determining expectation states for their performances; and it is just a short conceptual step to note that these expectation states also contain cognitions about the type and amount of resources that they should receive. Often it is not even particular persons who are used as a reference point because individuals often use abstract others – who represent an aver-age of what would constitute just shares for *this type* of person. This average becomes the just shares for all others, and it is used as a basis for comparison of actual shares to just shares.

These considerations reinforce my view that categoric units serve as reference points. In virtually all encounters, the categoric unit membership of others is noted, at least implicitly. Moreover, members of categoric units are differentially evaluated, with this evaluation also operating to provide a reference point for what would be a just share for members of this category vis-à-vis the categoric membership of the person making the justice assess-ment. Thus, a person who is a member of more valued categoric units (say, a white male with many years of education) will perceive that his just share is greater than the just shares for a person who is a member of less highly valued categoric units (black female with few years of education); and if it turns out that his rewards meet expectations for his and her relative rewards, then this male will feel that justice prevails. If, however, either his rewards do not meet expectations for what a just share means for him, or even if his rewards meet his just shares while the female's shares exceed what would be a just share for her, this male will experience negative emotions, mostly revolving around variants of first-order elaborations of anger.

Expectation-states' theorizing has emphasized individuals' relative power and prestige in the division of labor as influencing expectations for perfor-mance and, by extension, for rewards relative to others (Berger *et al.*, 1972, 1977, 1992). My view is that in the real world, outside the experimental laboratory, individuals make more global calculations about what would be just shares for individuals at different locations within the division of labor of a corpo-rate unit. These calculations may indeed be those of power and prestige at the level of the encounter, but I think that individuals also make assessments about the division of labor *as a whole* and the *subsets of persons* at different places in the division of labor. For example, professors make assessments of their shares of resources relative to those at ranks above and below them rather than the specific rank of a person in a particular encounter. The just share is thus *an average* of what variously ranked professors should receive in general within a particular corporate unit, and the assessment of fairness uses as a reference point these averages for the just shares of subsets of persons at different points in the division of labor. Moreover, individuals often compare corporate units to each other in their assessments of justice. For example, a top-level professor at a small liberal arts college may feel that his just share of resources is different than the just shares for a high-level professor at a prestigious research university. People thus not only use the relative status and prestige of persons (or average of persons in structurally equivalent positions) in a specific encounter as a reference point, but they also use subsets of persons in the larger division of labor or even the relative prestige among corporate units as a whole to establish what is a just share of resources.

Another kind of reference point is abstracted distributions. Individuals often formulate what would be a just share of resources in reference to more meso- and macro-level distributions of resources. The extreme case would be an implicit sense of the Gini coefficient for income distribution in which a person uses the degree of deviation from the straight line of perfect equality to determine what would be a just share, or alternatively, the person may use the line of perfect equality to establish what a just share is. For example, poor individuals often feel that injustice prevails because their place in this larger distribution of resources compares so unfavorably with those who are at higher points in this distribution; and when they feel angry, they are using not only the shares of resources of those in their local encounters but also the general level of inequality in a society or some subunit, implicitly believing that the rich get more than their just share and that poor persons do not get their just share.

Yet another kind of comparison point is what Thibaut and Kelley (1959) termed the "comparison level of alternatives." People will often use their alternative sources of resources and what they might expect from these alternatives as the reference point in determining what is their just share of resources in their current situation. Often, this comparison level is inflated, with a person believing unrealistically that they would secure a certain level of resources in exchanges with alternative others and, under these conditions, they are more likely to inflate their just shares in the current situation. For instance, a college professor may feel that she could earn more at another university, even though no job offer has been tendered, and be angry that current shares do not correspond to the shares perceived to be available elsewhere. Should a job offer from another university be lower than expected, this professor may be angry at this university not only because it has not lived up to her expectations for a just share but also because the less than expected offer will force her to recalibrate what is a just share in her current position.

In sum, then, the various reference points that I have listed – others, categoric units, corporate units, abstracted distributions, and comparison levels of alternatives – can all be part of the expectation states that a person has for resources in an encounter. Depending upon *which configuration* of these reference points is invoked, individuals will establish different formulations of what constitutes a just share and, in turn, the specifics of the configuration will influence emotional arousal. If others are used as a comparison point in establishing expectations as to the just shares for both self and other, the result will be high salience of justice calculations. Under these conditions, under-rewards for a person will generate envy, whereas over-reward will lead to guilt, especially if self's over-reward is perceived to cause other's under-reward. When the reference point is the division of labor or corporate unit as a whole (perhaps in comparison to other similar corporate units), the emotional reaction to under-reward will involve anger, fear, and sadness that eventually coalesce into the second-order elaboration leading to alienation from the culture and structure of the corporate unit. If this alienation is experienced collectively by individuals at the same place in the division of labor of a corporate unit, the anger in this alienation may emerge as collective anger at the injustice of the division of labor. If the reference point is an abstracted other or a categoric unit, anger is the likely response, with this anger developing in a more diffuse anger at, and negative prejudices toward, members of categoric units. If an abstracted distribution, and especially one that is society-wide, becomes the reference point, then diffuse anger at the institutional domains involved in resource distributions (e.g. economy, polity, education) and upper classes in the stratification system will emerge. If an alternative source of resources is used as the comparison point, then the person experiencing injustice will feel angry at others at key positions in the division of labor of corporate units who are perceived, by virtue of their place in the division of labor, to be responsible for under-reward relative to perceived just shares. Moreover, because it is persons within the division of labor of the corporate unit who are targeted, the structure and culture of the corporate unit may also be targeted; and when individuals feel angry at this structure, sad about its effects on them, and fearful of the consequences to them, they will generally experience alienation from the culture and structure of the corporate unit in which this perceived under-reward occurs.

Thus, somewhat different emotions are aroused by invoking varying reference points to formulate a conception of just shares and expectations for rewards in encounters. This combination of diverse reference points and arousal of different emotions leads individuals to target different objects as attribution processes play out. I will need to return to these considerations later but, for the present, let me outline the other key ingredient of expectation states: moral codes.

Moral codes and expectations

There are many potential rules of justice, but they fall into two basic categories: (1) those about distributions of resources among individuals and (2) those about the procedures by which these distributions are made. Among distributive rules are two subtypes: (1a) rules of equity stating that resources should be distributed on the basis of individuals' respective contributions to outcomes and their relative costs/investments and (1b) rules of equality asserting that resources should be divided up equally. These rules are "moral" in the sense that they state what *should* be the basis for individuals' rights to resources; and in most encounters these moral codes are part of the expectations that individuals have for resource distribution. Moreover, the broader culture of corporate units and macrostructures often enshrines justice rules in more general justice ideologies. For example, in American society people firmly believe that income should come from work and that shares of resources should roughly correspond to the distribution of individuals' talents, abilities, and contributions to society; or the culture of most business corporations at the meso level emphasizes that resources – such as money – should go to those who make the key decisions. When the culture of institutional spheres in a society reveals powerful ideologies about distributions of resources, these filter down into the ideologies and norms of meso-level structures, thus generating expectations states for the encounters embedded in these structures (see Figure 3.2).

When distributions conform to the moral rules, procedural rules are generally considered fair, or at least they do not arouse a powerful sense of injustice, as long as the actual distribution corresponds to what is seen as each individual's "just share." When, however, the distribution is viewed as unjust, procedural rules will also be considered unfair, even if they are the same rules that operated to produce "fair" distributions in the past. The general reaction to perceptions that the moral rules of distribution and procedures have been violated is variants of anger and first-order elaborations of anger such as righteousness (anger mixed with happiness). Moral codes add an extra potential for extreme emotional responses because morality is something that people tend to hold as an absolute expectation that *must* be met. Anger at moral injustice is a heat-seeking missile, to borrow the metaphor from the last chapter, but just how this emotional missive is targeted depends upon the reference point(s) used to establish just shares and upon attributions for why justice does not prevail. An additional complication is that any moral code that is violated in a situation – even if it is not part of the normal calculation of just shares – will generally lead individuals to see both the distribution of resources and the procedures by which this distribution occurs as unfair (Mullen and Skitka, 2006; Skitka, 2002). Moral codes in general, then, have broad powers to distort justice calculations.

The relationship between emotional arousal and moral codes is complicated by a number of factors. One is that a person's existing "mood" (low-key, diffuse affective state) has large effects on the distributive norms invoked and to perceptions of whether justice or injustice is seen to prevail (Mullen, 2007). There are data documenting, for instance, that positive moods lead individuals to invoke norms of equality over equity, at least in some circumstances (Sinclair and Mark, 1991, 1992), whereas a negative mood causes them to use equity rules in calculating just shares (O'Malley and Davies, 1984; Sinclair and Mark, 1991). Moreover, negative moods cause persons to perceive differences between social categories (i.e. categoric unit membership and status differences become more salient); and this cognitive tendency reinforces the propensity of negative moods to arouse rules of equity. Similarly, as is the case for diffuse moods, discrete emotions such as anger, sadness, happiness, shame, guilt, and other affective states also influence people's perceptions of justice, in much the same pattern as moods influence perceptions of justice.

Diffuse moods versus specific states of emotional arousal lead to very different cognitive processes revolving around attributions (Forgas *et al.*, 1990), memory (Adolphs and Damasio, 2001; Bower, 1991; Eich and Macaulay, 2000), attitudes (Petty *et al.*, 2001; Ito and Cacioppo, 2001), interpretations of behavior, assessing performances, and making judgments (Forgas, 1992, 1995, 2000). Anger will generally lead individuals to see any distribution of resources as unjust and to make external attributions for this injustice, whereas negative moods or emotions like sadness cause persons to be more deliberative and to seek out the causes of injustice (Bless, 2000; Bless and Schwarz, 1999; Isen, 1984).

There is, then, "a priming effect" of existing emotional arousal on the justice rules invoked and the reactions to violations in these rules (Mullen, 2007). There is also a complex feedback effect. The data show that individuals make moral evaluations very rapidly (Haidt, 2001; Damasio, 1994; Greene and Haidt, 2002) and, hence, experience immediate emotional arousal that then becomes the emotional prime for all subsequent moral assessments. There is some controversy over whether people become cognitively aware of injustice and then emit the appropriate emotion or experience emotional arousal that prompts cognition. In either case, the emotional arousal biases cognitions that, in turn, affect *which* moral codes are invoked and *how* they are interpreted. Thus, people who are in a constant state of anger, shame, alienation, guilt, happiness, or sadness will literally see the world somewhat differently, invoke potentially different moral rules of justice, and react both emotionally and cognitively to justice and injustice in somewhat different ways. Similarly, if emotions are aroused before cognition or in concert with cognitive appraisals, the initial emotion that is aroused – anger, sadness, fear, shame, guilt – will have effects on which moral codes become salient and how evaluations of justice proceed. How, then, are we to get a handle on these complex interaction effects between moods, emotions, justice rules, and cognitions?

Sadness, shame, and guilt are self-referencing emotions; and if repression is avoided, these emotions will lead individuals to reflection and assessment over the train of events that led to the failure to meet expectations for resource shares; and once this path of assessment is undertaken, the likelihood of self-attributions increases. If, however, shame and guilt are repressed, then the anger portion of these emotions will generally intensify and lead to external attributions. Whether as the by-product of repression and trans-mutation or as simply the mood or the discrete emotion aroused, anger inevitably leads to external attributions because it is not an emotion of reflection but of action outward, away from self. If anger becomes suf-ficiently intense, it will often become a first-order elaboration like righteous anger or a desire for vengeance which are typically directed even further outward, beyond the encounter to mesostructures and potentially mac-rostructures. If shame and anger play themselves out, the emerging emotion is often alienation; and, under these conditions, the target of alienation is typically the structure and culture of the corporate unit in which iterated encounters are embedded.

Any form of negative emotional arousal from the failure to meet expecta-tions for exchange payoffs escalates the costs of the exchange, thereby adding yet another source of negative emotional arousal. Thus, even if a person realizes a profit in an exchange, but does not realize *expected* profit, the narrowing margin of profit is made even more narrow or transformed into a loss as negative emotions are aroused over the less-than-expected payoff. As profit declines, whatever negative emotions are aroused will lower commit-ments to the exchange; and if individuals can leave the exchange they will. If they must remain in the exchange for lack of alternatives, negative emotions will gravitate toward alienation, but at times more intense variations of anger are sustained. Under these conditions, individuals will increasingly blame corporate units or members of categoric units, developing diffuse anger toward the latter often as a form of displacement of anger at self.

On the positive side of the emotional spectrum, the fact that positive moods and emotions tend to prime moral judgments toward equality over equity has interesting implications. Equality in resource distribution increases the likelihood that all participants to an encounter will meet expectations and be positively sanctioned which, in turn, activates the processes described in principles 4 and 6a. And once interaction rituals generate increased soli-darity, the positive emotions themselves become yet another resource to be exchanged; and, to the degree that emotions are distributed equally, the emotional energy behind solidarity encourages the symbolization of this mood in totems toward which rituals can be directed in actions and thoughts. And, if this process is repeated across encounters in diverse cor-porate units within different institutional domains and across social classes, then the positive emotions aroused will begin to migrate out from local encounters to corporate and categoric units and, potentially, to macrostruc-tures, thereby increasing commitments to, and the legitimacy of, institutional domains and the stratification system.

If, however, considerations of equity are invoked, for any reason, in encounters, they can have the effect of increasing the salience of differences and unequal distributions of resources – including the positive emotional energy aroused from interaction rituals. Once equity rules emerge, individuals will shift gears, with differences becoming more salient and with calculations of just shares using not only moral codes of equity but also reference points that emphasize differences among others, positions in the division of labor within corporate units, categoric unit membership, and even society-wide abstract distributions. In the context of previously equal disbursements of resources, and the positive interaction rituals that are thereby set into motion (and that increase the emotional profits for all participants to an encounter), it is inevitable that some will feel that they have not received their just share when new reference points and moral codes are invoked; and when expectations, particularly morally charged expectations, are not realized, emotions can quickly turn negative, activating one of the outcomes described above.

In general, embedding of encounters in corporate and categoric units, particularly units clearly embedded within the institutional domains and the stratification system of a society, will increase the clarity of expectations for resources and the consensus over just shares for individuals at different places in the division of labor of corporate units and for members of differentially evaluated categoric units. Most of the dynamics that follow from embedding are captured in the large literature from the expectation-state theoretical research programs. When diffuse status characteristics are discrete and differentially evaluated (in my terms, discrete categoric units) and when positions in the division of labor reveal hierarchical lines of power and prestige, expectation states are generally clear and, moreover, the dynamics of expectation states will generally work to sustain the status system. At the same time, there will generally be consensus over perceptions of what is a just share for individuals in various positions or for individuals revealing diverse diffuse status characteristics, with actual distributions of resources corresponding to these perceptions. If, however, status is ambiguous or if some challenge the status order, then so are the rules about procedures and distributions challenged, as are perceptions of just and actual shares. And, when this situation prevails, negative emotional arousal will unleash the dynamics summarized above and in principles 3, 5, and 6b.

Needs for group inclusion

Humans have needs to feel part of the ongoing interpersonal flow in encounters. Feeling included is very different, however, from having high levels of interpersonal solidarity. Solidarity generates positive emotions and thereby increases the likelihood that self will be verified and that each person will receive profits in exchanges of resources; and so, it should not be surprising that people are drawn to encounters where interaction rituals generate these effects (see principles 1, 2, and 6a in Chapter 9). Still, as a number of theorists have pointed out (e.g. Markovsky and Lawler, 1994), people also recoil from engulfment whereby self is overwhelmed and subordinated to the collective goals of the group.

Humans are, after all, still an ape; and, as I emphasized in Chapter 2, apes do not reveal propensities for strong ties and high levels of group solidarity. There is, in fact, a constant tension among humans that is the result of the cross-wiring in their neurology. On the one hand, natural selection worked to enhance needs for strong group bonds through increasing hominids' and then humans' emotional capacities but, on the other hand, this neurology is laid over the wiring for individualism, mobility, and weak-tie behavioral tendencies (Turner, 2002; Maryanski and Turner, 1992; Turner and Maryanski, 2005). The conflict that we often see in ideologies – e.g. collectivism vs. individualism – is a conflict that simply mirrors what occurs in our neurology.

If humans sought high solidarity in every encounter, they would be disappointed, especially in complex differentiated societies where mobility across a larger web of affiliations is common. Moreover, because humans use emotions to build solidarities, the energy needed for ritual practices building up solidarity and group symbols would lead to exhaustion, if these extended rituals were necessary in every encounter. Instead, as a basic strategy, humans are highly selective as to *which* encounters embedded in *which* corporate units and *which* categoric units will be worthy of a full ritual response. Most of the time, individuals only need to feel included – that is, as part of the interpersonal flow. When individuals do not sense that they are part of the flow, they will experience negative emotions. They may feel sad; they may become angry; they may feel fearful about what being excluded means. And, if they experience all of these emotions together, they may feel shame. They may also experience guilt if group inclusion is defined in moral terms. Over time, if they continue to experience all three negative emotions together and if they cannot withdraw from encounters where they do not feel fully engaged in the interpersonal flow, the three negative emotions will transmute to alienation from the encounter and, in all likelihood, the corporate and categoric units in which it is embedded.

Embedding generally works to increase a sense of group inclusion in encounters because embedding increases the likelihood that people will know what to expect and how to receive sanctions marking inclusion. However, inequalities can reduce this sense of inclusion, particularly for members of devalued categoric units but also for individuals at lower levels in the hierarchical division of labor. Typically, there are interpersonal rituals that smooth over inequalities (Collins, 1975) and, at the same time, provide a sense that each person is part of the interpersonal flow, but inequalities also increase distances between high-ranking and low-ranking persons. Moreover, if high-ranking individuals use their advantages to exclude low-ranking persons from the interpersonal flow, then needs for minimal levels of group inclusion may not be met, thereby increasing negative emotional arousal among the low-ranking.

Less embedded encounters make it even more likely that needs for group inclusion may not be realized because expectations are often ambiguous about what will transpire in the encounter. Since people will first pay attention to self-confirmation and profits from the exchange of resources, some may overlook the needs of others to feel included in the group. Moreover, ambiguity about status can set off status competition among individuals in these amorphous encounters; and if status competition causes individuals to raise their status by dominating conversations, some individuals will inevitably feel left out as they sink to the bottom of the status hierarchy. While virtually all studies on the emergence of expectation states for performance are conducted on task groups (in order to provide a clear marker of performance), the same dynamics occur in non-task groups. In fact, they are more likely to result in some being left out of the interpersonal flow when status competition occurs over issues beyond simple task performance.

If self is highly salient in an encounter and a person feels "left out" of the interpersonal flow, the negative emotions aroused will be that much more intense. And if certain resources marking group inclusion and hence self-verification are not received, the failure to verify self will be compounded by the inability to receive what a person may have come to expect as a just share. This person may feel only sad, mad, or fearful, but once self is highly salient, especially as deeper levels of self become salient, shame and perhaps guilt (if the situation is defined as moral) will be more likely to emerge. If the individual does not repress the shame and makes accurate attributions for the sense of being excluded, then this individual will feel sad if self-attributions are made and mad at specific individuals if external attributions are made. Individuals may also be fearful and anxiety-ridden if they feel that, no matter what they do, the experience of feeling excluded will be repeated as the encounter is iterated; and, if they can, excluded persons will seek to leave the encounter and the units in which it is embedded.

If a person who feels excluded does not repress this emotion, perhaps he or she can make adjustments, leave the group, or find an alternative group. However, if this person must experience a chronic sense of being excluded from groups, then shame may emerge; and if the shame is sufficiently painful, the individual will activate defense mechanisms and thus change the emotional dynamics. Any one of the emotions that make up shame – that is, sadness, anger, fear – can emerge in intensified spikes which generally breach the interaction and make the person feel even more excluded and hence shameful.

Group inclusion as a need operates somewhat differently than other needs in that repression intensifies the emotions and can transmute them into any of the three constituent emotions of shame. Sadness is the most likely emotion to emerge because sadness is already the dominant emotion of shame, whereas anger is the least likely to emerge because to vent anger only breaches the interaction further and makes one feel even more marginal. Anxiety is also likely because, if individuals cannot escape interactions, they will be fearful. Shame is more likely, I believe, to transmute into alienation which is composed of sadness, anger at others or social units, and some fear; in a sense, alienation allows for the anger to be quietly "expressed" in a passive-aggressive way: through a blasé attitude toward the group and its members, through role-distance, or through a feigned unwillingness to seek its approval from others.

Thus, the failure to meet needs for group inclusion does not have the same volatile consequences of intensifying the anger alone, or pulling out the anger component of shame in acts of direct aggression. Achieving a sense of group inclusion generates mild positive emotions, while failing to feel included leads to less aggressive negative emotions like sadness, anxiety, and alienation. Failure to meet needs for group inclusion does not, therefore, rip apart social relations, nor does this failure pose threats to social structures. Yet, the emotions aroused lower commitments and decrease the willingness of individuals to invest self and resources in the interpersonal flow and, hence, in the social structures in which the encounter is embedded. And, failure to realize needs for group inclusion motivates individuals to leave the structures in which they feel unappreciated and, if alienated, to withdraw from these structures and the institutional domains in which they are embedded (as is the case when devalued ethnic categories drop out of high school). The failure to meet needs for group inclusion can, therefore, have large effects on mesostructures and macrostructures when larger numbers of individuals potentially experience this sense of exclusion from mesostructures that are used to build institutional domains.

Needs for trust

I have grouped under the rubric of trust need-states that appear in a number of general sociological theories. Humans have a set of needs that, in the end, generates a sense of trust in others and the encounter. One need is for predictability of behaviors; humans need to feel that, through role-taking and through consensus over expectations, that the behaviors of others can be understood and anticipated. Another related need is for rhythmic synchronization of talk and body language; the rhythmic flow of interaction is critical to sustaining a sense of predictability and, more generally, that others can be trusted (Collins, 2004). Finally, humans need to feel that others are being sincere and honest, while at the same time respecting one's dignity (Habermas, 1970), thereby enabling a person to trust others.

These sub-needs all coalesce around a basic need to trust others; and when a person cannot derive this sense in an encounter, negative emotions will emerge. If a situation is important to a person, the negative emotions will revolve around variants of fear, coupled with anger. Without trust, other transactional needs cannot be realized. We cannot trust others to verify self, now and in the future, nor can we be assured that the exchange of resources will meet expectations for just shares, now and in the future. And, if we cannot trust others, our sense of group inclusion will be, at best, tenuous. When we experience trust, other needs are more readily met, thus ratcheting up the positive emotions that come from not only trusting others but also from feeling that self will be verified, that exchanges of resources will realize a profit, and that a sense of group inclusion will be achieved, and that the situation is as it appears (facticity).

Embedding has large effects on trust because the structure and culture of corporate and categoric units generally make expectations more explicit and, thereby, allow individuals to act in predictable, rhythmic, and sincere ways. Still, trust can be easily broken if others are not predictable, are not able to rhythmically synchronize talk and body, and are not able to appear sincere. No amount of structure can overcome a lack of trust at the face-to-face level; and when individuals do not meet this need, they become fearful and angry, seeking to leave the encounter and avoid future encounters if they can. Because a sense of trust is generated in the immediate, moment-by-moment interactions of individuals reading face, body, and voice, attributions for the failure to meet this need are generally external and are directed at others who are perceived to be unpredictable, out of rhythmic synchronization, or insincere. At times, individuals will blame categories of others as untrustworthy, experiencing anger and perhaps some fear about members of these categories and almost always developing negative prejudicial beliefs about the characteristics of members in untrustworthy categories.

If individuals cannot leave encounters where others or categories of others act in ways to thwart meeting needs for trust, then interaction with others will become highly ritualized and stilted. Often, negative personality characteristics will be imputed to others who are unpredictable, out of rhythmic synchronization, or insincere; and if these individuals are members of categoric units, negative prejudices toward such members may intensify if the correlation between categoric unit membership and failure to achieve trust is sustained over time and across diverse encounters. Moreover, if individuals feel sadness along with their anxiety and anger, they will become alienated from these others and, typically, from the encounter as a whole as well as the structure and culture in which this encounter is embedded. For once all three negative emotions are operative, and with the anger portion of alienation becoming more active, individuals will typically generalize their failure to achieve a sense of trust to the culture and structure of the corporate unit.

Needs for facticity

As part of what Alfred Schutz (1967 [1932]) termed intersubjecivity is the need for people to feel that they and others in an encounter are experiencing a common world. Ethnomethodology (Garfinkel, 1967) picked up on this basic idea, emphasizing that individuals employ folk methods to create accounts of reality. Anthony Giddens (1984) added to this point of emphasis an idea borrowed from philosophy in his view that humans seek ontological security that allows them to feel that "things are as they appear." These diverse approaches all converge on a view of humans as needing to sense that (1) they share a common world for the purposes of an interaction, (2) they perceive reality of the situation as it appears, and (3) they assume reality has an obdurate character for the duration of the interaction. I term these related need-states "facticity" because for an encounter to flow smoothly its participants must sense that they experience and share a sense of a common factual world (Turner, 1987, 1988, 2002:133–5).

Ethnomethodologists' (Garfinkel, 1967) early use of "breaching experiments" gives us data on the emotions aroused when people do not meet needs for facticity. Individuals would become angry at experimenters who had deliberately breached the interaction and forced others to use folk methods to try and reconstruct assumption of a shared reality. Like needs for trust, meeting needs for facticity is highly contingent on what transpires in the immediate situation, as individuals mutually role-take and present self. When needs are not met under these conditions, individuals are most likely to make external attributions to others in the encounter and direct variants of mild-to-moderate anger at these others.

Embedding increases the likelihood that individuals will meet needs for facticity because the culture and structure of corporate and categoric units provide guidelines for what is real, with individuals simply filling in needed details in encounters. If, however, an encounter is not embedded or if the structure and culture of the units in which an encounter are embedded is ambiguous, then individuals will have to work very hard at establishing a sense of a common reality. For example, an interaction among individuals from diverse but not clearly demarcated categoric units (high and moderate levels of education, for example), or who are members of several categoric units (e.g. poor white male and educated African American female), will usually have to devote considerable interpersonal energy to establish a sense of common reality. Initial interactions will be highly ritualized and stilted, with individuals probing each other as they try to build up a sense of a common world.

When individuals cannot achieve a sense of facticity, meeting other transactional needs becomes more problematic. It is difficult to feel that self has been verified when participants do not sense a common reality; it is equally difficult to know what resources are in play and whether or not people have received their just shares; it is hard to achieve a sense of group inclusion when the very nature of the common reality is up in the air; and trust is not likely to occur when questions about the nature of the reality in the situation are unresolved. This is why, I believe, individuals get frustrated (a mild variant of anger) in interactions that do not establish a sense of facticity; a lot more is on the line than just a common sense of what is real. Meeting other needs is being thwarted, and those who seem to be in the way invite anger from others.

If the situation is important to individuals and if needs for facticity are not met, then other emotions like fear can also emerge. Negative emotions work to make the situation even more problematic because, however these emotions are expressed, they will tend to breach the interaction and create an even more acute sense that needs for facticity have not been realized. Thus, what can sometimes seem like trivial occasions can become highly charged emotionally when individuals sense that they do not experience, even for the purposes of a short encounter, a common external world.

Conclusion

I have offered many propositions in this chapter that follow from those in the last chapter. I could present the full package of generalizations here, but the inventory of propositions would be long and complex, as it has been in other works on micro–social processes (e.g. Turner, 2002). This time around, my goal is to sustain the main line of theorizing, and so I will conclude with two relatively simple propositions that summarize the general thrust of my argument. Each transactional need has somewhat different emotional effects on individuals, but there is a general pattern to these effects that is summarized in principles 7 and 8 below.

7   *Humans possess at least five transactional needs for verification of self, profitable exchange payoffs, group inclusion, trust, and facticity, all of which generate expectation states in an encounter; and the more these expectation states generated by transactional needs are met, especially needs for self-verification and profitable exchange payoffs, the more likely are individuals to experience positive emotions and make self-attributions, while giving off positive emotions to others that initiates solidarity-generating interaction rituals (as described in propositions 1 and 4).*

   A   *The more others are seen as facilitating the meeting of transactional needs, the more likely will the giving off of positive emotions also involve the expression of gratitude.*

   B   *The more the structure and culture of the corporate unit are seen as facilitating the meeting of transactional needs, the more likely will individuals develop commitments to this culture and structure.*

   C   *The more members of categoric units are seen as facilitating the meeting of transactional needs, the more likely will individuals develop favorable prejudices toward members of these categoric units.*

8   *The less expectation states generated by transactional needs are met in an encounter, and especially needs for self-verification and profitable exchange payoffs, the more individuals will also perceive this failure to meet expectations as negative sanctions from others and, hence, the more intense will be their*

negative emotional arousal; and the more intense is the level of negative emotional arousal, the more likely will defense mechanisms be activated and lead to external attributions (see propositions 3 and 6b).

A   To the degree that individuals make self-attributions for failing to meet transactional needs in an encounter, the more likely will they experience all three negative emotions; and the more they experience these emotions simultaneously, the more likely are they to experience shame; and if moral cultural codes are invoked to evaluate self under these conditions, the more likely will they experience guilt as well.

B   The more individuals consistently experience shame and, to a lesser extent, guilt in iterated encounters, the more likely are they to employ defensive strategies and defense mechanisms, and the more they activate defense mechanisms, the more likely are external attributions revolving around transmuted and intensified negative emotions to be made.

1   If others are targeted, individuals will experience and express anger toward these others; and if shame is the repressed emotion, the more intense will this anger be.

2   If corporate units in which an encounter is embedded are targeted, individuals will experience and express anger toward this unit, thereby reducing commitments to the structure and culture of this unit; and if repressed shame and, to a lesser extent, guilt are fueling this anger, the more likely will this anger transmute further into alienation from the culture and structure of the corporate unit and, potentially, the culture and structure of the more inclusive institutional domain as well.

3   If categoric units in which an encounter is embedded are targeted, individuals will experience and express anger at, and develop negative prejudices toward, members of these units and, potentially, the more inclusive institutional domains or locations in the stratification system generating these categoric units.

6   Social structure and emotional arousal

At the level of face-to-face encounters, social structure impinges on individuals via the micro-dynamic forces of status, roles, ecology, and demography (see Table 3.1). Individuals generally occupy status positions that carry varying levels of resources, such as power and prestige; and by virtue of status and the resources associated with status, people seek to play particular roles; and, conversely, individuals seek to claim or affirm status through role-making efforts. Encounters are also driven by ecological forces revolving around the physical space, partitions, and props available as well as by the demography of space concerning the number of persons co-present, their memberships in categoric units, and their movements in and out of the encounter. Much of the effect of corporate and categoric units on the dynamics of encounters thus revolves around how these meso-level units structure (1) the vertical and horizontal divisions of labor as these affect status and role dynamics, (2) the amount and configuration of space as well as the props available to individuals, and (3) the number and nature of the people present as well as their movements in space. As might be expected, a considerable amount of sociological research and theorizing has been conducted on these micro-dynamic forces, particularly status, but surprisingly little work has been done on how the corporate and categoric units in which encounters are embedded determine the nature of status, roles, ecology, and demography. Similarly, comparatively little research and theory exists on how institutional domains and stratification systems exert effects on micro encounters via corporate and categoric units.

Status, roles, ecology, and demography are the conduits by which mesostructures and macrostructures exert pressure on encounters; and so, if we are to analyze how these micro-dynamic forces drive the formation and operation of encounters, we must also recognize that these micro-level forces are the contact points between individuals, on the one side, and the larger-scale structures of society, on the other side. As these forces operate, the emotions aroused have consequences not just for the interpersonal flow in the encounter but also for the mesostructures and, potentially, macrostructures in which the encounter is embedded.

Mesostructures and clarity of expectations

The operation of micro-dynamic forces is, as I have emphasized, constrained by embedding. As principle 2 B outlines,[1] encounters embedded in corporate and categoric units (which, in turn, are embedded in institutional domains and stratification systems) are more likely to generate clearer expectations than those which are not embedded (principle 3 B). These two principles are, however, rather general; and it is time to add some necessary detail about what *specific properties* of corporate and categoric units generate clarity of expectation states for individuals. I am pausing to add this specificity here because structural forces in encounters revolving around status, roles, ecology, and demography are directly affected by key structural conditions in corporate and categoric units that increase the clarity of expectations.

Specific structural conditions increasing clarity of expectations in corporate units

Certain conditions increase the degree of coherence in the structure of corporate units and, hence, in the expectations that they generate. A concise list is given in Table 6.1 for easy reference. One condition is the visibility of the boundaries of a corporate unit and the existence of "entrance and exit rules," as Niklas Luhmann (1982) has called them. When units are bounded and when individuals understand when and how they are to enter or exit the corporate unit, they also bring with them understandings about the culture, structure, and expectations on them. In contrast, corporate units that do not have clear boundaries, along with entrance and exit rules, can be ambiguous and amorphous, with individuals not entirely sure if they are in or out of the unit and unclear as to what expectations are salient and when they are to be invoked.

Table 6.1 Conditions in corporate units increasing clarity of expectations

1 Visibility of boundaries of a corporate unit and existence of entrance and exit rules.
2 Explicitness of goals of the corporate unit.
3 Embedding of a corporate unit in clearly differentiated institutional domain with an explicit ideology.
4 Explicitness of the vertical and horizontal divisions of labor within the corporate unit.
5 Formality of the structure within the corporate unit.
6 Explicitness of norms attached to positions in the division of labor as well as consistency between norms and corporate unit ideologies.
7 Degree of correlation between positions in the division of labor of a corporate unit and the distribution of members of discrete categoric units in these positions.

---

1   The complete list of theoretical principles is given in Chapter 9.

A second condition is the explicitness of the goals of the corporate unit. When goals are clear and, indeed, when the unit is focused on these goals, this focus will be evident in an explicit division of labor and in the ideologies and norms designed to realize the unit's goals. Again, when goals are amorphous or vague, they cannot provide guidance in how to structure the division of labor or in the formation of cultural codes. Without clear guidance by structure and culture, individuals are left to work matters out at the level of the encounter. The result is that expectations will be unclear, ambiguous, or even in conflict.

A third condition increasing the clarity of expectations is, as principle 2 C emphasized, the embedding of a corporate unit in a differentiated macro-level institutional domain revealing an explicit ideology. When an institutional domain is separated from other institutional systems and when it has clear beliefs about what should and ought to occur in this domain, the structure and culture of this more autonomous domain constrain to a high degree the structure and culture of corporate units. The specific organizational ideologies will represent applications of the broader institutional ideology; the unit will be more likely to have boundaries as well as rules for entering and exiting; and it will be more likely to have clear goals to secure resources within the resource niches generated by the institutional domain.

A fourth condition is the explicitness of the vertical and horizontal divisions of labor within a corporate unit, which is more likely under the above conditions. When the status structure is unambiguous, then expectations in general and, more specifically, the expectations attached to norms and roles will also be clear. Individuals will know what positions they can occupy and what range of roles they can play; and they are more likely to understand the expectations on them and others in the division of labor.

A fifth condition is the formality of the structure in a corporate unit. In general, vertical divisions of labor increase formality as they generate relations of authority; and while authority often creates tensions associated with inequalities, the clarity of expectations is nonetheless increased. Those in superordinate and subordinate positions are more likely to understand what they are to do and how they are to perform their tasks.

A sixth condition is the clarity of norms attached to positions in the division of labor within the corporate unit as well as the degree of consistency between corporate unit ideologies and norms. When ideologies are implemented through norms that are consistent with the mandates of the ideologies, then expectations are not only more explicit, they are also given a moral character which raises their salience and power.

A final condition increasing the clarity of expectations in corporate units is the degree of correlation between positions in the division of labor, on the one side, and membership in discrete categoric units, on the other. If structurally equivalent positions in the division of labor are occupied disproportionately by members of a discrete categoric unit (e.g. women are secretaries, men are managers; slaves are black, owners of plantations are white), then the norms (and the underlying ideology) attached to positions in the division of labor and the differential evaluations of incumbents in the division of labor and of members in categoric units generate convergent sets of expectations that specify how people are supposed to behave. Conversely, when there is a low or no correlation between categoric unit memberships and location in the division of labor, expectations can work at cross-purposes and indeed can generate ambiguity over expectations (e.g. the burdens of women managers having authority over men).

Each of these conditions, alone, increases clarity of expectations, but a corporate unit revealing all of these conditions will have very explicit expectations which individuals will understand and try to meet, as long as the inequalities in the division of labor and its correlation with memberships in discrete categoric units do not systematically generate negative emotions that cause conflict and change the division of labor, goals, and culture of the unit. In fact, at times the conditions increasing clarity can also work to increase inequalities that, in turn, produce negative emotions that mobilize individuals to change the culture and structure of the corporate unit.

Conditions increasing the clarity of expectations for categoric units

In Table 6.2, the conditions increasing the clarity of expectations attached to categoric units are listed. One condition is the discreteness of the boundaries defining categoric unit membership, or what Peter Blau (1977) termed "nominal parameters." Discreteness draws a line; one is either in or out of the categoric unit. For example, people are denoted as either male or female (true, even this line can become fuzzy) or as black or white (even when the line between "black" and "white" is vague). At times, discreteness is lost as markers become more continuous or, in Blau's terms, "graduated parameters." For instance, skin color is treated as a graduated parameter in Brazil, while in the United States it still remains a nominal parameter (despite the wide variations in pigmentation of those categorized as "black"). Graduated parameters generally create more ambiguity of expectations because it may be difficult to determine where a person should be placed along the parameter. For example, age often creates a problem in categorizing individuals and,

Table 6.2 Conditions among categoric units increasing clarity of expectations

1 Discreteness of boundaries defining categoric unit membership.
2 Degree of consensus over relative evaluations of categoric units in broader society.
3 Embeddedness of categoric units within macro-level stratification system.
4 Homogeneity among members of a categoric unit.
5 The degree of correlation between membership in one categoric unit with memberships in other categoric units.
6 The degree of correlation of categoric unit membership with positions in the vertical and horizontal divisions of labor of corporate units within clearly differentiated institutional domains.

hence, in determining the expectations on them and those responding to this person. The extremes of the distribution – very old and very young – are clear enough and, in fact, can operate more like discrete categoric units with unambiguous expectations; moreover, there can be markers along the scale that re-categorize individuals, as is the case on their twenty-first birthday in the United States. Still, there will always be some ambiguity when people are arrayed across a graduated parameter, thus decreasing the clarity of expectations.

A second condition increasing clarity of expectations for categoric units is degree of consensus over the differential evaluation of categoric units and the ideologies that legitimize this differential evaluation. Thus, black slaves in the anti-bellum south in the United States were very clearly devalued next to whites, even poor whites, and there emerged an elaborate ideological justification for this differential evaluation (an ideology that changed over time but nonetheless sustained the devaluation of blacks; see Turner and Singleton, 1978; Turner *et al.*, 1984, for a history of the changing ideology). When differential evaluations of categoric units are not clear or subject to contestation, expectations become correspondingly unclear and ambiguous.

A third condition is the degree of embeddedness of categoric units within the macro-level stratification system and the degree of inequality in the distribution of resources in this system, as was emphasized in principle 2 C. When there are large differences in the resource levels of different social classes, class itself becomes a discrete categoric unit. Equally significant, if there are other categoric units that are over-represented in a class, then this association of a discrete categoric unit – say, ethnicity – with another discrete categoric unit – such as lower class – increases the discreteness of both and sustains the differential evaluation that, in turn, increases clarity of expectations. Because a stratification system distributes resources unequally, this distribution carries differential evaluation – i.e. those with resources are more valued than those without them – and it also creates distinct class cultures which also serve to demark people as members of categoric units. In contrast, when categoric units are more embedded within an institutional domain – such as the category of worker, mother, student, politician – this embeddedness is not so clearly associated with the differential evaluation associated with inequality and, as a result, it carries less power. However, to the extent that a categoric unit is defined by a status and role within a clearly differentiated institutional domain, the expectations for members of this unit will generally be quite clear, but they will not carry the same degree of differential evaluation as is the case when categoric units are generated by the stratification system.

A fourth condition increasing clarity of expectations is the homogeneity of individuals who are members of a categoric unit. If the lower classes in a society are all black, this distribution of ethnicity increases the clarity of expectations for blacks and lower-class individuals, whereas if blacks are equally spread across the class structure, while members of other ethnic subpopulations are also widely distributed across social classes, the clarity of expectations for both class and ethnicity become more complex and, generally, less explicit. Once homogeneity of membership declines, individuals will always need to calibrate expectations for more than one categoric unit because diversity of membership generally means that individuals will need to figure out just how to respond to each person by assessing his or her membership in other categoric units. For instance, in assessing how to respond to poor persons of both genders, it becomes necessary to have one set of expectations for poverty categories and another for gender categories. Or, to take another example, if whites and blacks are equally represented in the lower classes, then interaction will need to calibrate what it means to be black and wealthy as well as white and poor.

A fifth condition increasing clarity of expectations associated with categoric units is the degree of correlation of membership in one unit with membership in another categoric unit. As the example above of over-representation of an ethnic subpopulation in the lower class illustrates, the clarity of expectations increases significantly when the correlation is high. The expectations, in essence, double up, and specify what persons in this category are supposed to do and how others are to respond to them.

A final condition increasing explicitness of expectations is the degree of correlation of categoric unit membership with positions in the vertical and horizontal divisions of labor of corporate units within institutional domains. For instance, if all managers in a business corporation are male and all secretaries are female, expectations are more explicit, whereas when secretaries can be male and managers can be female, this correlation (which once was very high in most industrial societies) is lowered and, as a result, expectations will not be so clear for members of categoric units (in this case, males and females) and will, in essence, need to be calibrated "on the ground" during the course of an encounter.

Constraints on encounters

The micro-dynamic forces of status, role, ecology, and demography are all manifestations of the structure and culture of corporate and categoric units as they constrain the formation and operation of encounters. If the clarity of expectations emanating from corporate and categoric units is high, then it is more likely that people can meet these expectations and receive positive sanctions (principles 1 and 4), while avoiding the negative emotional arousal that comes with not meeting expectations (principle 3) and receiving negative sanctions from others (principle 5) which, in turn, will unleash complicated emotional reactions associated with defense mechanisms, intensification and transmutation of emotions, and external attributions (principle 6b). Thus, the more the conditions listed in tables 6.1 and 6.2 are met, the more explicit are expectations and, as a result, the more the structural forces of role, status, ecology, and demography operate in ways that increase positive emotional arousal that sustain the encounter and the mesostructures in which it is embedded. Conversely, the more these conditions do not exist, the more likely are these structural forces of role, status, ecology, and demography to arouse negative emotions that can breach the encounter and, if repressed, intensify and transmute into emotions that can change mesostructures and, potentially, macrostructures as well. Now, let me turn to each structural force – that is, role, status, ecology, and demography – and outline how each affect emotional dynamics in embedded encounters.

Roles and emotional arousal

The concept of role has a variety of meanings. One is that roles are the expectations for how people should behave in a situation (Moreno, 1953 [1934]); another is that roles are the behavioral component of status positions regulated by norms (Parsons, 1951); yet another is that roles are bundles of resources that individuals employ to emit behaviors that gain them access to status (Baker and Faulkner, 1991); still another is that roles are strategic presentations of self (Goffman, 1967; R. H. Turner, 1962); and a final view is that roles are cultural objects that signify who people are, what they are doing, and how they should be treated (Callero, 1994). These views are not contradictory, but they do suggest that roles have many facets that need to be incorporated into a theory of how roles and emotions are related.

The phenomenology of roles

Ralph Turner (1962, 1968, 2002) has introduced the idea that people operate under a "folk norm of consistency" or an implicit (gestalt) assumption that the gestures emitted by individuals in an encounter are consistent with each other and mark an underlying role. Individuals assume, for the purposes at hand, that gestures constitute a syndrome of signs marking and embodying a role, and they are motivated to discover each other's roles. Once role-taking (Mead, 1934) allows individuals to discover this underlying role, the complementary role is orchestrated (role-making) so that cooperation can ensue. If, however, an individual cannot discover the underlying role, a person will experience negative emotional arousal – typically mild anger like annoyance or, if the other is powerful, variants of fear. Thus, humans are programmed by their neuroanatomy (by gestalt propensities) to search for the pattern among gestures and, if they can, to discover the roles being played by others.

   Since humans do not have the same level of innate bonding mechanisms as most other mammals, these phenomenological and gestalt dynamics are critical to sustaining the encounter. If the underlying role being played by another cannot be determined early in an encounter, an individual will then need to work extra hard to discover the role; and if these efforts prove futile, then it is very likely that the encounter will be breached, setting off a chain of negative emotional arousal. Breaches become less likely to the degree that individuals share common languages, particularly the language of emotions.

Speech does have effects on role-making, but as individuals make a role for themselves and as individuals role-take in order to discern this role, they rely more on "body language" and paralinguistic cues (inflections, tones) than on spoken words. The communication of emotions through gestures becomes the primary basis by which roles are made, taken, and verified; and even when social structure defines the range of roles that people can play in a situation, the language of emotion signals *which variant* within this range is being played by a person.

The cognitive basis of roles

Individuals carry inventories of roles in their stocks of knowledge (Turner, 1994a) which they access when role-taking with another. There are, I believe, four basic types of roles stored in these stocks of knowledge (Turner, 2002): preassembled roles, combinational roles, generalized roles, and trans-situational roles. Let me briefly discuss each.

Preassembled roles

These are widely known roles that are revealed by sets of gestures that are readily perceived and understood. When these gestures are observed in an encounter, individuals can immediately pull from their stocks of knowledge all elements of the role and adjust their conduct to play complementary roles. For example, the roles of mother, father, policeman, student, worker, lazy worker, serious student, and other roles generally associated with an institutional domain are well understood; and once gestures marking this role are observed, it is relatively easy for a person to scan stocks of knowledge and fill in the rest of the role.

Combinational roles

Individuals also carry in their stocks of knowledge conceptions of how roles can be combined in particular situations. What is involved is a conception of how two or more preassembled roles can be spliced together in certain situations. For instance, a woman hosting a family gathering plays both the role of host and the role associated with her place in the kinship institutional domain. Individuals already know this combination of roles and, hence, can easily make the necessary adjustments to the combined behaviors of both roles.

Generalized roles

Individuals also carry in their stocks of knowledge understandings of what certain syndromes mean in all types of situations. For example, people understand what syndromes mark being upbeat, assertive, gracious, shy, reserved, serious, and diligent. These generalized roles can be attached to almost any other role, as would be the case for a serious student, assertive worker, upbeat mother, and so on. The generalized role is known, and coupled with another role that is also known, a person easily role-takes and makes the necessary adjustments in his or her behaviors vis-à-vis another.

Trans-situational roles

For virtually every categoric unit there is also a set of behaviors that are expected from individuals in this categoric unit; and these roles are, in essence, carried from situation to situation and emitted, typically along with another role. For example, there are expected behaviors associated with being a woman or man as well as old or young; and the expectations for behaviors of individuals in these categoric units − that is, female, male, young, and old − can be easily blended with whatever other roles that individuals in these categories may be playing. For instance, a woman emits elements of her gendered role that she always carries and then blends this role with being a mother or worker; or a male carries the role of maleness from situation and then mixes this role with being a worker, father, or athlete. Individuals understand these trans-situational roles and generally the other roles that people assert in a situation; and on the basis of this understanding of the ways that these trans-situational roles can be combined with other roles, it becomes relatively easy to adjust behavior to play the appropriate complementary role.

Humans carry in their large neocortex vast inventories of these basic types of roles; and if we think about the process of role-taking for a moment, this must be the case because individuals ascertain the role of others rather quickly and without great agony. If we had to search for the unique or idiosyncratic roles of others in each and every encounter, individuals would exhaust themselves. Moreover, people would be constantly experiencing mild fear in all situations as they frantically scanned gestures to see what role a person might be constructing in a situation. By having a large inventory of roles already stored in stocks of knowledge, individuals can see the initial gestures marking a role, quickly scan the inventory, and pick out the role that is being asserted in a situation. In most situations this process occurs rapidly and with great ease, but when we cannot "figure out where some-one is coming from," negative emotions are aroused because we are resentful that the other has not played a role that is stored in our stocks of knowledge. Much of this knowledgeability is implicit and, in fact, it is often difficult to verbalize just what the syndrome of gestures marking a role might be; still, most of the time, we have little trouble in discovering the role in our inventory, even if we cannot fully articulate its components.

The verification of roles

When individuals present self in a situation, they are also role-making, to use Ralph H. Turner's (1962) term; role-taking occurs by viewing the role-making efforts of others. Individuals always seek to have their roles verified by others because it is through role behaviors that transactional needs are realized. Role-identities are tied explicitly to others' verification of the role presented, but other levels of self (sub-identities and core self-conceptions) are also presented via roles; and so, individuals are highly motivated to have their roles verified because self is on the line. Similarly, many of the resources given to and received from others come via roles; and if these roles cannot be mutually verified, the flow of resources will be disrupted. Group inclusion is often achieved by others accepting the role being presented in a situation. Trust ensues when others verify a role because, once verification occurs, behaviors become more predictable and rhythmically synchronized; and markers of sincerity become clear. Facticity is achieved by individuals understanding each other's roles because, with mutual verification of roles, the situation becomes more obdurate, giving people a sense that they do indeed share a common world.

Thus, verifying a role has implications far beyond the role, per se. The ability to meet expectations arising from transactional needs is, by and large, achieved when roles are successfully made and verified. Similarly, other elements of culture and social structure as they set up expectations will also be realized via role-making and role verification.

In many ways, the expectations that arise from the syndromes of gestures that constitute a role provide a shorthand way to meet the more complex expectation states arising from transactional needs. Although roles add yet another layer of expectation states to the encounter, they also serve notice to others about the expectations for self, resources, group inclusion, trust, and facticity that are piggy-backed onto a role. Others see the gestures of a person, assume that these gestures are consistent and mark an underlying role, and scan their stocks of knowledge to discover the underlying role; in so doing, they derive a quick image of, or sense for, the broader array of expectation states a person carries into the situation.

Moreover, sanctioning generally occurs as others respond to the role-making efforts of a person. People offer positive sanctions when verifying a role presented by another and negative sanctions when not accepting or not understanding a role. An individual thus knows *immediately* where they stand when observing the reactions of others to role-making efforts; and with this implicit recognition comes a sense for whether or not other expectations are likely to be met (and if forthcoming sanctions will be positive or negative). The result is that roles provide a kind of early warning system about expectations and sanctions, allowing individuals a chance to make necessary adjustments before they become too vested in a role and operate under unrealistic expectations that, in the end, will cause more severe negative sanctions from others.

Because so much is at stake in the process of role verification, it should not be surprising that emotions can run high when roles are verified; and, of course, emotions will run even higher when roles are not verified. When a role is verified, and especially a role where self and critical resources are on the line, a person will experience variants of happiness and give off positive emotions (e.g. happiness, pride, gratitude) in accordance with the processes enumerated in principles 1 and 4.[2] The individual will sense that more than expectations associated with a role have been met; other expectation states associated with transactional needs, social structure, and culture are also likely to have been realized. Verification of roles also works as the ultimate positive sanction because so many expectation states are interwoven with the role being presented. Conversely, when individuals' roles are not verified, the negative emotions aroused can take many turns. The person may feel sad, angry, or fearful; and if these emotions are experienced simultaneously, this person may feel shame, and guilt if expectations from moral codes were tied up in a role. Over time, this simultaneous activation of all three negative emotions may shift to alienation, with an individual revealing distance from the role that this person has been forced to play as a substitute for the role that was not verified.

Attribution processes become a critical force in mediating the nature of the emotions aroused and the targets of these emotions. When individuals make self-attributions for the failure to verify a role, they will generally feel sad but if self is highly salient, they will probably experience shame. If they repress this shame, they will be more likely to make external attributions and display anger toward the objects of these attributions. The anger may target individuals, if these individuals are not powerful and cannot sanction back, but there is a general bias for anger fueled by repressed shame to leap-frog others in the local encounter and target corporate and categoric units (see principle 6b). The reason for this is that, ultimately, the face-to-face encounter is where people derive their positive emotions; and to "soil" the encounter with anger and rage assures that the person will experience negative sanctions, thus increasing the sense of shame. If, however, others in the encounter cannot fight back, then repressed shame may indeed target specific others (an example would be abusive husbands who take out their shame as rage against wives and children who are not in a strong position to impose effective negative sanctions). Still, if others in an encounter are important to a person and/or have some capacity to offer effective negative sanctions, then it becomes ever more likely that anger will bypass the encounter and move out to safer targets. It is far easier to protect self by (a) avoiding negative sanctions and (b) attacking structures that cannot directly "fight back."

---

2   See list of principles in Chapter 9.

If corporate units are targeted, individuals will express anger at the culture and structure of the corporate unit and, if this anger is experienced over a long time, the person may also begin to target the institutional domain in which the corporate unit is embedded. Also over time, this anger toward corporate units may transmute from shame-based anger to shame-based alienation, with the person displaying role-distance and low levels of commitment to the corporate unit and, if the alienation is sufficiently great, to the institutional domain. A person with a biography of shame experiences in encounters within a diversity of corporate units within an institutional domain will be increasingly likely to experience alienation not only from corporate units but from the larger macro-level institutional domain in which the corporate units generating shame are lodged. At times, however, shame can lead to reaction-formation and sublimation (see Table 4.1) where individuals display intense positive emotions toward corporate units that have brought shame. For example, a mother who has experienced nothing but failure and shame in school may push her children to do well in school and extol the ideology of this institutional domain. Such defense mechanisms are not as frequent, I believe, as repression and external attribution. And, when shame is chronic and consistently repressed, it generally emerges as intensified anger at social structures; and it is this tendency of attribution to direct anger outward that often poses problems in sustaining social structures and their culture, as will be explored later in Chapter 8 (see principles 6b, 16, and 17 in Chapter 9).

If categoric units are targeted, individuals will express anger toward, and develop negative prejudicial beliefs about, members of the targeted categoric unit. Negative stereotypes about members of categoric units have complicated effects on emotions. One effect is for the anger to become as persistent as the shame that drives this anger; the more shame a person experiences in daily routines, the more diffuse is the anger directed at members of categoric units. Ironically, as members of categoric units are portrayed in negative terms, this portrayal reaffirms reasons for being angry at them, but it also potentially increases the fear element of the shame which only intensifies the anger. This kind of negative stereotyping, especially when fueled by the anger arising from repressed shame, can have dramatic consequences for meso and macrostructures when individuals collectively organize to vent their anger on members of categoric units and the social structures in which these units are embedded.

Status and emotional arousal

The concept of status has a number of meanings. In some analyses, status denotes a position within a social structure; for other researchers, status refers to differences in power and authority; for still others, status only denotes prestige and honor. These different uses of the concept of status do not have to be contradictory; each simply emphasizes a particular dimension of status, while de-emphasizing other dimensions. For my purposes, status will be defined as a position in a network of positions, occupied by an individual, standing in relation to at least one other position, occupied by another individual (Turner, 2002:192). Status positions evidence many potential properties, the most important of which, I believe, are: (1) the clarity and discreteness of the position vis-à-vis other positions; (2) the network properties of positions, and while there are many possible network properties of positions, I will emphasize (2a) density or the degree of connectedness of positions up to the maximum of all positions being connected to each other and (2b) equivalence or the degree to which positions stand at the same or equivalent place in a network structure; (3) the level of power/authority attached to a position; and (4) the amount of prestige, honor, and positive evaluation associated with a position. Each of these properties has effects on emotional arousal, as I explore below.

Clarity and discreteness of status

The phenomenology of status

There is a phenomenology of status, just as there is for roles, because individuals signal to others their status, and especially so when the corporate or categoric units do not establish individuals' status relative to each other. Indeed, as the data from expectation states literature document (Ridgeway, 2001, 2006), individuals determine the status of self and others very rapidly in an encounter; and they do so through roles. As individuals emit gestures, they are not only signaling their respective roles, they are also making claims to status relative to the status of others. In fact, emotions are often used as a strategy to assert claims to status, as is the case when a person exhibits assertiveness and confidence to make claims to high prestige and/or authority in an encounter (Ridgeway, 2006). Moreover, as status cues are given off in role-making, these cues clarify and fine-tune the roles that people are making for themselves. There is, then, a dynamic interplay between roles and status; role cues signal not only the role that a person is making for self but also the status that they claim which, reciprocally, works to provide additional information about role-making.

Status-making efforts of individuals operate through role-making and provide critical information to others. Without information on status, it becomes more difficult to establish expectations for how transactional needs will be met, for what elements of culture are relevant, and even for what dimensions of social structure are salient. When individuals understand each other's status, they feel more comfortable in their roles; and, as I noted earlier, when people are able to mutually verify roles, expectations for self-verification, for profits from exchanges, for group inclusion, for trust, and for facticity are more likely to be realized, thereby setting off the dynamics of positive emotional arousal summarized in principles 1, 4, and 6a. Conversely, when status cannot be easily determined, or if there is ambiguity or contests over status, role verification becomes more problematic and sets off negative emotional arousal, as is summarized in principles 3, 5, and 6b. Moreover, as we will see in the next chapter, normatizing will also become difficult because individuals are unclear as to which aspects of culture they are to invoke and apply to the encounter.

Embedding and status

Embedding dramatically increases the clarity of status, under the conditions listed in tables 6.1 and 6.2. Within corporate units, hierarchy in the division of labor increases the clarity of status by establishing the relative amounts of power and prestige attached to positions in the social structure. Discreteness and differential evaluation of categoric units work to increase clarity of status by establishing the diffuse status characteristics of individuals. Under these conditions, expectation states are clear, increasing the chances that individuals will meet expectations generated by not only status but also by transactional needs and culture. When status is established by the hierarchy in the division of labor, the salience of diffuse status characteristics declines, unless there is a high correlation between the distribution of discrete categoric units and particular positions in the status hierarchy. When this latter condition situation exists, the clarity of both authority system and diffuse status characteristics increases. However, if there are no power or prestige differences in the division of labor of a corporate unit or if the positions are horizontal and/or structurally equivalent, then the salience of diffuse status characteristics increases and has a greater effect on the flow of interaction because these characteristics will now stand in the absence of inequality (see next section for a discussion of how time and iteration reduce the salience of diffuse status characteristics).

When discrete and differentially evaluated diffuse status characteristics are consistently correlated with locations in the hierarchical division of labor across diverse corporate units within different institutional domains, status beliefs emerge and become part of the broader culture that impinges on all encounters (Ridgeway, 2001, 2006; Ridgeway *et al.*, 1998). When these beliefs are consistently invoked across encounters, they operate to affirm differences between members of discrete categoric units and to codify ideologies justifying differential evaluation (Ridgeway and Erickson, 2000). When enshrined in beliefs and ideologies, the power of diffuse status characteristics is that much greater in any given encounter but, equally significantly, the differential evaluation of diffuse status characteristics becomes salient in virtually all encounters across a wide range of corporate units in diverse institutional domains.

Iteration, time, and status differentiation

The expectation states literature emphasizes the processes whereby status differences are affirmed and reaffirmed, but I think that this consistent finding is partly an artifact of the experimental nature of task groups and the short duration of the interactions in these groups. In real-world groups that are built up from iterated encounters over time, the initial effects of status decline as individuals interact and generate positive emotions. This decline will be greater for diffuse status characteristics as individuals come to know each other and discount elements of status beliefs that justify differences in the evaluation of categoric units.

I must qualify this generalization by emphasizing that the dynamics summarized in the expectation states literature may work against this lessening of the differences in status, particularly in highly focused task groups where variations in performances remain highly relevant. Another force working against lessening of status differences is the way in which authority is used. If those in positions of authority frustrate subordinates in meeting expectations, consistently mete out negative sanctions on subordinates, and force subordinates to constantly readjust their actions, status differences will be highlighted. However, this kind of abusive use of authority will also generate anger that, in turn, may lead subordinates to mobilize and challenge positions of authority, thus eroding legitimacy of superordinates if not the authority system itself. Thus, actions by superordinates that arouse anger in subordinates may highlight status differences, but they may also set into motion conflicts that erode status differences.

My view, then, is that there is a propensity for iterated encounters, even those embedded in hierarchically organized corporate units and differentially evaluated (by status beliefs) categoric units to reduce the effects of status, unless the encounter remains highly instrumental and unless the holders of authority use their power in abusive ways. There is, however, an important consequence of reducing status differences, or at least pushing them to the background: expectations become more ambiguous and increase the likelihood that individuals will feel mild anxiety about how to respond appropriately in the encounters. Moreover, breaches become more likely, thus operating as a negative sanction to others, while inviting negative sanctions in return from others. One of the few virtues of inequalities in status – whether from positions in the division of labor or from differentially evaluated categoric units – is that inequalities increase the clarity of status and expectations associated with status as well as with transactional needs and culture. Iterations of the encounter over time reduce the clarity that comes with inequality and increase, for a time, uncertainty that opens the door to breaches and negative emotional arousal.

Mitigating this potential is the very process by which status differences are reduced: interaction rituals generating the reciprocal flow of positive emotions. As positive emotions flow, in accordance with the processes summarized in principles 1, 4, and 6a, new kinds of emotional expectation states are established; and if the interaction rituals are iterated over time, the enhanced solidarity and its symbolization with totems (toward which rituals are directed in thoughts and actions) generate a new set of expectation states that replace or diminish the salience of those revolving around status differences.

Once these ritual processes increase solidarity and group symbols, failure to meet the new emotional expectation states will arouse even more negative emotions. Individuals will generally be angry at those who breach the positive emotional flow and mete out negative sanctions, while those who have breached the encounter will feel sad and fearful. And, if they are also angry with themselves, they will experience shame and, if they feel that they have violated the moral symbols of the group, they will experience guilt as well. If defense mechanisms kick in, however, they may become angry and make external attributions or, if these only bring more negative sanctioning from others, they may become alienated and seek to withdraw from the encounter or, if withdrawal is not possible, to display role-distance. If these dynamics revolving around negative emotional arousal persist, they will tend to destroy the solidarity of the group, and indeed the group formed by the iterated encounters may disband. If this group is lodged inside of a corporate unit, then the original status differences may once again become salient and direct the flow of encounters revealing lower levels of social solidarity.

Networks and status

Network density and emotions

The more dense are the ties among positions, the greater will be the effects of status on the initial flow of interaction. Individuals will be sensitive to differences in expectation states revolving around variations in authority and prestige, roles, culture, and transactional needs. Eventually, the effects of iteration on interaction rituals and the flow of positive emotions will kick in and reduce the salience of status, but when positions are connected to each other to a high degree, individuals tend to be especially alert to status and particularly to status differences. When positions are not densely connected, individuals will generally pay less attention to differences. Compare, for example, how a soldier acts on an army base (where density is high) with behavior off the base (where density is low), or how a customer treats a clerk in a store compared to how the clerk acts with fellow employees and managers in the store. When density is low (soldier off base, customer–clerk), individuals will only pay attention to status in a perfunctory manner. Similarly, when diverse categoric units are not related in dense ties, individuals will typically only pay attention to differences if they are threatened by and, hence, fearful of members in a particular categoric unit; otherwise, diffuse status characteristics will be ignored and not have large effects on interaction.

The potential for emotional arousal increases with high density because any breach will radiate across the network, arousing negative emotions at each node in the network and inviting negative sanctions that reduce solidarity and, potentially, break the network apart. If such breaches reduce the clarity of status and lead to failures to verify roles (and, in turn, to meet transactional needs), then the negative emotional arousal will be more intense and activate the processes described in principles 3, 5, and 6b.

Attributions become important once negative emotions are aroused in dense networks. If self is blamed, then a person will feel sad, but if this person also experiences fear about the consequences of the breach to self, along with anger at self for causing the breach, then shame is aroused and, if moral codes are invoked, so is guilt. If the person does not repress this shame or guilt, then repair rituals and apologies are likely to be emitted, with the consequence of restoring the interpersonal flow in the breached interaction and, thereby, reconstituting the network. If a person blames others for the breach, anger will cause negative sanctioning; and if a category of others is blamed, then the breach may initiate new, or reinforce old, prejudices that are part of all status beliefs. If shame is repressed, then others may become more angry at the lack of contrition from a person or persons who have breached the encounter, setting off a conflict spiral in which the repressed shame comes out as anger and negative sanctions that is matched by increased anger and negative sanctioning from others who become outraged over the lack of contrition.

If a dense network reveals differences in authority or prestige, these dynamics are altered somewhat. Higher-status persons will be freer to express their anger, while lower-status individuals will be reluctant to express anger toward those with authority or with high prestige. And, fellow lower-status persons may also sanction a lower-status person who negatively sanctions a higher-status figure or who fails to meet expectation states for subordinates in the network. Yet, a subordinate or set of subordinates who cannot express anger at superordinates are exhibiting fear; and they will often be sad about their plight, but if anger is combined with this fear and sadness, shame will be aroused and be repressed, intensifying the anger component of shame. If superordinates can be placed into a categoric unit, then negative prejudices will emerge among subordinates toward members of this categoric unit; and if enough others similarly experience shame and anger, cliques among subordinates will positively sanction expressions of anger and prejudice that, potentially, can build up solidarity and symbols among subordinates and, as one potential outcome, lead to their mobilization for conflict that disrupts the corporate unit in which the hostile clique is embedded.

Structural equivalence and emotional arousal

Individuals standing at the same place in a network will often have high rates of interaction; or if they stand at structurally equivalent positions in different networks they will exhibit relative ease with each other when they meet in an encounter. The reason for this ease of interaction is that individuals will have had similar experiences in the larger status system and will have met expectations in similar ways. Equivalence raises the salience of hierarchy if those in the same positions are constantly forced to interact with superiors but, more typically, those in equivalent positions develop beliefs about superordinates through the process of clique formation described above. But equivalence, per se, regardless of any relationship to authority, will increase the flow of positive emotions among those in structurally equivalent positions. If discrete and differentially evaluated diffuse status characteristics are salient, however, these diffuse status characteristics will take on greater significance at initial phases of interaction, but over time, these differences will decline as the processes outlined in principles 1 and 4 unfold. If these processes revolving around the flow of positive emotions, entrainment of affect, solidarity, and symbolization of this solidarity are disrupted, the arousal of negative emotions will be more intense, just as it is for dense networks (since interaction among individuals who are structurally equivalent tends to increase clique formation and, hence, density of the clique). As a result the same emotional dynamics outlined for density are likely to unfold.

Ecology and emotional arousal

Encounters always reveal a spatial dimension, such as the amount of space available, the partitioning of space by architecture, and the number and nature of the props (chairs, desks, podiums, benches) that can be used by individuals. Most of the time, individuals understand what space, partitions, and props "mean"; and based upon these meanings in their stocks of knowledge, persons begin to establish expectations for what will transpire in the encounter. When the meanings of ecology are clear, individuals will better understand what emotions are appropriate, how transactional needs will be consummated, how roles are to be played, what status positions can be occupied or asserted, and how to normatize (bring culture to bear on) the encounter. If, however, the meanings of space are unclear or if there is conflict among meanings, then individuals will need to work much harder in the encounter. They will need to role-take, role-make, and monitor each other and the situation more closely in order to "figure out" what space, partitions, and props mean. Moreover, it becomes much more likely that at least some of the expectations associated with transactional needs, roles, status, and culture will not be met and that individuals will experience negative sanctions as they misinterpret the meanings tied to space. As a result, negative emotions will be aroused.

Most of the time, people know the meanings of the ecology of an encounter, and they experience mild positive emotions such as satisfaction when the expectations arising from these meanings are realized. But, lurking below the surface is the potential for seemingly disproportionate negative emotional arousal when these expectations are not realized. For instance, if you sit at the table in the student union that has been "reserved" by another student's backpack (who is off getting food), the negative emotional arousal will be pronounced when this student returns to find you in "her" space. Or, to intrude on a table where others are sitting and talking will similarly invite negative sanctions. The reason that these kinds of breaches of expectations associated with ecology can generate moderate-intensity negative emotions and perhaps equally negative sanctions is that ecology is one of the first forces of an encounter that comes into play.

People, in essence, situation-take before they role-take and role-make; they size up the meanings of space as a first step in an encounter, and if they make a misstep at this early stage of the encounter, all other forces driving the formation of encounters are thrown off. As a result, some expectations associated with transactional needs, roles, status, and culture will not be met, while the flow of negative sanctions will increase. And since other forces of the encounter operate through the ecology of place, making sure that each person understands the meanings of ecology becomes that much more critical.

Embedding increases the likelihood that individuals will share meanings over ecology. Entrance and exit rules, clarity in the division of labor, formality, and other features of corporate units listed in Table 6.1 work to increase clarity of what space, partitions, and props all mean and, as a result, what can be expected to transpire in the encounter. Similarly, if the organization of space is correlated with the distribution of categoric units, the meaning of both ecology and categoric units takes on greater clarity. In the old days of corporations, the "secretarial" pool was composed of women located in a particular place, separated by partitions from other places, and clearly marked with props such as desks and typewriters; as a result, the meaning of the ecology of the secretarial pool as well as the expectations associated with gender as a categoric unit both took on greater clarity and generated clear expectations for what would transpire. To take another example, corporations often seek to increase informality and interaction among workers; and one way they achieve this goal is to break down partitions and give all individuals the same props (desks, computers). Here the "democratization" of ecology in a corporate unit generates new kinds of expectations for how transactional needs, roles, status, and culture are to be realized, even when individuals occupy positions at different places in the division of labor and are members of different categoric units.

Demography and emotional arousal

Demography is the study of the number, characteristics, distribution, and movement of people; and so, the demography of an encounter concerns how many individuals are co-present, their categoric unit memberships and place in the division of labor, the relative numbers of people in different categoric units and status positions, and the movements of individuals in and out of the encounter. People carry in their stocks of knowledge information about what the demographic profile of an encounter "means"; and on the basis of these implicit meanings, they generate expectations for how transactional needs can be met, what roles can be played, what dimensions of status can be claimed, and what elements of structure and culture are relevant. Ecology has some effects on the demography of an encounter by imposing limits on how many people can occupy a space, how easy is it to move past partitions, and how many and what kinds of props are available for use during the course of the encounter.

One critical demographic feature of an encounter is the number of people co-present. Encounters all present a major bottleneck when individuals speak: speech is slow and sequential, and only one person at a time can speak. When encounters are small, it is relatively easy for all individuals to turn-take when speaking and thereby remain focused, but as the number of people increases, these limitations of encounters become more evident. To some degree, people can read body language and the emotions communicated through body language to compensate for the inherent limitations of sequential speech, but there are also limitations as to how many people can be visually scanned at the same time. As a result, large encounters generally reveal a pattern of migration in and out of the encounter and of formation of sub-encounters among subsets of members who can more readily maintain focus. Small encounters allow individuals to sustain focus and thereby activate the processes described in principles 1 and 4; and the more an encounter can be isolated by physical partitions, the more likely can these processes be sustained.

Diversity in the characteristics of participants has large effects on what transpires in an encounter. Diversity comes from varying memberships in different categoric units or from incumbency in different status positions in the division of labor of a corporate unit, or both. If location in the division of labor and the distribution of categoric unit memberships are highly correlated, it will be easier to establish expectations because place in the division of labor and categoric unit memberships will reinforce each other, thereby clarifying expectations. Conversely, if the place in the division of labor and distribution of categoric unit memberships are *not* highly correlated, individuals will need to spend more time and effort establishing expectations and avoiding inadvertent negative sanctioning in order to meet transactional needs, verify roles, claim status, and normatize (bring culture to bear on) the encounter. Moreover, when membership in categoric units and incumbency in the division of labor are uncorrelated, individuals will generally rely more upon status (in the division of labor) than diffuse status characteristics (as a result of categoric unit membership) in establishing expectations, but they still must work at reconciling any discrepancies between place in the hierarchical division of labor and differential evaluation of categoric units. Generally, people will use place in the division of labor as their "default" program for establishing expectations when the correlation between the division of labor and categoric unit memberships is low. As a consequence, it becomes more likely that expectations can be met, causing positive emotional arousal. And, if the encounter is iterated over time, the dynamics outlined in principles 1 and 4 will decrease the salience of categoric unit membership and, to a lesser degree, differences in status in the hierarchical division of labor.

The division of labor has additional effects on encounters. One effect is to increase focus of attention. In an encounter between low-ranking and high-ranking persons, the former will tend to remain focused on those with more power and be less likely to form sub-encounters or to migrate away from the encounter while it is still a going concern. Fear of negative sanctions and the effects that these sanctions would have on meeting transactional needs (especially verifying self and realizing profits in exchanges) keep people in line, even if they must "fake" attention. The same effect occurs – for somewhat different reasons – for individuals who are structurally equivalent. Here individuals share a common set of experiences that enable them to initiate and sustain interaction rituals that charge up positive emotions and, if sufficiently charged, lead to symbols marking group solidarity – all of which sustain focus when structurally equivalent individuals are co-present with each other.

Conclusion

Many of the forces driving the formation and operation of encounters (see Table 3.1) are structural and are imposed on encounters by virtue of the embeddedness of encounters in corporate and categoric units. The effects of status, roles, and ecology on the flow of an encounter is very much constrained by the properties of a corporate unit summarized in Table 6.1, while the demography of an encounter is often influenced not only by the structure of corporate units but also by the distribution of memberships in categoric units. Moreover, as we will see in the next chapter, the culture of an encounter as it directs normatization imposes itself via the conduits provided by social structures. Just what symbols are invoked and used to establish expectations is filtered by the properties of corporate and categoric units delineated in tables 6.1 and 6.2.

As I have emphasized, individuals are probably hard-wired to assume that gestures reveal congruence and mark an underlying role which can be retrieved from stocks of knowledge; and once retrieved and verified over the course of an encounter, the more expectations associated with roles will be realized. To some degree, consensus over the meanings and expectations associated with the ecology of an encounter (space, partitions, and props) facilitates processes of role-making, role-taking, and role verification; and the more unambiguous are the meanings of ecology, the more individuals will understand what roles can be made and verified in an encounter as well as what status can be claimed. Similarly, the demography of an encounter – the number of people, their positions in the division of labor, and their membership in categoric units – will create expectations that guide individuals in role-making, role verification, and status-claiming.

Thus, if roles can be effectively made and verified, then the expectations arising from transactional needs, status positions, and culture are more likely to be clear. Roles offer the initial clues to others about what each person expects in an interaction, and with mutual verification of roles, other expectations arising from status and culture become clearer. And, when expectations associated with transactional needs, status, and culture (see next chapter) are realized as individuals successfully play roles, individuals will experience positive emotional arousal, as outlined in principles 1 and 4; and as principle 6a emphasizes, they will be more likely to make self-attributions and give off positive sanctions to others in an encounter. Conversely, when ecology and demography do not provide clues about the range of roles that can be played, and when role-making and role verification do not ensue, expectations arising from other micro-dynamic forces are less likely to be met. Moreover, the failure to meet expectations will also involve perceptions of being negatively sanctioned by others, thus unleashing the dynamics summarized in principles 5 and 6b. When expectations are not realized, individuals will experience negative emotional arousal, activate defense mechanisms, especially when self and identity have been highly salient, and make external attributions.

As I have emphasized in principle 2 B, C and in more detail in Table 6.1, embedding increases the clarity of expectations; and the more encounters are embedded in corporate and categoric units, and the more meso-level units are embedded in institutional domains and stratification systems, then the greater will be the clarity of expectations attached to roles, status, ecology, and demography. And, hence, the more likely will individuals experience positive emotions and make self-attributions (principle 6a). Conversely, the less embedded an encounter is in corporate and categoric units and the less meso-level units are embedded in macro-level structures, the less clear are expectations for roles, status, ecology, and demography. As a result, individuals will be less likely to meet expectations and/or receive negative sanctions, causing them to experience negative emotions, activate defense mechanisms, and make external attributions.

The more self is salient in an encounter, the more intense will be the effects of either success or failure in meeting expectations and/or receiving positive or negative sanctions. Similarly, the more exchanges of resources, markers of group inclusion, trust, and facticity in an encounter are tied up in the verification of self (and the roles and status occupied by self), the more intense will be emotional reactions, whether positive or negative. If negative, individuals will experience shame and, if moral codes are invoked, guilt as well when expectations are not realized or when negative sanctions are experienced; and the more likely will these persons repress their shame and make external attributions revolving around anger. If the anger cannot be expressed in the encounter, it will target meso-level units. If the corporate unit is targeted, the anger will be directed at the culture and structure of this unit and, over time, the anger will be combined with the other negative emotions in shame to produce alienation. If categoric units are targeted, then anger will be directed at members of this categoric unit and will lead to the codification of negative stereotypes and prejudices about members of this categoric unit. When shame is consistently experienced across a wide range of encounters embedded in corporate units distributing resources (e.g. polity, economy, and education), the negative emotions will be ever more likely to target macrostructures.

This basic line of argument is the complex core of my theory but, in concluding, I should summarize this argument in relatively simple principles:

9   *The clarity of expectations for all dimensions of social structure in encounters – that is, roles, status, ecology, and demography – is a positive function of the degree to which an encounter is embedded in corporate and categoric units.*

    A   *The clarity of expectations in corporate units is an additive function of:*

        1   *The visibility of boundaries of the corporate unit and the existence of entrance and exit rules.*

        2   *The explicitness of goals and the degree of focus by a corporate unit on these goals.*

        3   *The level of differentiation of the institutional domain in which a corporate unit is embedded.*

        4   *The explicitness of the vertical and horizontal divisions of labor in the corporate unit.*

        5   *The formality of the structure of the corporate unit.*

        6   *The level of consistency among ideologies, generalized symbolic media, and norms governing the operation of the corporate unit.*

        7   *The degree of correlation between positions in the division of labor, particularly in the vertical division of labor, with memberships in discrete categoric units.*

    B   *The clarity of expectations associated with categoric units is an additive function of:*

        1   *The degree of discreteness of the boundaries defining membership in a categoric unit.*

        2   *The degree of consensus over the relative evaluation of categoric units and the ideologies used to form this evaluation.*

        3   *The degree of embeddedness of categoric units in the macro-level stratification system and the level of inequality in this system.*

        4   *The homogeneity among individuals who are members of a categoric unit.*

5 The degree of correlation of membership in one categoric unit with membership in other categoric units.

6 The degree of correlation of membership in categoric units with diverse positions in the vertical and horizontal divisions of labor in corporate units embedded in differentiated institutional domains, especially domains distributing valued resources.

10 The more individuals employ similar languages, particularly the language of emotions, the more likely will they be successful in mutual role-making, role-taking, and role verification; and the more they can successfully role-make and role-take, the more likely are they to communicate the expectations associated with their respective roles and relative status which, in turn, makes it more likely that they will understand and meet expectations generated by transactional needs and culture.

11 The more individuals understand the meanings associated with the ecology and demography of an encounter, the more likely are they to successively role-make and role-take, and thereby successfully verify each other's roles and status which, in turn, will increase the likelihood that they will understand and meet expectations generated by transactional needs and culture.

12 The less individuals successfully role-take, role-make, and verify roles, the less likely are expectations associated with status, ecology, demography, and culture to be fully understood, thereby increasing the likelihood that individuals will fail to meet expectations, while increasing the likelihood that they will experience negative sanctions.

13 To the degree that self is highly salient and to the extent that core self-conceptions are implicated in efforts to verify a role-identity, the greater will be the potential for more intense emotional arousal, whether positive or negative.

A The more expectations for self are verified in a role, the more intense will be the level of positive emotional arousal, and the more likely will the dynamics outlined in principles 1, 4, 6a, and 7 be initiated.

B The less expectations for self are verified in a role, the more intense will be the level of negative emotional arousal, and the more likely will the dynamics outlined in principles 3, 5, 6b, and 8 be activated.

7   Culture and emotional arousal

Humans rely upon systems of symbols to direct face-to-face interaction; and ultimately, larger-scale social structures are constructed from blueprints provided by cultural symbols. As Table 3.1 summarizes, humans normatize encounters, creating expectations for how people and the situation are to be categorized, what frames are to be imposed, how talk is to proceed, what rituals are to be employed, what constitutes a just share of resources, and what emotions should be felt and displayed.

Embedding provides the structural conduits for culture to impinge on an encounter. Conversely, as individuals in face-to-face interaction develop culture, meso-level structures provide paths for symbols arising from encounters to have potential effects on mesostructures and macrostructures. Thus, as individuals normatize an encounter, they draw upon cultural resources in corporate and categoric units in which the encounter is embedded; and these resources are, in turn, pulled into mesostructures from macrostructures. We need, therefore, a simple conceptualization of how culture travels across these levels of reality.

The culture of macrostructures

Culture and institutional domains

Societies and often inter-societal systems all reveal some basic values, which are abstract standards of good–bad, right–wrong, and appropriate–inappropriate. They are abstract because they provide highly general moral codes that can be applied to many diverse situations. At the level of institutional domains, values are transformed into ideologies that apply general values to a specific domain, whether the economy, kinship, polity, religion, science, education, law, education, or medicine. For example, a general value of "achievement" becomes in the economy an ideology of just how, within this domain, individuals and collective actors are to do well and succeed. Similarly, this value will be an element in another ideology of how to achieve as a parent or child in the kinship domain. Ideologies thus are moral standards of what ought to occur within a particular institutional domain.

Institutional norms are the general expectations for individuals occupying key positions in the corporate units of a particular institutional domain. For instance, the expectations for how mothers, fathers, and children are supposed to act are well known in any society (as what Affect Control Theory terms "fundamental sentiments"), as are other key roles such as worker, religious worshiper, politicians or voter, teacher or student, and all of the basic positions and roles that make an institutional domain distinctive. Institutional norms always carry general cultural values via ideologies to the specific positions and roles; and it is through institutional norms that moral codes impose expectations on individuals in corporate units within a domain. There will, of course, be more specific norms associated with the division of labor within corporate units, and while these provide instructions and expectations for what individuals are supposed to do by virtue of occupying a position in the division of labor, they also carry some of the moral content of institutional norms as the latter translates ideologies into concrete expectations for behaviors and performances.

I do not want to connote an overly Parsonsian view that there is a neat and clear hierarchy of cultural codes; in reality, there is considerable slippage among values, ideologies, institutional norms, and norms tied to the division of labor in corporate units. Moreover, these dimensions of culture can often be in conflict or inconsistent with each other, thereby reducing the clarity of expectations. But, to the degree that values, ideologies, institutional norms, and division of labor norms are consistent, expectations for how individuals should normatize an encounter will be clear and, as a consequence, increase the likelihood that the processes outlined in principles 1, 4, and 6a will be activated.

A final dimension of culture within institutional domains is even more problematic and vague than my portrayal of values, ideologies, and norms. Despite this ambiguity and imprecision of the concept of "generalized symbolic media," I think that this is an important force that must be addressed. Georg Simmel (1990 [1907]) was perhaps the first to fully recognize the importance of symbolic media in his analysis of how money changes the orientations, behaviors, interactions, and social relations among individuals. Later, Talcott Parsons (1963a, b, 1970) introduced the notion of these media, an idea further developed by Niklas Luhmann (1982). None of these elaborations of the notion of generalized symbolic media is very precise, and yet, there is an important set of dynamics denoted by the concept of generalized symbolic media.

One of the features that differentiates an institutional domain is the specific generalized symbolic medium that individual and collective actors use in communication and in exchange relationships. Without providing a detailed taxonomy of symbolic media, Table 7.1 presents my views of what the dominant media are for key institutional domains. When institutional domains are differentiated from each other, they will exhibit a distinctive symbolic medium or set of media by which communication and

Table 7.1 Generalized symbolic media of institutional domains

1	Economy	*Money* and other metrics of value that can be converted into money
2	Polity	*Power* or the capacity to control the actions of other actors
3	Law	*Influence* or the capacity to define what is just and right for actors as well as the ability to adjudicate social relations among actors
4	Religion	*Sacred/supernatural* or the ability to explain events in terms of the power and influence of non-observable forces
5	Education	*Transmission of knowledge* or the capacity to impart knowledge to actors
6	Kinship	*Love/loyalty* or the use of strong affective states to engender strong attachments and commitments among kin
7	Science	*Verifiable knowledge/truth* or the search for knowledge in the empirical world revealing truths about the operation of this world
8	Medicine	*Health* or the ability to sustain the normal functioning of the human body

transactions are conducted. These media will reveal a number of properties. First, there is always an evaluative element embodied in a medium, an evaluation that follows from the ideologies of an institutional domain. For example, the ideology of capitalism adds an evaluative element to money: the use and accumulation of money, per se, is a worthy goal. The ideology of the family domain assures that the medium of love/loyalty becomes a moral goal to be pursued by family members. Or, the medium of power in polity is heavily infused with the ideology of the political domain (say, "checks and balances" on power are needed to assure democracy; or "might makes right" in a warlord system). Thus, symbolic media are not morally neutral; they always embody the ideologies that dominate a domain.

Second, discourse within an institutional domain is conducted, to a large degree, with the generalized symbolic medium of the domain. The symbolic media structure communication and, as Luhmann (1982) has emphasized, they become the media by which "thematization" of a domain occurs. For instance, money is the primary topic of conversation in a capitalist economy, as can be see on any given day with the large number of television programs (particularly on cable TV) and business sections in newspapers devoted to discursive talk about money. Similarly, the medium of science for truth and knowledge is the primary topic of those working in this domain, and it has been thematized in many different ways, as is illustrated by idealized portrayals of "the scientific method."

Third, the symbolic medium of an institutional domain is also the resource that is exchanged among actors within a domain. Money is the medium of exchange in the economy, power in the polity, truth and know-ledge in science, or love and loyalty in kinship. In exchanges *within* an institutional domain, some form of an institutional domain's symbolic medium is generally given up for another form of this symbolic medium. For example, love of a particular type is given by a parent to a child in exchange for childhood loyalty and love in return; money is "invested" to gain more wealth (defined by the metric of money) in a capitalist economy; power over one set of events is given over to others in return for power over another set of events. It is the flow of a symbolic medium as a "currency" of utility and reward that adds to its capacity to dominate discourse and, hence, to become thematicized.

Fourth, as Parsons and Smelser (1956) illustrated, exchanges across institutional domains can often involve the giving of one symbolic medium for another. For example, parents are given control (power) over family activities in exchange for loyalty (if not love) to polity (thereby legitimating the use of power by polity); family members give loyalty to employers in exchange for money which is used to purchase products that, the producer hopes, will make family members loyal customers; polity uses its powers, such as those for taxation and redistribution, to make capital selectively available to the economy which, in turn, provides the money necessary to run the polity; or government uses its power to organize the public school system that, in return, transmits knowledge legitimating polity.

Fifth, symbolic media always contain a normative element, above and beyond the evaluative element. Media provide instructions and expectations for how they are to be used by individual and collective actions. For instance, money carries expectations for how it is to be used in various contexts; love is codified into normative expectations for how to be a loving parent or a devoted offspring. Power is generally transformed into authority that contains expectations for how such authority is to be employed in various contexts. Knowledge and truth in science are translated into some version of the scientific method and other expectations for how the search of knowledge is to occur.

Sixth, some media are more evaluative and normative than others, and this fact has important implications for how they operate in social relations. As Simmel first noted, money is a neutral medium in that it is highly generalized and can be used in a variety of settings, whereas an alternative medium, such as love or knowledge, is more evaluative and normative; as a consequence, these media cannot be used in many settings. Similarly, power has some of the properties of money and can be mobilized in just about all social settings. As Habermas (1973) has argued, money and power can "colonize" the "lifeworld" because they can penetrate institutional domains that rely upon other distinctive media.

This facility of media to move into other institutional domains will often make expectations unclear and ambiguous. For example, when parents seek to "buy their kids' love" with money, expectations become ambiguous in the family since money and love are conflated; or if private companies fund scientific research in universities, the mixing of money, truth, and knowledge creates normative ambiguity; or if sacredness from religion is imported into the polity, the rules of power-use are altered and often become more ambiguous. Thus, to the degree that an institutional domain reveals a mix of symbolic media for evaluation, discourse and communication, normative regulation, and exchange, expectations for actions within this domain will become somewhat ambiguous, even actions at the level of the encounter. The fact that money and power can readily move into other institutional domains signals that these "cool" media will often be mixed with "hot" media such as love, loyalty, truth, sacredness, and knowledge, thereby conflating expectations associated with these hotter media.

Granted, this kind of argument has been made before; and my rendering reveals the same level of ambiguity as has been evident with others such as Simmel, Parsons, and Luhmann. Nonetheless, sociologists need to take the properties of the social world denoted by symbolic media more seriously, incorporating them into theories and research. I have not developed a theory or even a very precise conceptualization of symbolic media, but this is not my goal here. Rather, I want to make a more general theoretical point: the more an institutional domain is dominated by one symbolic medium, and to the degree that the evaluational and normative content of this medium is consistent with general societal values and, more specifically, institutional ideologies and norms, expectations within corporate units and at the level of the encounter will be clear; and, as a result, the encounter is more likely to be successfully normatized.

Culture and stratification systems

The unequal distribution of valued resources in a society is an outcome of the dynamics operating in key institutional domains, in several senses. First, the resources themselves that are distributed unequally are typically the generalized symbolic media of particular institutional domains – money from the economy, power from polity, knowledge leading to prestige from education, or health from medicine. Second, the operation of institutional domains determines how much of any given resource various subpopulations in a society will receive. For example, a manorial agrarian economic system, coupled with the political structure of feudalism, assure that wealth, power, and prestige will be highly concentrated in the hands of a few elites, with the vast majority of the population having very little of these resources. In contrast, a market economy, regulated by a democratically elected state and universal education, will operate to reduce inequality in the distribution of resources – power, money, educational credentials, or access to medical care. Third, the ideologies of institutional domains distributing resources will also serve as the legitimating ideologies for unequal distribution of resources in the stratification system as well as the moral standards by which classes and factions within classes are differentially evaluated. For example, if the ideology of capitalism dominates (e.g. people should work hard and accumulate wealth), then those with money will be given honor and prestige over those who do not possess money, and those with money will be seen (however inaccurately or unfairly) as deserving their wealth through their (presumed) work. Or, if the ideology of education is strong – learning and knowledge are desirable as measured by educational credentials – this ideology will justify those with more education receiving more prestige, power, and money than those with less education. Naturally, the ideologies of different domains can intersect in ways that complicate the ideologies justifying inequality, but this fact only underscores the degree to which the ideologies of the class system in a society are composed of the ideologies of the institutional domains distributing resources unequally. In a post-industrial society, the key domains are economy, polity, and education because they are the most directly involved in resource distribution; hence, the ideologies of these domains will be the underpinnings of a meta–ideology justifying the class system in a society.

As institutional domains systematically distribute resources, the shape of the distribution determines the structure of classes and factions within each class (Bourdieu,1984). If money, power, and prestige are highly concentrated among a relatively small pool of elites, with the majority of the population having few resources, then the class system will reveal few classes and factions within classes, whereas if there is less inequality in the overall distribution of resources and if individuals receive varying amounts of different resources, then there will be more classes, mobility across class boundaries, and factions within classes.

Bourdieu (1984, 1989) has argued that stratification systems distribute four kinds of "capital" – economic capital (money and property bought with money), cultural capital (taste, knowledge, manners, skills, habits, and lifestyles), social capital (positions, network ties, status in corporate units), and symbolic capital (symbols that can be used to legitimate the possession of other forms of capital). The unequal distribution of these forms of capital not only determines the overall class structure but also the distinctive factions within classes. The dominant class, for instance, has more of all forms of capital, but factions within the dominant class have varying configurations of these resources (the dominant faction has the most economic capital, the dominated faction within the dominant class has more cultural relative to other forms of capital). There is a homologous dimension to a stratification system because each social class will reveal a dominant, intermediate, and dominated faction, with the dominant always having the most economic, the intermediate having less economic capital than the dominant faction and moderate amounts of social, cultural, and symbolic capital, and the dominated possessing comparatively low levels of economic but having high levels of cultural and symbolic capital. In fact, factions within different classes often have more in common than they do with the factions within their class (e.g. elite college professors with high levels of cultural capital in the dominant class may find that they have more in common with school teachers in the middle class).

The culture of each class and the factions within classes are, therefore, related to the relative amounts of various forms of capital. We need not lay out the complete picture in Bourdieu's theory to come to a simple general-ization: the culture of the stratification system, and the classes and factions within classes, are a mixture of the evaluative dimensions of generalized symbolic media of institutional spheres, the ideologies of these spheres, and the forms of capital − economic, social, symbolic, and cultural − that sub-populations possess. From this mix comes a general level of evaluation of different social classes and factions within classes; and to the extent that these evaluations are associated with categoric units, they impinge on status processes as diffuse status characteristics and on dynamics of normatization in a face-to-face encounter. There is, obviously, a great deal of conceptual and empirical work to be done on how these various symbol systems inter-act to generate class cultures and subcultures associated with class factions as these lead to differential evaluation of people located at different points in the stratification system. This culture will generally have some effects on normatization in encounters, but most of this effect at the level of the encounter comes from the differential evaluation of categoric units at the meso level of social reality.

The formation of categoric units and beliefs about the characteristics and worth of members in these units are partially tied to the culture of insti-tutional domains directly, to the structure of the class system (as an outcome of the structure of institutional domains distributing resources), and to indi-viduals' location in the division of labor of corporate units (as these are constrained by institutional domains). Yet, the more a categoric unit is gen-erated by class dynamics, the more likely will status beliefs reveal differential evaluations and the more salient will these evaluations be during interaction in an encounter, at least initially. Thus, although categoric unit differen-tiation can come from a variety of sources, the salience of a categoric unit increases significantly when it is generated by the macro-level stratification system and meso-level class distinctions.

Macro-level culture and justice

Transactional needs for profitable exchange payoffs (see Chapter 5) are realized when individuals perceive that the shares of resources received in an encounter meet perceptions of a "just" or "fair" share. As I have emphasized, just shares are calculated by assessing the degree to which the costs and investments of a person relative to the costs and investments of others are proportionate to the respective rewards received by individuals in an encounter. This process of calculating justice is greatly constrained by general cultural ideologies and, to a lesser extent, generalized symbolic media. Contained in virtually all ideologies and generalized media are just-ice assumptions that are often translated into justice norms for corporate and categoric units and, by extension, the encounters embedded in these units. For example, the ideology that people should "work for their money" contains an implicit notion that the amount of work is the criterion for establishing individuals' respective costs and investments; and, hence, those who work hard should receive more shares of money than those who do not. Similarly, there is an implicit norm of justice in the symbolic medium of love and loyalty in the kinship system which, in essence, states that those who give love to other family members (costs, investments) should reap more love and loyalty in return than those who do not give as much love to members of their families.

Thus, ideologies and generalized symbolic media provide some of the important guidelines for how to establish just shares and, then, how to assess costs and investments of self and others relative to their respective rewards. Individuals carry in their stocks of knowledge implicit conceptions of just shares in a wide variety of situations – work, school, family, politics, religion, community, and many other corporate units embedded in macrostructures. The clarity of these conceptions of just shares increases, I believe, when the ideologies and symbolic media of institutional domains are explicit and consistent with each other. Conversely, when ideologies are vague or a symbolic medium does not wholly dominate an institutional domain, conceptions of just shares of resources will correspondingly be less clear. For instance, if the ideology of romantic love is confounded by the ideology of profit-making from a capitalist economy, and if the generalized media of love is conflated with money, then determining individuals' "just shares" becomes difficult. Does the amount of money spent to secure the love of another take precedence over the amount of love and loyalty given to this other, or does some combination of love and money go into calculations of costs, investments, returns, and just shares?

To some degree, institutional norms help to clarify "just shares" by providing, in essence, instructions for how persons should behave to receive appropriate levels of rewards. In a capitalist economy, for example, there are general norms about work – amount of time spent at work, attitudes at work, energy given to work – that also define what workers should receive for meeting these normative obligations. Similarly, there are norms about how parents in the kinship system are to behave – amount of time they should spend with children, the amount of love and affection given, and the sacrifices to be made – which also contain implicit calculations about what would be a "just share" of rewards for meeting these general institutional norms of kinship. Thus culture has large effects on people's perceptions as to whether or not they have made a profit and met this fundamental transactional needs because ideologies, generalized symbolic media, and institutional norms all provide information about what would constitute a "just" or "fair" return on costs and investments.

As emphasized above, the ideologies and symbolic media of institutional domains have significant effects on the ideologies of the stratification system, particularly those ideologies and symbolic media that determine people's life chances for money, power, prestige, knowledge, and credentials certifying knowledge. One's place in the stratification system is considered "just" and "fair" if individuals have abided by the ideologies and norms of institutional domains. Thus, those in the upper classes will be perceived (whether accurately or not) as having worked hard to gain wealth, power, and prestige whereas those in the lower classes will be perceived as not working hard enough or as not having acquired the skills (via education) to justify high income or power. Thus, ideologies and symbolic media always become part of the ideologies legitimating or, potentially, challenging or de-legitimating the stratification system. And, as they operate in this manner, they provide yet another point of triangulation on what would constitute a "just" or "fair" share of resources.

These macro-level cultural processes constrain people's perceptions of justice in virtually all situations. These culturally defined conceptions of justice are learned early and constantly reinforced in discourse and actual interaction, and they become part of an extensive inventory of knowledge stocks about what is fair in a situation. These macro-level elements of culture can operate somewhat independently of meso-level structures because they are carried to, and then invoked, in specific encounters. However, these conceptions of justice are also given specificity and focus by meso-level corporate and categoric units that determine how these generalized ideologies, symbolic media, and institutional norms are to be applied to encounters embedded in these meso-level units. For example, the norms attached to the division of labor in a corporate unit embedded in the economy specify just how much work of what kind and duration is to lead to how much income, power, and prestige; these norms provide a more finely tuned calculus for determining what is a just share of resources.

The culture of mesostructures

Culture and corporate units

A corporate unit will have more explicit entrance and exit rules, goals, divisions of labor, and culture when it is embedded within a differentiated institutional domain with a clear ideology, set of institutional norms, and dominant symbolic medium. Conversely, when a corporate unit is not embedded in an autonomous institutional domain or in a domain that overlaps with another domain (e.g. law and polity) or one that has a mixture of symbolic media (e.g. science for sale to the highest bidder), the structure and culture of the corporate unit will be less explicit.

In general, I see the substance of the culture of a corporate unit as an additive function of the goals of the unit, the ideology of the institutional domain in which this unit is embedded, the vertical and horizontal divisions of labor, and the symbolic medium or media used in discourse, thematization, and exchange within the unit as well as between this unit and those in another institutional domain. For example, an organization with explicit goals (producing a specific commodity), guided by the ideology of profit-making, organized in clear hierarchy of authority, and concerned solely with making money will reveal a culture that is very different than a non-profit organization that, for instance, also has a less hierarchical division of labor. Moreover, the exchange between these two corporate units and their workers/members will be different, with the former inspiring less loyalty than the latter.

The culture of a corporate unit is also affected by the specific norms attached to the division of labor, especially with respect to entrance and exit rules, expectations for performance, range of roles available for performances, affect expectation states, and rules for evaluation and sanctioning of performances. A corporate unit, for example, that does not require incumbents to come and go at specific times and places, does not impose clear performance goals for each incumbent, tolerates a wide range of role-playing styles, and reveals ambiguous rules for evaluation and sanctioning will reveal a very different culture than one exhibiting the converse normative structure. Thus, even if two corporate units reveal similar goals, employ the same institutional ideology, evidence a similar profile in the hierarchical and horizontal divisions of labor, their respective cultures will differ if the norms attached to the division of labor vary with respect to entrances and exits, performances, and evaluation of performances. In turn, these differences in culture will be reflected in the clarity of expectations for face-to-face encounters and the arousal of emotions in encounters as individuals seek to meet transactional needs, play roles, claim status, and normatize the situation.

Culture and categoric units

Categoric units can be generated, as noted above, via a number of routes: from the division of labor in corporate units embedded in institutional domains (worker, manager, student, priest), from place in the stratification system (lower class, poor), from basic differences among individuals (gender, age, ethnicity), or from some combination of these. Categoric units take on more visibility and salience when they are correlated with positions in the division of labor and locations in the class system. For example, gender as a categoric unit is generated not only by biological differences between men and women, but also by the shares of resources secured in the stratification system and positions in corporate units within institutional domains like economy and kinship. If gender is correlated with positions in corporate units (e.g. nurses, secretaries, and elementary school teachers are overwhelmingly women) and with the stratification system (women on average earn less money and have less power than men), then the status beliefs about women will be more explicit and involve differential evaluations (compared to men) than would be the case where women were equally distributed across positions in corporate units and secured the same level of resources as men. Under the latter conditions, only beliefs about differences between the sexes would be used to form status beliefs about the characteristics of women and the evaluations of these characteristics. Similarly, an ethnic subpopulation that is distinctive by virtue of its history and culture will be characterized by status beliefs tied to the distinctiveness of its culture, but if members of this ethnic subpopulation are over-represented at certain places in the division of labor of corporate units (say, as farm workers for agribusiness), secure few resources from key institutional domains (money from economy, power from polity, or credentials from education), and occupy the poverty categories in the lower classes of the stratification system, the characterization of this categoric unit will be much broader and involve higher levels of differential evaluation. As a result, expectation states for this "diffuse status characteristic" at the level of the encounter will be very different than would be the case if only ethnic background were salient. As a general rule, when there is only one basis for defining individuals as a member of a categoric unit – say, gender or ethnicity – and members of this unit are distributed in proportion with their numbers across the division of labor in corporate units, across classes and class factions, and across the distributions of money, power, and prestige, then status beliefs will be less powerful; and these beliefs will reveal dramatically reduced levels of differential evaluation. As a consequence, categoric unit membership will be less salient and have fewer effects on the normatization of the encounter.

Justice calculations in meso-level units

The division of labor in corporate units and the differential evaluation of categoric units provide additional information about justice. As noted earlier, the norms of the division of labor specify the kinds of role behaviors that will yield particular rewards – whether money, love, authority, or any other reward – and in so doing, the division of labor helps establish what a "just share" is. Norms guiding the division of labor say, in essence, "this much work and effort entitles a person to this much share of the available resources." Similarly, the differential evaluation of categoric units also provides a measuring stick for determining a just share of resources. Less-valued categoric units are entitled to less money, power, prestige, or any other resource than more valued categoric units. And so, as people make calculations of justice in encounters, they implicitly use the calipers provided by the norms of the division of labor of corporate units and the differential evaluation of categoric units to fine-tune their perceptions of what a just share would be in the encounter.

Normatizing encounters

I employ the term normatizing to denote a specific set of expectation states that emerge in all encounters as individuals invoke the cultural systems, typically attached to corporate and categoric units. To some degree, the expectations associated with transactional needs and social structure are also part of this normatizing process, but in addition to these sources of expectations are those that come from values, ideologies, symbolic media, and norms. This latter set of expectations may be connected to status, roles, ecology, and demography or they may be invoked in seeking to meet transactional needs, but they also reveal properties that are distinctively cultural.

Normatizing is a key force in an encounter because the culture of institutional domains, stratification systems, corporate units, and categoric units is often rather diffuse and ambiguous. Individuals often must *work at applying culture to a specific situation*, and as they do so they are normatizing the encounter. Imagine, for example, an encounter among diverse individuals occupying different status positions and playing a number of roles in an encounter within a university − say, a professor, secretary, dean, and maintenance worker. For the encounter to proceed smoothly, additional expectations need to be developed, above and beyond those associated with transactional needs, status, roles, ecology, or demography. The status, roles, ecology, and demography of social structure will facilitate the process by delimiting the range of options, but still, additional interpersonal work must also be performed to bring relevant dimensions of culture to bear on the interpersonal flow in this encounter. Thus, many extra elements of culture − technologies, texts, values, ideologies, symbolic media, and institutional norms − will often *need to be assembled* to supplement expectations associated with transactional needs and social structures. As in most encounters, embedding will facilitate this process, but still, further interpersonal work must also be performed to fully normatize the encounter, as the professor, secretary, dean, and maintenance worker would soon realize.

Culture is thus something that must *constantly be assembled* in encounters. At times, situations are so tightly structured that culture is pre-assembled, but in large complex societies revealing many diverse kinds of corporate and categoric units within differentiated institutional domains and stratification systems, many encounters are initially ambiguous about what people expect to occur. There are simply too many potential combinations of expectations associated with needs, culture, and structure to provide all of the necessary information; additional interpersonal work must be performed on the ground to assemble culture, and I am denoting this work as the basic micro-level force of normatization (see Table 3.1). Table 7.2 summarizes the dimensions along which normatization occurs, and Figure 7.1 outlines the causal effects among these normatizing dynamics.

Categorization

Individuals categorize each other and the situation along a number of dimensions. As Affect Control Theory emphasizes, individuals have "fundamental sentiments" about actor, other, behavior, and situation. I borrow more from Schutz (1967 [1932]) and Goffman (1967) in pointing to a similar

Table 7.2 Axes of normatizing

1 **Categorizing**	The process of developing expectations by virtue of (a) placing self and others in categoric units, (b) typifying the situation in terms of the relative amounts of work-practical, social, and ceremonial activity, and (c) determining if others are to be treated as personages, persons, or intimates.
2 **Framing**	The process of developing expectations by determining what is to be included and excluded for the purposes of interaction, particularly with respect to (a) the values and evaluative beliefs that will be relevant, (b) the persons to be included and their distribution of others in space, (c) the portions of bodies and biographies to be displayed, (d) the stages and props to be used, and (e) the categoric and corporate units to be used as a point of reference.
3 **Communicating**	The process of developing expectations for the forms of talk and nonverbal gesturing to be employed during the course of the interaction.
4 **Ritualizing**	The process of developing expectations for the stereotypical sequences of gestures to be used in (a) opening, (b) closing, (c) forming, (d) symbolizing and totemizing, and (e) repairing the interaction.
5 **Justice**	The process of calculating just shares of resources for self and others.
6 **Feeling**	The process of developing expectations for (a) what emotions are to be experienced and expressed, (b) at what level of intensity they are to be experienced and expressed, and (c) when they are to be experienced and expressed.

dynamic. The first axis of categorization occurs with respect to diffuse status characteristics that, in turn, follow from categoric unit membership. The expectations associated with diffuse status characteristics can be highlighted or diminished by roles and status in corporate units, but individuals will first scan situations to determine the distribution of diffuse status characteristics and assemble in their minds the appropriate set of expectation states for members of specific categoric units. The second axis of categorization is the nature of the situation as predominately work-practical, social, or ceremonial (Goffman, 1967; Collins, 1975). Rarely are situations wholly of one type; encounters reveal relative amounts of work-practical, social, or ceremonial content, with individuals scanning a situation to determine these relative amounts and, then, invoking the relevant expectation states. Moreover, the relative amounts of work-practical, social, and ceremonial content can change over the course of the encounter or across iterated encounters. For example, the amount of social content will generally increase, and the ceremonial aspects will decrease or become more informal in work groups over time. As this process unfolds, individuals will need to re-assemble cultural expectations. The third axis of categorization is the degree of intimacy to be achieved in an encounter. Following Schutz (1967 [1932]), I see three levels

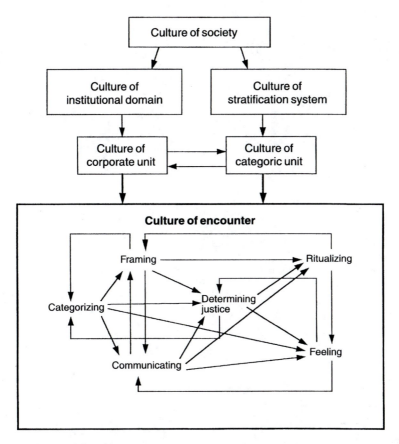

Figure 7.1 Normatizing the encounter.

of intimacy: (1) expectations for treatment of people as "personages" or relative strangers occupying positions or social categories (e.g. a brief encounter between a sales clerk and customer); (2) expectations for assessment of self and others as persons with unique characteristics; and (3) expectations for viewing others as intimates about whom a great deal is known. Categorization of situations as work–practical, social, and ceremonial leads to somewhat different expectations for treatment of individuals as personages, persons, or intimates, as outlined in Table 7.3. Each box in Table 7.3 generates a different set of expectations that will need to be assembled if the encounter is to proceed smoothly. This range of potential expectations is also overlaid with expectations associated with categoric units and for status and roles in corporate units. What is most remarkable, I believe, is how effortlessly people are able to make complex calibrations along these many dimensions and successfully categorize self, others, and the situation; and in so doing, an additional layer of expectation states is added to the encounter.

Table 7.3 Categorizing situations and intimacy

Levels of intimacy	Types of situations		
	Work/Practical	Ceremonial	Social
Personages	Others as functionaries whose behaviors are relevant to achieving a specific task or goal and who, for the purposes at hand, can be treated as strangers	Others as representatives of a larger collective enterprise toward whom highly stylized responses owed as a means of expressing their joint activity	Others as strangers toward whom superficially informal, polite, and responsive gestures are owed
Persons	Others as functionaries whose behaviors are relevant to achieving a specific task or goal but who, at the same time, must be treated as unique individuals in their own right	Others as fellow participants of a larger collective enterprise toward whom stylized responses are owed as a means of expressing their joint activity and recognition of each other as individuals in their own right	Others as familiar individuals toward whom informal, polite, and responsive gestures are owed
Intimates	Others as close friends whose behaviors are relevant to achieving a specific task or goal and toward whom emotional responsiveness is owed	Others as close friends who are fellow participants in a collective enterprise and toward whom a combination of stylized and personalized responses are owed as a means of expressing their joint activity and sense of mutual understanding	Others as close friends toward whom informal and emotionally responsive gestures are owed

Embedding helps simplify this process by delimiting the range of options. An encounter embedded in a workplace will easily be categorized as predominately work-practical, with elements of sociality and ceremony added; the division of labor will establish individuals' relative status and constrain the roles that can be played; and if categoric units are salient (especially when correlated with positions in the division of labor), the expectations associated with diffuse status characteristics will be clear. The norms attached to the division of labor will also further constrain the categorization of the encounter, and the ideologies and culture of the corporate unit as they follow from more general ideologies and symbolic media of the institutional domain will define the morality of all expectation states arising from the categorization of people and situations.

When encounters are not successfully categorized, individuals will need to work harder to create and sustain the rhythmic flow; and, indeed, it is more likely that breaches in this flow will occur, thus activating negative emotions. If individuals blame themselves for failure to properly categorize others and the situation, they will experience variants of shame ranging from embarrassment at the low-intensity end to humiliation at the high-intensity end. If the situation was important to a person or if others were powerful, the fear component of shame may be pulled out with individuals experiencing anxiety and, over time, if repairs have not been made or have not been accepted, the person may increasingly feel sad. If others are blamed for the failure to categorize, then variants of anger – ranging from annoyance to rage – are likely outcomes, although if others are powerful, this anger will need to be repressed and may be transmuted into sadness or fear. And if sadness, fear, and anger are combined, alienation may emerge if the encounter must be iterated and if the failure to categorize self, other(s), and situation persists.

When encounters cannot be successfully categorized, the process of normatization is disrupted because so many of the expectations guiding the interpersonal flow depend upon the initial categorization of self, others, and situation. People will now have to work especially hard, and they will do so by rituals designed to establish frames. For, as categorization breaks down, individuals will generally seek to compensate by successfully framing the situation so as to generate a new set of expectations that, hopefully, may help them re-categorize the encounter.

Framing

Erving Goffman's (1974) analysis of frames and framing added more precision to his earlier views on "definition of the situation" (Goffman, 1959) but, in some respects, his frame analysis went too far into the phenomenology of the mind. My view on frames is much simpler than Goffman's and argues that individuals seek to establish expectation states for what is to be included and excluded in an encounter. Individuals use rituals –

stereotypical sequences of talk and body language – to establish or "key" a frame and to re-key the frame. Categorization greatly facilitates this process, but if categorization fails, individuals will use rituals to see if they can establish frames that will guide the interaction (in fact, the use of rituals to key a frame in the absence of successful categorization often makes the encounter ever more ceremonial). If categorization is successful, however, frames are not only more readily drawn but they reinforce categorization in a mutual process that makes establishing expectation states for the encounter much easier (as outlined in Figure 7.1).

Individuals frame, I argue, along several axes, as outlined in Figure 7.2 (Turner, 1988, 1994a, 2002). In many ways, structure and culture impose themselves on an encounter via framing. Individuals use frames to pull from culture and social structures those elements of institutional spheres, corporate units, categoric units, symbolic media, ideologies, and norms that will be salient in the interaction. At times these are given by culture and structure, but most of the time the amount of structure and culture in play for an encounter is far greater than can ever be used. Indeed, without framing, it is difficult to know *which* elements of culture, social structure, and person are

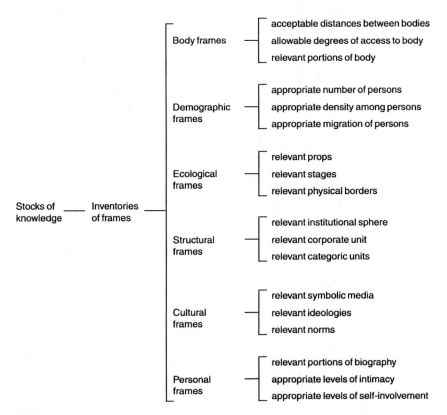

Figure 7.2 Dimensions of framing.

relevant to the interaction. Frames establish expectations for what elements of bodies, person, demography, ecology, social structure, and culture are to guide an interaction; and without successful framing, individuals are not given sufficient guidance and, as a result, are likely to feel anxious and breach the interaction which, in turn, will arouse additional negative emotions.

Much like roles, individuals carry vast inventories of frames in their stocks of knowledge. Not only do people implicitly understand a wide range of frames, they also understand the "grammars" by which they are communicated through talk and body language. Much initial role behavior in an encounter works to categorize and frame the interaction; and, in this way, individuals know what cultural expectations associated with what aspect of person, body, ecology, demography, culture, and social structure will guide the interpersonal flow. If framing is unsuccessful, however, individuals will use highly stylized ritual grammars to seek out common understandings about frames. In this process, they will experience anxiety and other variants of fear. If they blame others for their incompetence in establishing frames, they will also experience anger; and if they blame themselves for not clueing into the frame, they will experience sadness, and perhaps shame if they have also felt anger (at self) and fear (about the consequences to self) of the failure to establish a frame.

Communication

Individuals communicate via the auditory and visual channels and, at times, along the haptic channel (touch). Categorization and framing establish the proper "forms" of communication, setting up expectations for the proper form of talk, body gesturing, and touching. If categorization and framing have guided the assembling of expectations for communication, then actual talk, facial expressions and body movements, and touching will reinforce categories and frames. If, however, communication fails in that people do not understand each other's talk, body expressions, and patterns of touching or, even worse, breach expectations for the proper form of communication, then other normatizing processes will be in jeopardy.

Individuals will use stylized rituals to put the encounter back on track as they search for the proper forms of communication and seek to key new frames and impose new categories on the interaction. Like all other breaches of normatization, anxiety is typically aroused when communication fails, but individuals can also become angry if they perceive that others are simply not following the proper form of communication in a situation. People can also feel sadness, if not shame, when they come to realize that they have violated expectations for communication.

Since interaction is mediated by communication, to use an inappropriate form of talk, to employ improper facial and body language, or to touch inappropriately is highly disruptive to the encounter. All other normatizing processes are immediately called into question; and, as a result, individuals will now need to devote extra ritual effort at normatization. People will generally be resentful of having to make this extra effort, but if the encounter is important to them or if others have power, then they will experience more intense forms of fear because not only will categories and frames be called into question but just how to meet transactional needs, how to play what roles, and what status to claim will all become problematic. Typically, people will avoid encounters where communication breaks down, but if they cannot, they must work hard to sustain at least the illusion that the encounter is operating normally – an effort that can arouse fear, anger, and sadness. And once these three emotions are aroused together, shame, guilt (if values and ideologies are salient), and alienation all become possible emotional reactions.

The culture of corporate and categoric units has large effects on forms of communication. When an encounter is embedded in a corporate unit, the norms associated with the division of labor, the ideologies, and the symbolic media used in the corporate unit all dictate what is to be communicated and the form of communication. For example, an encounter embedded in a corporate unit with a lineal/vertical division of labor, an ideology emphasizing conformity to orders, and a symbolic medium revolving around power (e.g. the military) will be normatized very differently than one in a corporate unit with a horizontal division of labor, ideologies emphasizing the importance of knowledge for its own sake, and a generalized medium revolving around truth and knowledge (e.g. research in higher education). Similarly, categoric units constrain forms of communication. For instance, an encounter embedded in ethnic or class categories will exhibit patterns of communication reflecting the ideologies justifying differential evaluation of social classes or ethnic groups, by norms or expectations for how people in these categories should act, and by any generalized symbolic media (e.g. money, power) that are implicated in the inequalities among people in different classes or ethnic categories. This kind of embedding generally makes it clearer how to communicate, but when breaches occur, the emotional reaction is that much greater because at least some individuals will have presumed that the expectations had been sufficiently clear. Moreover, when inequalities in status or categoric unit membership are part of the encounter, the more generalized and diffuse anger over these inequalities can increase the likelihood that low-status and low-evaluation categoric unit members will breach the encounter by communicating in forms that violate the status order – thereby setting off cycles of anger–anger/fear–anger that can make it very difficult to successfully normatize the encounter.

Ritualizing

Frames are keyed and forms of communication are established through rituals – stereotyped sequences of talk and body language. Figure 7.3

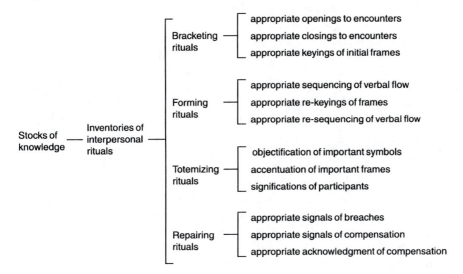

Figure 7.3 Dimensions of ritualizing.

delineates what I see as the basic types of rituals. There are always expect-ation states for what kinds of rituals can be used in an encounter, and then these rituals are employed in establishing other expectation states that guide the subsequent flow of interaction in an encounter. Bracketing rituals open and close interactions, establishing the initial forms of talk, frames, and feeling/display rules for emotions in an encounter; and, with closing ritual sequences come expectations for frames, forms of talk, and emotions in subsequent encounters. When bracketing rituals are not conducted properly or fail to key frames, forms of talk, and emotional mood, the encounter will become very awkward, with new rituals emitted to see if indeed the inter-action can get back on track. Similarly, if the closing rituals do not meet expectations, then the next iteration of the interaction will be awkward and tentative, until rituals can put it on track.

Depending upon what expectations have been generated by opening and closing rituals, as well as by all other sources of expectation states from transactional needs, social structure, and culture, forming rituals will be selected and then used to structure the flow of communication in an encounter. Different forming rituals will be expected under varying condi-tions imposed by individuals' transactional needs, by social structure, and by elements of culture; and if the proper bracketing rituals were used, then the expectations for the appropriate forming rituals will be more readily understood, with the result that these forming rituals will be effective in structuring the flow of interaction. But, if the wrong bracketing and/or forming rituals are invoked, the interaction will be breached. For example, if the bracketing rituals were highly effusive and initiated high levels of inter-personal animation, the use of a forming ritual that breaks this mood (e.g. "enough of this, time to get to work") may prove ineffective at best and breach the interaction at worst.

Repair rituals signal a breach and a readiness to offer compensation for the breach. Depending upon the profile of expectations guiding an encounter, additional expectations always emerge as to which rituals would be appropriate for repairing breaches. If the wrong repair ritual is used and breaks with expectations, however, the repair ritual itself adds to the existing breach. For example, if a person offers an apology ritual in a sarcastic manner – e.g. "soooorry!" – under conditions where more solemnity is required, the repair becomes yet one more breach, setting up expectations for an extra-special repair ritual (assuming that a person wants to repair the breach). A successful repair sequence involves an initial ritual calling attention to a breach, a ritual signaling of an apology and offer of compensation, and an acceptance of the apology and compensation. Generally, the apology and compensation are mixed together as is the case when a person indicates that they "are truly sorry" and "will make it up" to the offended party.

Totemizing rituals are directed toward symbols marking the solidarity of the encounter or social structure in which an encounter is embedded. As principles 1 and 4 emphasize, the arousal of positive emotional energy sets into motion a more inclusive interaction ritual revolving around rhythmic synchronization, emotional entrainment, enhanced solidarity, and symbolization of this solidarity (Collins, 2004). Once symbolization has occurred, expectations for rituals directed at these symbols or totems emerge, with the stereotyped sequence arousing the emotion generated in the encounter and reinforcing the symbols. Sometimes the totem can be confined to just a few people. For instance, when one of two lovers says "I love you," the expected ritual replay is something like "I love you too"; both rituals are directed at an implicit totem – the sacredness of the love relationship – and the couple's rituals are directed at this totem and thereby arouse the positive emotions associated with "their love." Street gang symbols – dress, forms of address, and demeanor – can also be seen as totems of the solidarity of the gang, with stereotypical gestures operating as totemizing rituals directed at the sacred symbols of the gang.

Expectations for rituals of all kinds are constrained by embedding and the culture associated with corporate and categoric units. The ideologies and generalized symbolic media that filter through mesostructures to encounters generate expectations for certain types of rituals; and then the emission of the rituals structures the interpersonal flow of the encounter. For example, an encounter that is embedded in corporate units in which control of others is part of the ideology of the unit and in which power is the dominant symbolic media will reveal very different expectations for rituals than an encounter embedded in units where sociality is the goal and where the dominant symbolic medium is loyalty. The ritual expectation states for these two encounters – i.e. the rituals that bracket them, the rituals that structure the interpersonal flow, the rituals directed at totems, and the rituals used to repair breaches – will not be the same. Similarly, norms associated with the division of labor of corporate units or the expectations for behaviors among members of categoric units will also create expectations for certain types of rituals that can be used to key frames, form talk, calculate just shares, and arouse emotions.

Like all expectation states, failure to emit the expected rituals violates expectations and also serves as a negative sanction – thus initiating the processes summarized in principles 2, 5, and 6b. Because rituals are the tracking mechanisms for getting interactions started and keeping them flowing in the expected manner, failure to emit the proper rituals intensifies the breach. If the mechanisms for preventing breaches and for repairing them are, themselves, breached, then the negative emotional arousal will be even more intense. And, as a result, finding and using the "right" repair ritual to mend the breach becomes that much more difficult. If a person blames self for using the wrong ritual, then this individual will likely experience shame and, if possible, initiate a repair sequence – using, this time, the proper ritual. If a person blames others for failing to meet ritual expectation states, then anger is the most likely emotion, unless the situation is an important source for meeting transactional needs or the others are powerful. Under these latter conditions, fear is also likely to emerge. Interactions that cannot be ritualized will always be stressful because, without rituals, expectation states from transactional needs, culture, and social structure become ambiguous and, hence, more difficult to meet. As a result, individuals will leave such encounters if they can, but if they are forced to stay in the encounter, they will likely experience alienation and exhibit role-distance, offering rituals in only the most perfunctory manner.

Rules of justice

When individuals enter an encounter, particularly one that is highly embedded in the vertical and horizontal divisions of labor of a corporate unit and the differential evaluation of categoric units, they may have already calibrated a rough sense of their "just share" of resources in the encounter. They have expectation states for what they and others should receive; and, as the encounter unfolds, they will fine-tune their expectations during the process of normatization. In this case, the expectation states will indicate that, given how the encounter has unfolded in terms of categorization, framing, forms of communication, and ritual enactments, a just share of resources would be x amount. When they realize this amount, they will feel positive emotions and continue to accept the categorization, frames, forms of communication, and rituals. If, however, expectations for just shares are not realized, then the arousal of negative emotions may lead to a breach in the encounter as individuals make claims for more resources – thereby forcing re-normatization of the encounter. Of course, if others are powerful, a person may have to repress anger over injustice; and if an individual must persistently do so, these persons may come to feel sad and fearful of the consequences to self for not being able to meet expectations for just shares. If a person experiences all of these negative emotions, he or she may also feel shame and, if the expectations for just shares carry high moral content, guilt about their inability to secure resources. Or, this person may readjust perceptions of what will be a just share in this particular encounter, but this re-calibration will not generally eliminate the negative emotions. Individuals will likely remain angry, sad, fearful, shamed, and guilty even as they deny that they are upset because of the injustice done to them.

Feeling rules

As Hochschild (1983) was first to emphasize, interactions are guided by feeling and display rules that reflect feeling ideologies. Thus, every encounter is guided by expectations that individuals should feel and express particular emotions. These rules are often dictated by ideologies of the meso-level structures in which encounters are embedded. For instance, an ideology emphasizing individual achievement will require individuals to feel satisfaction and quiet pride for success and shame for failure; or an encounter lodged in mesostructures emphasizing power and control might direct individuals to feel triumphant when control is achieved and, again, shamed or alienated when control has not been forthcoming. Symbolic media also have this capacity to arouse emotions because there is almost always an evaluative element attached to a medium. For instance, if money is the medium of exchange, people feel sad or shameful if they do not have much money, whereas they will feel pride and satisfaction when they have money (with the implicit evaluative element being that if money is the medium, it is best to have more of it). When ideology and symbolic media are combined, as they often are, the constraints on feeling and displaying emotions are that much greater. If money is the symbolic medium and the ideology argues that money is also a sign of worth, then persons with money are entitled to feel and display pride, whereas those who do not have money should feel sad, if not shameful, and display these emotions, especially in the presence of those who have money and are hence "better."

Other features of embedding also generate expectation states for feeling. A hierarchical division of labor (in a corporate unit) or differentially evaluated diffuse status characteristics (arising from categoric unit membership) will set up expectation for high- and low-status individuals; and, in so doing, those in high positions should feel satisfaction while those in lower positions should feel sad or shameful if they violate expectations. Moreover, individuals in high-status positions are entitled to feel angry at those in low positions who challenge their superordination, while those who have violated expectation states by challenging inequalities of status are to feel sad, if not ashamed.

Often there will be explicit norms associated with status that direct feeling rules. Here, the feeling rule is also part of the normative expectation for performance for a person in a status position, as is the case when a student is to feel and express shame at not doing well on an examination if this student did not study (a rule that is often violated because students often make external attributions and blame professors for their poor performance on an exam). Or, a worshiper who has not lived up to the tenets of a religion is expected to feel shame, to express this shame and guilt (since religion is always moral), and then to abide by expectations for repair rituals.

Other aspects of normatizing also set up expectations for feeling and displaying emotions. Categorization sets up expectations for the emotions to be displayed in any of the nine cells in Table 7.3. For example, there will be different feeling and display rules for individuals in work–practical vs. social or ceremonial situations, and there will be further differentiation of feeling and display rules associated with whether others are personages, persons, or intimates. Moreover, classification of individuals in categoric units not only invokes the relative evaluations of these units and the expectations for how members of these units should act but also how they should feel and the manner in which their emotions should be displayed. For example, there are different feeling and display rules for those in higher and lower social classes, for those in valued vs. devalued ethnic minorities, for old and young, and most dramatically for men and women (with women having a much greater burden to "feel" sympathetic emotions than men). And, when expectations for these emotions are not realized in actual feelings and displays, individuals will experience sadness, if not shame and guilt if these feeling rules invoked moral codes from values and ideologies.

Framing also constrains feeling and display rules. Frames establish what is to be included and excluded; and, in so doing, they also establish which emotions are to be included and excluded from an encounter. Indeed, "breaking frame" is often the result of individuals feeling and expressing emotions that have been excluded by the frame, thereby breaching the encounter and forcing costly repair ritual sequences. In the same manner, forms of communication also constrain the kinds of emotions that are to be felt and displayed. Since so much communication is accomplished via body language – the language of emotions, as I emphasized in Chapter 2 – communication, per se, restricts emotional arousal and display. As individuals seek to use the proper form of communication, they necessarily attempt to manage emotional displays, if not feelings. Such is particularly likely for body language where expressive control is more difficult to sustain; and should *in*appropriate emotions be displayed, then the proper form of communication is breached, forcing repair rituals or perhaps a re-keying of the frame as new emotions are introduced into the encounter. For example, a father who "loses it" around his kid and displays intense anger is forced to re-key the interaction or offer elaborate apologies which might go against his role as father and his higher status as a father and adult. Thus, the proper form of fatherly communication to a son operates to restrict emotional displays and, presumably, the underlying feelings; and if a parent does not feel the emotions that he or she is forced to display as part of the parent and adult roles, then the emotion work requirement is indeed high, and it is likely that the real emotions will break out in weak moments, prompting shame and also guilt at having violated the (moral) expectations arising from parent roles, ideologies of how to be a good parent, and symbolic media revolving around love and loyalty.

Expectations for justice have very large effects on feeling and display rules in an encounter. At one level, expectations for "just shares" indicate how much of what resource a person should receive to experience happiness and satisfaction, with any amount below this perception of "just shares" indicating that a person should be angry, if not sad, fearful, shamed, or guilty. Thus, feeling rules and rules of justice are often interwoven, signaling to a person the kind and level of emotion they should feel and display. On another level, feeling rules also specify how an individual is to manage the emotions that come with meeting, or failing to meet, expectations for just shares. Rules may prohibit displays of emotions when injustice occurs, or they may be more relaxed; and rules may not sanction even the feeling of injustice, much less its display to others, or it may encourage both the feeling and display. To the degree that feeling rules require high levels of emotion work to hide or, if possible, to eliminate feelings of injustice, they work to encourage repression of the negative emotions which, in turn, will generate an underlying tension in the encounter that periodically may be breached as intensified and transmuted emotions erupt, often making persons who breach the encounter feel shame and guilt for violating expectations for how they should feel and act.

Whatever their source – whether from explicit feeling ideologies and rules, evaluative elements of symbolic media, expectations associated with categories, frames, forms of communication, status and roles, or norms of justice – violating feeling rules almost always leads individuals to experience shame, even if only mild shame such as embarrassment. If the shame is acknowledged, then repair rituals can be initiated and lead to the arousal of positive emotions. If, however, the shame is repressed, it will transmute into anger and target the persons or situation in which feeling rules were violated. If this shame is chronic, shame–anger–shame cycles may operate, or the individual will become ever more depressed and/or alienated from the situation. Emotions that violate emotion rules thus pose a kind of double burden: the person is not supposed to feel or display emotions that are felt, and if these emotions escape cortical censorship, the negative emotions aroused for violating a feeling rule are piled upon the ones that were not supposed to be felt or displayed in the first place, thereby compounding the emotional agony of the person. Since a feeling rule has been violated, and especially a feeling rule tied to a feeling ideology about what is right and wrong in a particular sphere, the person may not only experience shame but guilt as well. Guilt may lead a person to initiate repair rituals, but if guilt is combined with shame, it will compound the shame – thus increasing the likelihood of repression and transmutation into anger leading to anger–shame/guilt–anger cycles or to severe depression and/or alienation.

Conclusion

The expectations arising from transactional needs and social structure are, for all their robust complexity, insufficient in directing individuals in face-to-face interaction. Additional elements of culture need to be assembled in most encounters to assure the smooth flow of interaction; and, for want of a better label, I have termed the processes by which these elements of culture are brought to an encounter, normatization. Normatization is both a sequential and simultaneous process. Initial role-taking focuses on categorization of self, other, and situation which, in turn, provides guidance for the bracketing and forming rituals that will key the frame; and together, categorization and framing provide guidance for subsequent forming and bracketing rituals as well as forms of communication, assessments of justice, and feeling rules. At any point, a breach can occur if the individuals do not successfully normatize the encounter and, thus, come to implicit agreements about the expectation states that will be added by culture as it filters into encounters from macrostructures via corporate and categoric units.

At the macro-level of social organization, general societal values as these become instantiated in the ideologies of institutional domains and stratification systems provide one source of cultural input into the encounter. Another source of input comes from the generalized symbolic media of institutional domains that serve as a resource to be exchanged and distributed as well as a medium of discourse and thematization within a domain. Moreover, since it is institutional structures that distribute resources unequally in the stratification system, it should not be surprising that the ideologies of this system are couched in terms of symbolic media and that the very resources distributed unequally are the symbolic media themselves, particularly money and power. Ideologies and symbolic media always contain evaluative premises about what is right, good, proper, and their opposite. Thus, much of the moral content of an encounter is provided by ideologies and symbolic media as these are filtered through mesostructures down to the encounter.

Institutional norms for domains also come to encounters directly and, frequently, via the norms of the division of labor of corporate units. Similarly, normative expectations for individuals incumbent in classes and class factions come to encounters via these categoric units, as well as categoric units formed by other distinctions, such as those associated with gender, age, and ethnicity.

These normative systems operating at the meso level almost always carry evaluational content. Division of labor norms are derived from institutional norms, ideologies, and symbolic media; as a result, they contain the evaluative content of these elements of culture. Expectations for people in categories created by classes and class factions carry the evaluative content of the meta-ideologies legitimating the class system, plus the cultural content of the institutional domains that distribute resources (including symbolic media) unequally. The same is true with categoric distinctions revolving around other dimensions such as age, gender, and ethnicity; these categoric distinctions almost always carry differential evaluations from associations with locations in the stratification system or from institutional domains or corporate units in these domains that contribute to creating or sustaining the salience of these categoric distinctions.

In general, the more evaluative content that filters into the encounter from values, ideologies, symbolic media, and normative systems, the greater is the potential for more intense emotional arousal. Individuals not only evaluate themselves as they role-take with specific others in front of them, but they also compare their and others' actions to the moral yardsticks of culture. As a result, categorization, framing, ritualizing, communicating, sensing justice, and feeling become not just run-of-the-mill expectations but, instead, are super-charged as moral expectations. Categorizing others and the situation correctly, framing the situation accurately, using the proper form of talk and body language, employing the appropriate rituals, calculating justice, and feeling as well as displaying the right emotions all take on greater moral significance when the evaluative content of values, ideologies, symbolic media, and norms is high. As a result, the positive emotions that are aroused when an encounter is successfully normatized will be more intense, and particularly so if self was on the line in role-making and claiming status; and, conversely, the negative emotions will be more intense and almost always involve shame and guilt when the encounter fails to be normatized. Moreover, the emotions aroused will be doubly affected by the fact that a failure to meet expectations associated with the process of normatization will also be seen by individuals as negative sanctions on self, thus increasing the salience of self in the encounter and, hence, the emotions aroused.

Embedding increases the moral content of an encounter through normatization because mesostructures become the conduit by which values, ideologies, symbolic media, and evaluative institutional norms reach the encounter. An encounter in a school or family, for example, will almost always have more moral content than one in a shopping mall or any public place because of the clear embedding of the encounter within a corporate unit within an institutional domain. An encounter among people in discrete categoric units will typically have more moral content when these units are associated with places in the division of labor of a corporate unit in particular institutional domains and classes or class factions embedded in the society-wide stratification system. Outside these macrostructures and mesostructures, however, the moral content of membership in different categoric units will decline, as is evident in public places where representatives of diverse categoric units move, although the salience of membership may dramatically increase if members of one or more categoric units use public places to make role and status claims.

Like most of the forces driving encounters, the nature and intensity of the emotional arousal arising from normatization is related to the level of moral content, the salience of self, and the specific phase of normatization involved. As a general rule, the more salient is self and the higher is the emotional content, the more intense are the emotions aroused, whether positive or negative, during the process of normatization. Breaches at any point in the process of normatization will, under these conditions, almost always arouse righteous anger at those who are seen as responsible for the breach, and shame and guilt if individuals perceive that they have been responsible for the breach. Of course, the processes of repression, intensification, and transmutation can make these relationships much more complex because people will often repress shame and, to a lesser extent, guilt, while exhibiting righteous anger and making external attributions for their own repressed shame and guilt. In turn, those who feel unjustly sanctioned by this anger will, themselves, become angry and sanction the sanctioner in a conflict spiral that can break the encounter apart.

When somewhat less morality is on the line and where self is not so salient, the emotional reactions are less intense. A person may feel only sad that they have breached a phase of normatization, or fearful if others in the encounter are powerful. If anger at self is also present, then mild shame like embarrassment may emerge; and if shame is chronic, it will often transmute into alienation. Those who blame others for breaches may only be mildly annoyed, or if these others are powerful, then annoyance may turn to fear; and if anger and fear emotions are supplemented by sadness, then alienation may become the dominant emotion for those who are angry at, fearful of, and sad about the way others have breached the encounter.

Some phases of normatization have more emotional potential than others. If categorization cannot occur, other phases of the encounter will become more difficult to normatize. And, if rituals used to key frames in an attempt to arrive at categorization also prove unsuccessful, then appropriate forms of communication, justice calculations, and feeling rules will likely be violated. Rituals are, in many respects, the key to re-normatizing an encounter that is off track; by using rituals to remake roles and reclaim status, it is sometimes possible to re-calibrate categories, frames, forms of communication, justice calculations, and appropriate feelings. Since roles and status will be more explicit when an encounter is embedded in mesostructures, this route to re-normatizing is likely to be more successful when embedding exists. For encounters without the framework of explicit roles and status provided by embedding, however, rituals will be less successful unless they immediately get categorization and framing correct. If rituals can be successful in categorizing and framing, then it is likely that normatization of forms of communication and feeling rules can be achieved.

There are many potential generalizations that can be offered along the lines, but let me conclude with a simple principle that can subsume the many specific hypotheses that I have offered in this chapter.

14   *The more an encounter is embedded in meso-level structures and the more these mesostructures are embedded in institutional domains and/or society-wide stratification systems, the greater will be the moral content from values, ideologies, generalized symbolic media, and norms penetrating the encounter; and the higher the level of moral content penetrating the encounter, the more intense will be the emotions aroused, whether positive or negative, during the process of normatization.*

   A   *The more self is salient under conditions of high moral content, the more expectations for categorization, framing, ritualizing, communicating, justice calculations, and feelings will become implicated in the process of verification of self and, hence, the more intense will be the emotions aroused, whether positive or negative, during the process of normatization.*

      1   *The more self is verified during each phase of normatization, the more likely will the processes outlined in principles 1, 4, 6a, and 7 be initiated.*

      2   *The less self is verified during each phase of normatization, the more likely will failure to meet expectations also be viewed as negative sanctions to self and, hence, the more likely will a person experience shame and guilt.*

      3   *The more shame or guilt is repressed, the more likely will these emotions be transmuted into anger and, hence, the more likely will the processes outlined in principles 3, 5, 6b, and 8 be operative.*

   B   *The more initial phases of normatizing, particularly categorization and framing, prove successful, the more likely will other phases of normatizing (ritualizing, forms of communication, justice calculations, and agreements on emotion rules) be achieved; and, conversely, the less successful are initial phases of normatizing, the more pronounced will be ritual sequences among individuals and the more problematic will normatizing become, unless these ritual efforts can establish a frame which, in turn, can lead to successful categorization.*

8   Emotions and social change

Societies are ultimately held together by the positive emotions that people feel toward social structures and culture; and, conversely, societies can be torn apart and changed by the arousal of both negative and positive emotions. Indeed, if there is a micro basis of social order and change, it is the arousal of emotions among individuals as they navigate encounters lodged within mesostructures and macrostructures. Emotions are the energy that sustains or changes social reality, and while much human energy is generated by biological and by transactional needs, emotions are nonetheless implicated in meeting these biosocial needs. More importantly, emotions represent an independent source of motivational energy – above and beyond biosocial needs – that has large effects on the structures and cultures of a society. Thus, we require some generalizations about how emotions emerging at the micro level of social reality can, under specifiable conditions, generate pressures for stasis or change in social structure and culture.

Emotional energy and commitments to social structures and culture

Positive emotional arousal has a proximal bias, as outlined in principle 6a; as a result, positive emotional energy tends to circulate within the local encounter, as summarized in principles 1 and 4. This fact of emotional life poses a dilemma because if positive emotions are critical to people's commitments to macrostructures – that is, institutional domains, stratification systems, societies, and even inter-societal systems – how is positive emotion to "break free" from the centripetal forces of the local encounter? To restate this question more theoretically: What conditions increase the probability that positive emotions will target mesostructures and macrostructures, thereby increasing commitments to these structures and their attendant cultures?

Humans did not evolve macrostructures; indeed, the small band and nuclear family units were humans' only structures for well over 90 percent of our history. And so, for early humans, the dilemma of how to move positive emotions outward beyond micro-level structures did not exist, because macrostructures did not exist. True, there may have been a sense of a regional population of bands sharing a common culture (just as there is among chimpanzees), but commitments were to the nuclear family and band. But as the scale of society grew and as macrostructures became more remote, problems of how to generate attachments to these structures increased dramatically. To some degree, the processes outlined in interaction ritual theory (Collins, 2004 and Figure 4.1) get us part of the way in that humans may be hard-wired to engage in emotion-arousing rituals that build up solidarity and group symbols. Moreover, like their chimpanzee cousins, humans may also be wired to perceive, and develop commitments to, a larger region and its population. Once the group can be symbolized and once rituals directed at these symbols produce solidarity, more remote mesostructures and macrostructres can similarly be symbolized and become targets of emotional attachment. In many ways, Émile Durkheim's (1965 [1912]) analysis of the elementary forms of the religious life came to this same conclusion. For, as mechanical solidarity built around dense networks and common culture could no longer organize large, differentiated populations, the solution to the problem of integration was to make culture more abstract and general so that individuals located at different places in the complex division of labor could hold common symbols (Durkheim, 1997 [1893]) and, within local encounters and groups, engage in ritual practices that aroused emotions directed at these symbols. Thus, as network density declines, orientations to common symbols become ever more critical to sustaining the larger, differentiated population (Maryanski, n.d.; Hammond, 2006).

Indeed, the differentiation of culture among values, ideologies, generalized symbolic media, and various levels of norms provides a variety of targets at different levels of social reality toward which solidarity-generating rituals can be enacted. Still, if positive emotions reveal a proximal bias (principle 6a), there is no guarantee that the positive emotions will be directed outward toward these differentiated symbol systems and the structures in which they are instantiated. Having a micro-level propensity to symbolize local solidarities does not mean that people will naturally do the same thing to macrostructures. In fact, it is clear that humans do not easily develop commitments to macrostructures and culture because the "problem of legitimacy" for polity as an institutional domain, the problem of alienation in the economic and educational domains, the tensions over inequalities, and the many other flashpoints of large, complex societies indicate that achieving attachments to macrostructures is often tenuous and, in the long run, likely to break down. We require, then, some additional theorizing on what conditions increase commitments to social structures and cultures outside the local encounter.

Commitments to mesostructures

Commitments to corporate units

Although positive emotional arousal stemming from meeting expectations and receiving positive sanctions has a propensity to stay local and circulate in iterated encounters, individuals do make external attributions for their positive feelings. They will experience gratitude toward those whom they perceive to have helped them meet expectations and receive positive sanctions; and they will exhibit the same tendency toward mesostructures. If a corporate unit is perceived to facilitate individuals in meeting expectations and receiving positive sanctions, then some of the positive emotional energy directed at self and others may well spill out to the corporate unit. This "spillover" effect is more likely in corporate units revealing low levels of hierarchy and authority, although some hierarchical corporate units, such as churches, have memberships that are highly committed (probably because of the constant use of rituals targeting the symbols of the church, thereby raising intensity of positive emotions directed at the church and its culture). But in general, hierarchy creates the potential for negative sanctioning and shaming which erode positive emotional energy and, hence, the likelihood that commitments will be strong − unless rituals are *constantly* enacted to channel emotions toward the totems of the group.

Another condition increasing commitments to mesostructures and their cultures is the ability to meet expectations that they impose and to receive positive sanctions by virtue of successfully claiming status and playing roles in these structures. When expectations are defined by the culture and structure of a corporate unit, meeting these expectations automatically makes the corporate unit highly salient and an easier target for the outflow of positive emotions from self, others, and local encounter to the structure and culture of the meso unit. Similarly, when a corporate unit is built around positive sanctioning of performances that meet expectations imposed by the structure and culture of this unit, the sanctions are seen to come from the structure and culture of the meso unit as much as they are from particular individuals; and, as a consequence, commitments to the meso unit become more likely.

The converse of these processes also holds true. If the structure and culture of the unit are perceived to be punitive and to impose unrealistic expectations, negative emotions will readily be directed at the corporate unit. True, there is a built-in distal bias for negative emotions (principle 6b), but this bias is facilitated by the structure of the corporate unit in which encounters are embedded. When the structure and culture operate to assure that individuals will fail at meeting expectations attached to the division of labor and/or that individuals will be sanctioned by those in authority, external attributions are given an added boost outward. Under these conditions, the proximal bias of whatever positive emotions aroused in encounters will tend to stay local, often becoming a basis for solidarities that oppose the culture of the larger corporate unit (as is the case in prisons and other kinds of authoritarian corporate units).

Commitments to categoric units

When membership in a categoric unit is perceived to have facilitated meeting expectations and receiving positive sanctions, then the proximal bias of positive emotions is easily extended to the social identity of a person as a member of a particular category. For example, if being male is seen as partly responsible for positive emotional arousal, then commitments to this social category increase as a natural matter of course. The same process can work in developing commitments to other categoric units. When a person perceives that members of another distinctive categoric unit have been responsible for positive emotional arousal, this person will develop positive stereotypes about members of this categoric unit, giving them a high evaluation and developing commitments to members in this categoric unit. For instance, upper-class individuals often develop positive sentiments toward their servants not only as persons (due to high rates of interaction rituals) but also as members of categoric units because these servants facilitate meeting expectations and receiving positive sanctions from fellow upper-class persons. Yet, if high levels of inequality in power and authority exist between two categoric units, there is almost always tension (especially from those in the less-valued categoric unit) that works against this kind of commitment since those in less-valued categories often do not meet expectations and must endure in silence negative sanctions from those with more social "worth" and with more power, money, and prestige.

Just as is the case with corporate units, the converse of these processes can erode commitments. When members of categoric units are perceived (whether or not accurately) to have frustrated meeting expectations or to have been directly or indirectly responsible for negative sanctions, then negative prejudices toward members of these categoric units will emerge, and individuals will express anger toward their members. If Jews, for example, could be blamed for the economic problems of Germany in the 1930s, then this anger could be mobilized and used to exterminate this "enemy" – the ultimate indicator of a lack of commitment.

Commitments to macrostructures

More intriguing than commitments to meso units are commitments to macrostructures and their cultures. In many ways, commitments to the culture and structure of macro-level structures are an extension of the processes generating attachments to mesostructures. If expectations have been realized and positive sanctions received across many encounters embedded in diverse corporate units and categoric units of macrostructures, the positive emotions aroused will move outward toward these macrostructures. For example, if a person has been consistently successful in schools − that is, encounters in classes embedded in primary, secondary, and university corporate units − it is likely that this person will develop commitments to the culture and structure of education as an institutional domain and to the ideology and structure of a stratification system that, in part, uses educational credentials to determine people's life chances to gain access to the resources. Similarly, people who have enjoyed success in business in a capitalist economic system or who have been able to secure high wages in this system will believe in the ideology, use the symbolic medium, and abide by institutional norms of this system because they will have a biography of meeting expectations and receiving positive sanctions in a variety of corporate units. To take another example, those who have money, power, and prestige and who are members of upper classes and upper factions within classes will generally feel that the larger stratification system is legitimate because they consistently meet expectations and, given their power, money and prestige, receive positive sanctions in deference rituals. The same is true of middle-class individuals because they too will have consistently met expectations and received positive sanctions. Even lower-class persons may give legitimacy to the system if they had realistic expectations and been able to meet them in corporate units where they also received positive sanctions.

Thus, the key dynamic here revolves around the consistent activation of positive emotions in meso-level units over a longer time frame. When institutional domains and stratification systems are built from these meso units, the positive emotions aroused will target macrostructures. Consistent reinforcement arouses positive emotions toward self and others in the encounter, but this pattern of reinforcement also generates a sufficient surplus of positive emotions that moves out to the meso-level units and beyond to macrostructures. And, this external attribution process becomes even more likely when the individual defines self in terms of the roles that can be successfully played in a range of encounters within corporate and categoric units. Confirmation of role-identities adds extra levels of positive emotional energy because verification of self is, I believe, the most important transactional need. Also, when persons receive positive sanctions and meet expectations, they also will receive profitable exchange payoffs and meet other transactional needs − thereby adding extra layers of positive emotional energy that will migrate outward to macrostructures.

The structure of corporate and categoric units also influences the degree to which emotions will move outward to macrostructures. If expectations and sanctions in a corporate unit are clearly specified by the culture and if performances within the division of labor of the unit are rewarded when meeting expectations, positive emotional arousal will increase commitments to this unit, as noted above. Moreover, if this unit is embedded in a clearly differentiated institutional domain with a distinctive generalized medium of exchange, clear ideologies, and explicit institutional norms, this close coupling between the culture and structure of a corporate unit and an institutional domain leads individuals to see not only the meso unit as facilitating success, but also, if this success is consistently repeated across a number of corporate units within this domain, the positive emotions will increasingly be directed outward to the culture and structure of the institutional domain. The converse of this process is also important: a lack of clear embedding of a corporate unit in an institutional domain works to localize the positive emotions aroused at the level of the encounter or at corporate structure rather than moving outward toward macrostructures.

The same coupling processes also operate with categoric units. If a categoric unit is discrete and commands a clear level of evaluation in terms of class or class faction within a lineal stratification system, success in meeting expectations and receiving positive sanctions in encounters where categoric unit membership is salient will increase not only commitments to this unit but also to the macrostructural stratification system in which this categoric unit is embedded. The same is true for a categoric unit that is also discrete and embedded in an institutional domain. For example, successful "managers" as a categoric unit develop commitments not only to the stratification system but the institutional domain of the economy. The converse of these processes is also important because when people do not experience positive emotions with those in more highly evaluated categoric units, the negative emotional energy generates anger at members of these categoric units, thereby decreasing commitments to the stratification system and/or institutional domains generating these units. Thus, if blue-collar workers or the poor do not meet expectations or, as is more likely, must endure negative sanctions from managers or rich people, commitments to either the institutional domain or stratification system will be low. Indeed, these persons may become sufficiently angry to seek change in social structure and culture.

Perhaps this is all a long-winded way of saying that those who do well in a society reveal higher levels of commitment to the structure and culture of a society than those who do not. But, the process is more nuanced than this broad generalization would indicate. If we are to understand the level of commitment to specific institutional domains or to the class system in a society or, potentially, a system of societies, we need to see *how consistently* expectations and sanctioning have been tied to the structure of corporate and categoric units and how embedded these mesostructures are in the culture and structure of institutional domains and stratification systems. But more is required; we must also know the degree to which the culture and structure of meso units increases or decreases the likelihood that persons will be positively sanctioned and will meet expectations defined by the culture of the meso unit and the macro-level unit in which it is embedded. Further, we will need to know the number of meso units in which members of a population have participated, and the degree of success they have had across diverse meso units embedded in different institutional domains and in the classes and class–factions of the stratification system. Once data of this nature are secured, then it becomes possible to predict the extent to which the positive or negative emotions aroused will move out from the meso unit and target macrostructures.

Since negative emotional arousal has a built–in distal bias, negative emotions are far more likely to move out and target macrostructures – whether an institutional domain or the stratification system and, potentially, society as a whole or system of societies. When negative emotions are consistently aroused across many diverse mesostructures among large numbers of individuals, then it is likely that change in macrostructures will occur, as I will outline shortly. When positive emotions are consistently aroused among many individuals across many diverse mesostructures, commitments to institutional domains and the existing stratification system become ever more likely, making change generated by emotional arousal less probable. By knowing *which* mesostructures in *which* macrostructures generate positive or negative emotions among *how many* persons will also allow for predictions about *which* institutional domain and *which* element of the stratification system will be targeted for change. True, there is some blow-over effect with emotion in one domain or point in the stratification system affecting emotions about other domains and locations in the stratification system. Still, commitments to, anger at, or alienation from macrostructures can also be more institution-specific, as when a person hates religion or universities but is committed to the political and economic domains, as well as the stratification system.

Thus, the more people experience positive emotional arousal across encounters within mesostructures, the more some of this emotion will be externalized to the structure and culture of this meso unit, whether a corporate or categoric unit. And, the more people consistently experience positive emotional arousal across a number of meso units lodged in macrostructures that are clearly differentiated by their structure and culture, the more likely will positive emotional energy break the centripetal hold of the proximal bias and lead individuals to make commitment and to assign legitimacy to macrostructures, whether an institutional domain or a stratification system. And if most institutional domains and classes in the stratification system are given legitimacy, then it is likely that the society as a whole and the inter-societal system in which it is embedded will also receive commitments and legitimacy.

The stratification of emotions

As I have emphasized, attachments to social structures come from consistent arousal of positive emotions in encounters embedded within mesostructures that, in turn, are lodged within clearly differentiated macrostructures. When individuals experience emotions in accordance with the process outlined in principles 1, 4, 6a, and 7, commitments to the encounter and, often, to the mesostructures and macrostructures in which the encounter is embedded will increase. Conversely, when the processes described in principles 2, 5, 6b, and 8 are operative, commitments will decline.

Another way to look at emotions and social structures is in terms of the distribution of emotions across a population. Different sectors of a population have habitually experienced more or less positive and negative emotional arousal; and the cumulative effect is the unequal distribution of emotional energy and the formation of yet one more basis of social stratification. Those who have been successful in schools and jobs, for example, will not only have more money and prestige, but they will also have had consistent positive emotional arousal in these embedded corporate units, with the result that they will exhibit the confidence to secure more positive emotions along with other resources. In contrast, those who have been less successful will have biographies filled with negative emotional arousal – variants and elaborations of anger, fear, sadness, shame, and perhaps guilt – with the consequence that they will lack the necessary confidence to secure other resources, thereby perpetuating the emotions that accompany failure.

There should thus be a positive correlation among the distributions of material well-being, power, prestige, and positive emotional energy, as Collins (1975) noted long ago and as Kemper (1978) along with Collins (1990) have emphasized. When people meet expectations and gain power and prestige, they feel more confident; and this reservoir of positive emotions is yet one more resource that can be used and invested to secure additional resources. In contrast, when individuals do not meet expectations or lose power and prestige, they lack confidence and, as a result, are less likely to have the emotional reserves to secure other resources. Since a stratification system is built around the unequal distribution of resources, those in the higher classes or top factions within classes should not only have more economic, cultural, social, and symbolic capital (to use Bourdieu's typology), they should also have larger reserves of positive emotional energy. Conversely, those in lower classes or dominated factions within classes will have less of all forms of capital and positive emotional energy. *Emotional capital* – to invent yet one more type of capital in sociology's recent fascination with forms of "capital" – is thus unequally distributed within and across societies. The reason for this inequality is that high-ranking classes and dominant factions within classes will be inhabited by persons who have been successful in meeting expectations and receiving positive sanctions in encounters embedded in corporate units lodged in institutional domains distributing resources, whereas lower classes and dominated factions within classes will reveal biographies where negative emotions have been aroused in encounters lodged in corporate units of institutional domains distributing resources.

High- and low-ranking persons in the general stratification system will also be marked by memberships in differentially evaluated categoric units revolving around social class and, as result, they will enter most encounters with varying degrees of prestige, with those in more valued categoric units able to secure more resources than those in less valued categoric units. Indeed, the expectation states literature (e.g. Berger, 1988; Berger *et al.*, 1972; Berger and Zelditch, 1985) clearly documents the advantages of high-value diffuse status characteristics over those with low-value status characteristics.

The above generalizations need considerable qualification, however. First, individuals in all social classes may experience positive emotions in many encounters in corporate units lodged in institutional domains that are less directly related to the distribution of power, money, and prestige. For example, a person who has not been successful in either the educational or economic domains may nonetheless have a biography of positive emotional arousal in other domains, such as kinship, religion, or sports. Thus, whatever the level of negative emotional energy that has accumulated as a result of not meeting expectations in corporate units lodged in some institutional domains, it is, to a degree, mitigated by positive emotional arousal stemming from positive sanctioning and meeting expectations in other domains. Of course, if a person has not been so compensated for failures in domains involved in resource distribution (i.e. economy, polity, education) by positive sanctioning in these other domains, then an even larger reserve of negative emotional arousal will be evident. Thus, for example, a poor person who has not succeeded in corporate units within the educational and economic domains and who has also had a difficult life within the kinship domain will have very high reserves of negative emotional energy and, potentially, be an agent of social change.

Second, when persons have experienced sadness, fear, and anger simultaneously, they become more likely to experience shame and guilt; and these painful emotions may be repressed. Once repressed, the emotions will intensify and transmute into new emotions, particularly anger if external attributions are made for failures in key institutional domains. If the anger component of shame, guilt, or even alienation is pulled out of these second-order elaborations of primary emotions (see Table 1.4), then emotions that typically cause withdrawal and inaction – emotions like fear and sadness, shame, and alienation – are converted into emotions that fuel aggressive behavior which, in turn, can lead to success in securing resources that can partially compensate for the shame that has come from failures in institutional domains directly involved in resource distribution. For instance, as Collins (2000) recently noted, lower-class people often dominate public places with their loud music and talk, bullying behavior, and hostility that forces higher-ranking people to withdraw. I suspect that much of this behavior is an outcome of repressed shame, whereby the anger component of shame emerges and is used in highly strategic ways to gain momentary power (over higher-ranking persons) and prestige (among one's fellows), while imposing negative emotions like fear on those who have been more successful in the stratification system. In a sense, the anger that comes from the shame experienced in *focused* encounters in corporate units lodged in distributive institutional domains is used to dominate *unfocused* encounters in public places.

Third, the operation of defense mechanisms thus complicates the picture of emotional stratification. Those who have persistently experienced sadness, fear, and anger as well as first- and second-order elaborations of these negative primary emotions like misery, grief, envy, bitterness, depression, betrayal, dread, wariness, shame, guilt, and alienation (see tables 1.3 and 1.4) will generally have repressed many of these emotions in order to protect self, causing them to experience a diffuse and persistent sense of anger, occasionally punctuated by sadness and fear. The result is that individuals in lower social classes should, on average, reveal considerably more anger, sadness, fear, shame, guilt, and alienation than those in upper social classes; and these diffuse emotions coupled with less commitment to mesostructures and macrostructures will pose a potential for not only individual but collective violence, at worst, or fuel social movements designed to change institutional domains, at best.

Negative emotional arousal across a cocktail of negative emotions can potentially be harnessed and used to secure more resources, including emotional resources like pride at having struck back at the stratification system and the institutional domains generating this system. Indeed, the transmutation of sadness, fear, anger, shame, alienation, and even guilt can operate as a positive force in redressing grievances and, perhaps, in changing the institutional domains and stratification system. Such is particularly likely to be the case if the anger component of first- and second-order elaborations of shame, alienation, and guilt is pulled out (by ideologies and leaders) and used to mobilize individuals to secure a more equitable distribution of resources.

Jack Barbalet (1998) and, to a lesser extent, Axel Honneth (1995) have made arguments similar to the one that I have presented above. Barbalet emphasizes that resentment is a moral emotion in which others are perceived to receive resources that they do not deserve, with classes or segments of classes that lose resources becoming resentful of those classes and segments that gain resources. When the resentment is conscious, it can lead to collective action, whereas when it is repressed, it will manifest itself in "crime, cruelty, deviance, and perversity." Vengefulness is, according to Barbalet, an emotion that arises when people believe that their basic rights to form meaningful social relationships are abridged by the use of power by others. Those at the bottom of the stratification system will be more likely to perceive that power has been used to deny them basic rights, leading to violent actions to redress their sense of outrage. Honneth (1995) draws the same conclusion when he argues that political protests are an outcome of a perceived lack of respect by elites and others in advantaged persons for the rights of dominated segments of a population to form affective bonds, experience a sense of autonomy, and to feel esteem.

In terms of my argument, Barbalet's and Honneth's generalization can be translated into a view that very intense and aggressive negative emotions like resentment, righteous anger, and vengeance are aroused by the repression of shame (and to a lesser extent, guilt) in encounters over a long period of time among segments of a population. This shame comes from the failure to meet expectations and from the receipt of negative sanctions within corporate units lodged in the distributive institutional domains. In particular, when self cannot be verified in roles and when exchange payoffs consistently fall below what a person perceives as a "just share," an individual will experience anger, but if fear and sadness are also evoked, then shame and alienation may also emerge – particularly if the failure to meet expectations and the receipt of negative sanctions in key institutional domains is habitual and long term. To protect self, shame is repressed and re-emerges as anger, but often this anger is further transmuted by mixing satisfaction-happiness with assertion-anger to form righteous anger and desires for vengeance (see Table 1.3).

For anger to become further transmuted into righteous anger and vengeance, it is necessary for individuals to frame their experiences in terms of "justice." William Gamson (1992) has argued that if righteous anger is to drive protest, "injustice frames" must first emerge, but before such frames lead to collective mobilization, subpopulations in a society must view their failure to verify self and receive "just rewards" in local encounters as unfair, leaving them with not only a diffuse sense of anger but an anger made more intense by a corresponding sense of injustice. At the level of the encounter, individuals must perform what Jasper (2006a,b) has termed "moral work" by translating their feelings of shame into perceptions of injustice. For this translation to occur, external attributions need to be made; that is, others or social structures must consistently be blamed for negative emotional arousal (Goodwin and Jasper, 2006).

What makes this process complex is that external attribution is both a defense mechanism and, I believe, a natural cognitive process built into human neuroanatomy. External attribution can be conscious and accurate, or it can emerge from repression and unconscious emotional forces. When used as a defense mechanism and when coupled with repression of shame and other negative emotions, external attribution allows a person to protect self and blame others or social structures. Thus, as people persistently cannot verify self in roles and must accept exchange payoffs below their sense of what is fair, their feeling may be a complex mix of anger, shame, sadness, indignation, guilt (if moral codes are invoked), and alienation. This emotional cocktail may not all remain conscious, nor need it be accurate, but it is likely some portion of this emotional cocktail may be repressed, particularly that part which could harm self. The result is that righteous anger may be fueled by a person's conscious indignation at unfair payoffs in encounters, coupled with repressed, intensified, and transmuted anger from repressed shame and guilt. In the end, the more repressed are the emotions that attack self, the more volatile will the emotional cocktail that fuels righteous anger and vengeance become; and the more these emotions will lead to external attributions that target not just other people but also larger-scale social structures that are perceived, through "moral work," to cause persistent negative emotional arousal in those institutional domains distributing valued resources. And, the more classes and class factions have persistently experienced negative emotions, imposed justice frames, and performed moral work, the more likely will the system of emotional stratification in a society be an impetus to social change.

Negative emotional arousal, social structure, and change

Negative emotional arousal and accurate attributions

As principles 2, 5, and 6b emphasize, individuals experience negative emotional arousal when expectations are not met and/or when negative sanctions are received (or at least perceived to have been meted out by others). The range of potential negative emotional arousal is quite wide because there are many variants of the three negative primary emotions, coupled with first-order and second-order elaborations of all primary emotions. In the approach that I advocate, the activation of defense mechanisms, particularly repression and attribution, become critical to understanding the intensity and direction of the emotional valences under conditions of negative emotional arousal (principle 8). If, however, defense mechanisms are *not* activated and a person makes self-attributions for the failure to meet expectations or for the receipt of negative sanctions, several potential paths of negative emotional arousal can ensue. One is a variant of disappointment–sadness (see Table 1.2) in which a person is sad about his or her performance, and if this person cannot leave the situation or make necessary adjustments to meet expectations and receive positive sanctions, it is likely that commitments to the local encounter and mesostructures in which this encounter is embedded will be low. Another route is to experience variants of shame (embarrassment at the low-intensity end of the continuum and humiliation at the high-intensity end). Eventually, this shame will transmute into alienation and lead to even lower commitments to social structures. When moral codes have been salient in a situation where a person has not met expectations, received negative sanctions, and made self-attributions for these failings, then this individual will experience guilt. And, if efforts to perform in ways that eliminate these feelings of guilt consistently fail, then guilt will also transmute into alienation, thereby lowering commitments to social structures.

Persons may also make *accurate* external attributions for their failure in encounters to meet expectations or receive positive sanctions. Under these conditions, individuals will generally experience anger toward others or, potentially, the social structures in which the encounter is embedded. If others are powerful, individuals may also experience fear when they make accurate external attributions. If the individual cannot adjust behaviors so as to receive positive emotional arousal because others or the structure of the situation block such efforts, anger and fear will also be accompanied by sadness about one's fate. In turn, if these three emotions are emitted simultaneously, a person will experience the second-order elaboration of alienation from others and social structures. If individuals perform "moral work" and accurately use "justice frames" to assess their failures, more intense variants of anger may emerge periodically; and this anger will be accurately directed at those persons or structural features of the situation that have frustrated efforts to meet expectations and receive positive sanctions.

However, if individuals cannot leave iterated encounters in which they experience negative emotional arousal and/or if others at whom anger is directed are powerful, it is likely that attributions will become distorted by repression. It is painful to see self as consistently responsible for failures; and in order to protect self, a person is likely to repress shame. Similarly, to experience persistent anger, especially anger fanned by a sense of injustice, is taxing and drains individuals emotionally; and if these persons cannot escape the encounters and social structures in which these encounters are embedded, it is likely that repression of anger will occur. This repression can be accompanied by a variety of additional defense mechanisms, such as denial, displacement, reaction–formation, projection, and sublimation (see Table 4.1). People will often deny that they are angry, only to have disproportionate anger suddenly emerge and breach an encounter, thereby increasing the likelihood that the person will experience shame and guilt. Individuals may displace their anger on others not in the encounter, or they may blame categoric units for their negative feelings about self and powerful others. They may also reverse the polarity of their emotions, seeing others and the structure that are frustrating them in highly positive terms.

The problem with these kinds of defense mechanisms is that they often break down. The repressed emotion will periodically erupt in episodes of intense fear (high anxiety, terror), anger (rage), and sadness (ennui, depression); and, typically, the arousal of a more intense form of a repressed emotion will breach and disrupt the encounter, often causing a person to experience shame or guilt at having done so. Moreover, the operation of these defense mechanisms will typically anger others who will negatively sanction a person, thus increasing the arousal of negative emotions and, in all likelihood, the repression of these emotions. As these cycles of repression and intense emotional displays of anger, anxiety, sadness, shame, or guilt ensue, the connection between the original sources of emotions aroused and the emotions felt and expressed will be broken, thus unleashing the intensifying dynamics that come with repression.

Negative emotional arousal, repression, and external attributions

As emphasized above, repressed shame will generally intensify and transmute into intense forms of anger (e.g. rage), particularly first-order elaborations of anger such as righteousness and vengeance (a combination of mostly anger coupled with lesser amounts of satisfaction-happiness). If shame is experienced over a long period of time in many diverse encounters, it can also transmute into sadness and anxiety, but the most common manifestation is alienation, punctuated by anger at the others and social structures from which a person is alienated.

To some degree, the nature of the target of alienation or anger is critical in determining the emotions aroused, and it is here that attribution processes feed into the general defenses employed to protect self. If corporate units are the targets of repressed shame, individuals will become angry at, and alienated from, the structure and culture of these units. If categoric units are the targets of repressed shame, persons will experience diffuse anger at, develop negative prejudices about, and be willing to commit discriminatory acts against members of these units. Of particular interest are shame–anger–shame cycles that can emerge once shame is repressed (Lewis, 1971; Scheff, 1988). If intense episodes of anger arising from repressed and transmuted shame breach encounters, individuals will likely experience more shame at having done this; and if this shame is repressed, anger will eventually emerge again, setting off yet another moment of shame that is repressed. As this cycle proceeds, the emotions involved will often intensify; and as the anger is ratcheted up, the anger may begin to target more distant macrostructures. Thus, repressed shame as it is transmuted into anger is, as Scheff and Retzinger (1991) and others (Volkan, 2004) have emphasized, the fuel of aggressive actions against social structures far removed from the encounters that originally generated the shame.

The more the biography of a person has involved repressed shame in corporate units within institutional domains distributing valued resources – e.g. economy, education, polity – the more distal will be the targets of anger and first-order elaborations of anger such as righteousness and vengeance. Negative emotions have a distal bias to begin with, and coupled with repression, intensification and transmutation, the emotions that emerge will likely reveal an even greater distal bias. There is also centrifugal force operating in microstructures that pushes negative emotions outward. Positive emotional arousal evidences a proximal bias, circulating among people in encounters as interaction rituals (see principles 1, 4, and 6a). To avoid breaching the encounter, negative emotions and particularly intense negative emotions like righteous anger are repressed within the encounter and pushed out to "safer" mesostructures and macrostructures. In this way, a person can sustain positive emotions at the level of the encounter and, at the same time, vent negative emotions at more remote targets. The likelihood that these dynamics will ensue is related to several conditions.

One condition is the degree to which the targets of external attributions can be symbolized in highly negative terms, in essence, becoming negative totems. Aggressive acts become more likely if negative ideologies about the "evils" of the targets of external attribution can emerge. Here leaders, media, and dense networks of others who share the ideology are critical to sustaining the righteous anger at distal targets, including the institutional systems of other societies (as is the case with terrorists).

Another condition is the focus of local networks on targets of external attribution. Particularly critical is positive sanctioning for articulation of the negative ideology about the evil characteristics of targets. This sanctioning can also work to enable individuals to perceive that they are meeting expectations for realizing the goals of the network, such as attacking (or thinking about attacking) the targets of external attributions. For example, terrorist cells often charge up the positive emotional energy and symbols by the very act of planning or just "thinking about" action, as individuals positively sanction each other and perceive that they have indeed met expectations. The planning of acts of aggression, per se, increases the positive emotional energy of the local encounters among people in a dense network, focusing positive energy on fellow travelers and combining this positive energy with anger at external targets, producing mixes of positive and negative emotions like righteousness and vengeance.

A third condition follows from the above. If individuals can charge up the positive symbols of the local network into an ideology legitimating their goals, and then juxtapose this positive ideology against the negative ideology demonizing the targets of external attribution, then each and every inter-action in an encounter reaffirms both the positive and negative symbols, keeping the positive emotions focused on the targets of external attribu-tions. Indeed, even thinking about external targets juxtaposes the positive and negative symbols in ways that sustain intense emotional arousal.

For these dynamics to target macrostructures, especially those of another society, the connection between the mesostructures originally generating shame must be severed by the activation of defense mechanisms or, alter-natively, must be manipulated by actors with an interest in displacing anger of individuals outward. Shame is produced locally in encounters lodged within mesostructures embedded in institutional domains and stratification systems; and so, for the anger emerging from repressed shame to target remote tar-gets, the connection between the local structures producing shame must be obscured or lost. Otherwise, individuals would target the real sources of their shame: the encounters in mesostructures where emotions are aroused. Repression facilitates this disconnection; and leaders, media, and other actors can further break the connection by portraying external targets in highly negative terms. Moreover, the positive emotions that people also experience in local encounters – family, neighborhood, friendship cliques, religious rit-uals, and the like – also operate as a kind of emotional high-pressure area that deflects negative emotions outward toward macrostructural targets. In this way, individuals can sustain the emotional highs that come with interaction rituals at the local level, while displacing outward their anger at targets at the more remote macrostructural level of social organization.

Along with the distal biases of negative emotional arousal, there are also resource mobilization dynamics that institutionalize this distal bias

(McCarthy and Zald, 1977; Tilly, 1978; Goodwin and Jasper, 2006). If corporate units, with a new ideology and symbolic medium of discourse and exchange, can emerge to recruit and channel collective anger toward remote targets, then the structure and culture of these units will assure that local encounters maintain the focus on external "enemies." The success of such corporate units – whether a social movement organization or a terrorist cell – depends not only on the symbolic resources (ideology and symbolic media) that can be mobilized, but also on material resources such as money, organizational expertise, and a ready pool of recruits among whom diffuse anger already exists as a result of persistent shaming or other forms of negative emotional arousal. Again, emotions are one of the key resources of any successful social movement.

As individuals develop ideologies justifying their anger at external targets, while demonizing these targets with negative ideologies, they have performed the "moral work" and generally imposed "justice frames" to focus emotional energy on remote external targets. To see a cause in moral terms intensifies the commitment; and to phrase the issues and goals of an emerging corporate unit organizing and channeling people's emotions in terms of "justice" legitimates whatever actions will be taken. People can feel variants of first-order elaborations of anger, such as indignation, loathing, disgust, bitterness, hate, wrath, fury, outrage, vengeance, pride, righteousness, revulsion, dislike, antagonism, and other emotions built around the anger that has been pulled out of repressed shame and often combined with satisfaction-happiness to forge a most dangerous emotional cocktail. This collage of emotions adds to the intensity of emotional arousal, while providing an emotional charge to the morality of a cause.

Even if individuals do not perceive that they will be successful in their acts against targets, the very framing of issues in terms of morality and justice allows them to experience positive emotions, such as pride, and to ratchet up the positive emotional flow through interaction rituals in ways sustaining a change-oriented organization. In this way, negative emotions like shame and variants of anger become positive emotions that add fuel to the emotional fire driving the formation of corporate units whose goal is to target mesostructures and macrostructures. Moreover, when the targets of external attributions are portrayed in highly negative terms, they become more threatening which, in turn, increases the intensity of the indignation and other moral emotions. As a consequence, individuals feel even more morally correct and prideful when they perceive that through their ideologies, use of symbolic media (revolving around justice and fairness), and planning for action they have "stood up" to an "evil" force (Stein, 2001; Gould, 2001, 2002).

As affective ties build up among members of a change-oriented corporate unit, these positive emotions can be used to recruit new members, to forge solidarity, to motivate participation (Lichterman, 1996), and to sustain a movement in "abeyance" during difficult times and strategic reversals (Rupp and Taylor, 1987; Taylor, 1989). Thus, positive emotions flowing in accordance with principles 1, 4, and 6a become a critical force in sustaining an organization, even as other resources needed for action become problematic. As Goodwin and Jasper (2006) have noted, resource mobilization theories tended to underemphasize emotions but, in fact, emotions and the interaction rituals that generate and sustain them are *a critical resource* for all collective action against social structures. Without emotional commitment to goals defined in terms of morality and justice, social movement organizations loose their driving force. Power, money, and organizational capacities alone can indeed change social structures, but power, money, organizational structures, *and* high levels of emotional arousal can typically generate even more social change.

Emotions and social transformation

Positive emotional energy and change

There are many forces causing change, and so we cannot see emotions as the only engine of social transformations. But, emotions are still an important ingredient of change. Positive emotional arousal will generally translate into commitments to corporate and categoric units and, by extension, the institutional domains and classes of the stratification system. As such, positive emotions work to sustain the status quo. However, when corporate units have goals that can potentially change macrostructures, attachments operate to sustain the division of labor of these units and their change-oriented goals. Whether an army revealing solidarity (Turchin, 2006), a social movement composed of committed persons, a focused political party, or a firm with a new technology, these change-oriented meso units require committed incumbents. Such commitments come when the structure is perceived to mete out sanctions and when role-making leading to self-verification and positive exchange payoffs are perceived to be facilitated by the structure and culture of the meso-level unit. And, the more such units can garner other resources such as power, economic capital, and social capital, the more they will be in a position to change macrostructures and their cultures.

Negative emotional energy and change

More interesting, perhaps, is the arousal of negative emotional energy and the more volatile dynamics that such energy can unleash. When negative and positive emotions are highly stratified, the potential for collective action by those with high reserves of negative emotional energy increases, *if* other resources such as ideology, leadership, money, and corporate units can be brought to bear on their grievances. Diffuse anger among a large segment of a population is often a powder keg waiting for a fuse and someone to light the fuse, but other emotions such as collective shame, guilt, grief, sadness, or even alienation can serve as the raw materials around which change-oriented movements can begin. One critical force is the imposition of justice frames so a broad spectrum of persons can be potentially mobilized.

Successful movements not only recruit those adversely affected by existing conditions but also sympathizers; and here the justice frames become essential. When an ideology can be articulated in terms of justice frames and morality, additional people can be recruited to join the movement; or if they do not actually join, their sympathy may reduce resistance to the movement or provide crucial resources. The civil rights movement in the United States is an excellent example of these dynamics. The movement framed the issue as one of justice, with support from elements of the legal system. Moreover, the fear, sadness, anger, and shame of those who had been oppressed were successively converted into pride at having confronted the system of racial and ethnic stratification, with the violence meted out by local political authorities used as a means for mobilizing sympathizers who, in turn, supported the movement in communities, halls of local and national power, schools, and economy. Political democracy is typically a critical condition for successful social movements because it allows channels of influence peddling, mobilization for political purposes, political dialogue and discourse, ideological conflict and ferment, and other important elements of successful movements.

In societies evidencing less democracy, movements often have difficulty emerging and prospering (as a consequence of coercive repression by centers of power), but if the anger is sufficiently widespread and the sense of injustice is increased through effective leadership and ideological articulation, then the diffuse anger can be mobilized – often at great risks – against centers of power. Initial engagement may lead to violence and even reversals, but if the collective engagement can be sustained, conflict becomes very much like a vortex, pulling in persons who have large reserves of anger and particularly persons whose anger is the surface manifestation of repressed shame and humiliation. Initially, this anger is mobilized to strike out at meso-level structures that are seen to have caused the arousal of negative emotions, but as the conflict is engaged, the mesostructures of the political, economic, educational, and religious institutional domains are pulled into the conflict.

And, once these mesostructures are defined as representatives of larger institutional domains and/or as responsible for the unequal distribution of resources in the stratification system, the conflict becomes one focused on changing macrostructures more than the local mesostructures in which people have experienced negative emotional arousal. The outcome of such conflicts often depends upon the relative resource levels of the contending parties, but often the emotional resources of those in change-oriented corporate units are just enough to tip the balance of the conflict, although at other times, the level of coercive power of the state is simply too great for even a movement drawing upon deep and diffuse anger.

When anger is repressed and when centers of power have sufficient resources to control collective mobilization, the shame that is often the root source of this anger may transmute into alienation. At other times, the anger may be pushed outward beyond a society's borders or it may target safe scapegoats, typically members of categoric units (ethnic subpopulations or members of a religion). In one sense, these dynamics can be seen as a kind of collective displacement of anger from the meso units of a society's institutional domains to safer targets that cannot so easily "fight back." As this process unfolds, the connection between the anger and its original source – meso units in a society's distributive institutional domains – is lost or distorted so that "outsiders" are now considered to have caused the negative emotions. In this way, local encounters in neighborhoods and communities are sustained in a positive mode, in accordance with principles 1, 4, and 6a. As such, these positive-valenced encounters operate to sustain the displacement of aggression outward to external enemies.

Terrorism is, I believe (Turner, 2006, 2007a, b), fueled by these dynamics, as centers of political power repress dissent and use media to deflect anger outward toward the "west" and its "corrupt" institutional systems. The intensity of religious ideologies, coupled with the flow of positive emotions in networks plotting to attack an enemy's institutional systems, create a deadly combination: intense positive emotional arousal in local networks combined with negative ideological portrayals of external enemies. This combination generates righteous anger and vengeance toward external targets, coupled with high levels of positive emotional arousal for planning or even thinking about attacking these targets (see Volkan 1999, 2004, and 2006 for an in-depth analysis of these dynamics). Under these conditions, people will often be willing to kill themselves in the name of a cause, deriving high levels of pride and other positive emotions for doing violence to others who are seen to represent evil institutional and stratification systems.

Conclusion

As with other chapters, I have offered many provisional propositions that can serve as hypotheses for research. Here, I present only the most important general propositions that can complete the theory that I have been developing.

15 *The more iterated encounters embedded within corporate and categoric units lead to consistent positive emotional arousal among their participants, the more likely are individuals to develop commitments to the structure and culture of these mesostructures; and the more individuals experience consistent positive emotional arousal across iterated encounters within diverse corporate and categoric units within clearly differentiated institutional domains with their own norms, ideologies, and generalized symbolic media and within differentiated classes and class factions with their own legitimating ideologies, the greater will be reserves of*

positive emotional energy and, hence, the more likely will the proximal bias of positive emotions be broken, allowing individuals to develop commitments to the structure and culture of macrostructures.

A   The more stratified is a society, and the more clear-cut class divisions and factions within classes, the more likely will the distribution of positive emotional energy among members of a population be correlated with the distribution of power, money, and prestige; and, hence, the more likely are those in the upper and middle classes and/or dominant factions within classes to have experienced positive emotional arousal in encounters, leading them to develop commitments to the system of stratification and the ideologies legitimating this system.

B   The more differentiated are institutional domains involved in distributing resources, the more likely are those experiencing positive emotional arousal in these domains to be in the upper and middle classes and/or dominant factions of classes; and, hence, the more likely are individuals in these classes and factions to have experienced positive emotional arousal in encounters, leading them to develop commitments to both the culture and structure of system of stratification and the institutional domains generating this system.

C   The more corporate units within institutional domains or class factions within the stratification system are mobilized for change-oriented action, and the greater has been the consistency of positive emotional arousal and the level of commitments among members of these units, the more likely will these corporate units or factions be successful in change-oriented activities, if they have other necessary material, organization, and symbolic resources.

16   *The more iterated encounters embedded within corporate and categoric units lead to consistent negative emotional arousal among their participants, the less likely are individuals to develop commitments to the structure and culture of these units; and the more individuals experience consistent negative emotional arousal across iterated encounters within diverse corporate and categoric units within clearly differentiated institutional domains and within clearly differentiated classes and class factions of the stratification system, the less will be their commitments to the structure and culture of macrostructures, and the more likely will their cumulative negative emotional arousal be mobilized in efforts to change the culture and structure of macrostructures.*

A   The more negative emotional arousal in mesostructures within distributive institutional domains is accompanied by consistent positive emotional arousal in non-distributive institutional domains, the less will be the mobilization potential of cumulative negative emotional arousal in the mesostructures of distributive institutional domains.

B   The more individuals experiencing negative emotional arousal in mesostructures within distributive institutional domains make self-attributions for their failures in these domains, the less will be the mobilization potential of cumulative negative emotional arousal.

C The more negative emotional arousal in mesostructures within institutional domains has evoked variants and first-order elaborations of fear, anger, and sadness, the more likely are individuals to have also experienced second-order elaboration of these negative emotions, particularly shame and alienation but also guilt if failures in these domains are evaluated in moral terms.

D The more individuals have experienced shame in mesostructures within distributive institutional domains, the more likely are they to have repressed this shame, particularly if they have been unable to verify self in roles and/or to receive just shares of resources; and the more repressed is this shame as well as other second-order emotions like guilt and alienation, the more likely will the anger component of these second-order elaborations of negative primary emotions surface and be part of external attributions, thereby increasing the level of anger at the structure and culture of mesostructures and macrostructures.

17 The more individuals have experienced diffuse anger, especially anger emerging from repressed second-order elaborations of negative primary emotions, the more likely will they make external attributions to macrostructures; and the more likely will they begin to experience intense first-order elaborations of anger such as righteous anger and vengeance at targets of external attribution.

A The more the connection between negative emotional arousal and the structures and persons causing this arousal become obscured, the more distal will the targets of external attributions become, and the more intense will the emotions accompanying these attributions be.

B The more available are resources — ideological, financial, political — and the more leaders can articulate grievances and use negative ideologies to sustain external attributions to macrostructures and the negative emotions accompanying these attributions, the more likely will intense forms of anger like righteous anger and vengeance be channeled into collective violence.

1 The more local networks and the encounters in them can sustain high levels of positive emotional energy for the planning and implementation of violence against enemies portrayed in negative ideologies, the more likely are individuals to experience and act upon their righteous anger and feelings of vengeance.

2 The more negative emotions can be framed in terms of justice and morality, the more intense will the negative ideologies about the targets of external attributions, and the more likely will local networks and encounters increase the intensity of righteous anger and feelings of vengeance, and the more likely will the goals of the corporate units formed by these networks be viewed in moral absolutes.

9 The theory reviewed

Unlike earlier works, where I developed too many highly complex principles, I have tried to keep the formal principles to a minimum; as a result, I offer seventeen principles, although it is obvious that these are still rather complex principles. Yet, as I emphasized at the beginning of this book, the power of a theory is in the propositions that it generates, with each generalization serving as a testable hypothesis. I have couched these principles in the language that I have employed over the last decade, but I think that they can be converted into the vocabularies of most other theories without significant loss of content. One does not read these principles, of course, without understanding the simple conceptual scheme on which they are hung, nor will the propositions be clear without at least some familiarity with the terms defining key concepts. Despite these limitations, I thought it useful to put all of the basic principles developed in each chapter in one place, if only for easy reference when reading the chapters. As I emphasized early on, I make frequent reference to some of these principles by their number, and so they are listed here for quick reference to refresh the reader's memory.

The theoretical principles

1 When expectations for self, other, and situation are met in an encounter, individuals will experience mild positive emotional arousal and will be more likely to give off positive sanctions to others (see principle 4 below); and if they had some fear about expectations being met, they will experience more intense variants and elaborations of positive emotions.

2 The likelihood that expectations will be met in an encounter is a positive function of the degree of clarity in expectations, which, in turn, is a positive and multiplicative function of:

   A   The degree to which participants to an encounter use the same emotional phonemes and syntax.

   B   The degree to which an encounter is embedded in corporate and categoric units.

C   The degree to which the meso-level corporate and categoric units are embedded in macro-level institutional domains and stratification systems.

D   The degree to which the cultural symbols of meso- and macro-level structural units are explicit and consistent.

E   The degree to which transactional needs generate expectation states that are consistent with A–D above.

3   When expectations for self, other, and situation are not met in an encounter, individuals will experience one or more negative emotions. The likelihood that expectations will not be met in an encounter is a positive and multiplicative function of:

A   The degree to which participants to an encounter do not use the same emotional phonemes and syntax.

B   The degree to which an encounter is not embedded in corporate and categoric units.

C   The degree to which an encounter is not clearly embedded in an institutional domain or a location in the stratification system.

D   The degree to which divergent or ambiguous cultural symbols are invoked by participants to an encounter.

E   The degree to which transactional needs are unclear, ambiguous, or unattainable in an encounter.

4   When individuals perceive that they have received positive sanctions from others, they will experience positive emotions and be more likely to give off positive sanctions to others in an escalating cycle that increases rhythmic synchronization of talk and body language, heightened mutual flow of positive sanctioning, increased sense of social solidarity, representation of this solidarity with symbols, and overt as well as covert ritual enactments toward these symbols. The likelihood that positive sanctions and these interaction rituals will occur is a positive function of the conditions listed under 2A–E above.

5   When individuals perceive that they have received negative sanctions from others, they will experience negative emotions; and the more negative these emotions, the more likely are defensive strategies and defense mechanisms revolving around repression, intensification, and transmutation to be unleashed, and the less will be the degree of solidarity in the encounter and, potentially, the less will be the commitments to the meso and macrostructures (and their respective cultures) in which the encounter is embedded. The likelihood that negative sanctions will have these effects is a positive function of the conditions listed under 3A–E and the intensity of transactional needs for self-verification.

6   When individuals experience either positive or negative emotional arousal, they will make attributions about the cause of their emotional

experiences to one or more of the following objects: self, others, structure of encounter, structure and culture of corporate unit, members of categoric units, institutional domain, stratification system, society, or system of societies. (a) Positive emotional arousal reveals a proximal bias, with individuals making self-attributions for meeting expectations and receiving positive sanctions, thereby initiating the ritual dynamics that sustain the flow of positive emotions (propositions 1 and 4), whereas (b) negative emotional arousal evidences a distal bias, with individuals making external attributions for the failure to meet expectations or for the receipt of negative sanctions, with a propensity to bypass others and the local encounter and target the structure and culture of corporate units and members of categoric units.

7   Humans possess at least five transactional needs for verification of self, profitable exchange payoffs, group inclusion, trust, and facticity, all of which generate expectation states in an encounter; and the more these expectation states generated by transactional needs are met, especially needs for self-verification and profitable exchange payoffs, the more likely are individuals to experience positive emotions and make self-attributions, while giving off positive emotions to others that initiates solidarity-generating interaction rituals (as described in propositions 1 and 4).

   A   The more others are seen as facilitating the meeting of transactional needs, the more likely will the giving off of positive emotions also involve the expression of gratitude.
   B   The more the structure and culture of the corporate unit are seen as facilitating the meeting of transactional needs, the more likely will individuals develop commitments to this culture and structure.
   C   The more members of categoric units are seen as facilitating the meeting of transactional needs, the more likely will individuals develop favorable prejudices toward members of these categoric units.

8   The less expectation states generated by transactional needs are met in an encounter, and especially needs for self-verification and profitable exchange payoffs, the more individuals will also perceive this failure to meet expectations as negative sanctions from others and, hence, the more intense will be their negative emotional arousal; and the more intense is the level of negative emotional arousal, the more likely will defense mechanisms be activated and lead to external attributions (see propositions 3 and 6b).

   A   To the degree that individuals make self-attributions for failing to meet transactional needs in an encounter, the more likely will they experience all three negative emotions; and the more they experience these emotions simultaneously, the more likely are they to experience shame; and if moral cultural codes are invoked to evaluate self under these conditions, the more likely will they experience guilt as well.

B The more individuals consistently experience shame and, to a lesser extent, guilt in iterated encounters, the more likely are they to employ defensive strategies and defense mechanisms, and the more they activate defense mechanisms, the more likely are external attributions revolving around transmuted and intensified negative emotions to be made.

   1 If others are targeted, individuals will experience and express anger toward these others; and if shame is the repressed emotion, the more intense will this anger be.

   2 If corporate units in which an encounter is embedded are targeted, individuals will experience and express anger toward this unit, thereby reducing commitments to the structure and culture of this unit; and if repressed shame and, to a lesser extent, guilt are fueling this anger, the more likely will this anger transmute further into alienation from the culture and structure of the corporate unit and, potentially, the culture and structure of the more inclusive institutional domain as well.

   3 If categoric units in which an encounter is embedded are targeted, individuals will experience and express anger at, and develop negative prejudices toward, members of these units and, potentially, the more inclusive institutional domains or locations in the stratification system generating these categoric units.

9 The clarity of expectations for all dimensions of social structure in encounters – that is, roles, status, ecology, and demography – is a positive function of the degree to which an encounter is embedded in corporate and categoric units.

A The clarity of expectations in corporate units is an additive function of:

   1 The visibility of boundaries of the corporate unit and the existence of entrance and exit rules.

   2 The explicitness of goals and the degree of focus by a corporate unit on these goals.

   3 The level of differentiation of the institutional domain in which a corporate unit is embedded.

   4 The explicitness of the vertical and horizontal divisions of labor in the corporate unit.

   5 The formality of the structure of the corporate unit.

   6 The level of consistency among ideologies, generalized symbolic media, and norms governing the operation of the corporate unit.

    7   The degree of correlation between positions in the division of labor, particularly in the vertical division of labor, with memberships in discrete categoric units.

B   The clarity of expectations associated with categoric units is an additive function of:

    1   The degree of discreteness of the boundaries defining membership in a categoric unit.

    2   The degree of consensus over the relative evaluation of categoric units and the ideologies used to form this evaluation.

    3   The degree of embeddedness of categoric units in the macro-level stratification system and the level of inequality in this system.

    4   The homogeneity among individuals who are members of a categoric unit.

    5   The degree of correlation of membership in one categoric unit with membership in other categoric units.

    6   The degree of correlation of membership in categoric units with diverse positions in the vertical and horizontal divisions of labor in corporate units embedded in differentiated institutional domains, especially domains distributing valued resources.

10 The more individuals employ similar languages, particularly the language of emotions, the more likely will they be successful in mutual role-making, role-taking, and role verification; and the more they can successfully role-make and role-take, the more likely are they to communicate the expectations associated with their respective roles and relative status which, in turn, makes it more likely that they will understand and meet expectations generated by transactional needs and culture.

11 The more individuals understand the meanings associated with the ecology and demography of an encounter, the more likely are they to successively role-make and role-take, and thereby successfully verify each other's roles and status which, in turn, will increase the likelihood that they will understand and meet expectations generated by transactional needs and culture.

12 The less individuals successfully role-take, role-make, and verify roles, the less likely are expectations associated with status, ecology, demography, and culture to be fully understood, thereby increasing the likelihood that individuals will fail to meet expectations, while increasing the likelihood that they will experience negative sanctions.

13 To the degree that self is highly salient and to the extent that core self-conceptions are implicated in efforts to verify a role-identity, the greater will be the potential for more intense emotional arousal, whether positive or negative.

A   The more expectations for self are verified in a role, the more intense will be the level of positive emotional arousal, and the more likely will the dynamics outlined in principles 1, 4, 6a, and 7 be initiated.

B   The less expectations for self are verified in a role, the more intense will be the level of negative emotional arousal, and the more likely will the dynamics outlined in principles 3, 5, 6b, and 8 be activated.

14 The more an encounter is embedded in meso-level structures and the more these mesostructures are embedded in institutional domains and/or society-wide stratification systems, the greater will be the moral content from values, ideologies, generalized symbolic media, and norms penetrating the encounter; and the higher the level of moral content penetrating the encounter, the more intense will be the emotions aroused, whether positive or negative, during the process of normatization.

A   The more self is salient under conditions of high moral content, the more expectations for categorization, framing, ritualizing, communicating, justice calculations, and feelings will become implicated in the process of verification of self and, hence, the more intense will be the emotions aroused, whether positive or negative, during the process of normatization.

1   The more self is verified during each phase of normatization, the more likely will the processes outlined in principles 1, 4, 6a, and 7 be initiated.

2   The less self is verified during each phase of normatization, the more likely will failure to meet expectations also be viewed as negative sanctions to self and, hence, the more likely will a person experience shame and guilt.

3   The more shame or guilt is repressed, the more likely will these emotions be transmuted into anger and, hence, the more likely will the processes outlined in principles 3, 5, 6b, and 8 be operative.

B   The more initial phases of normatizing, particularly categorization and framing, prove successful, the more likely will other phases of normatizing (ritualizing, forms of communication, justice calculations, and agreements on emotion rules) be achieved; and, conversely, the less successful are initial phases of normatizing, the more pronounced will be ritual sequences among individuals and the more problematic will normatizing become, unless these ritual efforts can establish a frame which, in turn, can lead to successful categorization.

15 The more iterated encounters embedded within corporate and cat-
    egoric units lead to consistent positive emotional arousal among their
    participants, the more likely are individuals to develop commitments to
    the structure and culture of these mesostructures; and the more indi-
    viduals experience consistent positive emotional arousal across iterated
    encounters within diverse corporate and categoric units within clearly
    differentiated institutional domains with their own norms, ideologies,
    and generalized symbolic media and within differentiated classes and
    class factions with their own legitimating ideologies, the greater will be
    reserves of positive emotional energy and, hence, the more likely will the
    proximal bias of positive emotions be broken, allowing individuals to
    develop commitments to the structure and culture of macrostructures.

    A   The more stratified is a society, and the more clear-cut class divi-
        sions and factions within classes, the more likely will the distribu-
        tion of positive emotional energy among members of a population
        be correlated with the distribution of power, money, and prestige;
        and, hence, the more likely are those in the upper and middle classes
        and/or dominant factions within classes to have experienced posi-
        tive emotional arousal in encounters, leading them to develop
        commitments to the system of stratification and the ideologies
        legitimating this system.

    B   The more differentiated are institutional domains involved in dis-
        tributing resources, the more likely are those experiencing positive
        emotional arousal in these domains to be in the upper and middle
        classes and/or dominant factions of classes; and, hence, the more
        likely are individuals in these classes and factions to have experi-
        enced positive emotional arousal in encounters, leading them to
        develop commitments to both the culture and structure of system of
        stratification and the institutional domains generating this system.

    C   The more corporate units within institutional domains or class
        factions within the stratification system are mobilized for change-
        oriented action, and the greater has been the consistency of positive
        emotional arousal and the level of commitments among members
        of these units, the more likely will these corporate units or fac-
        tions be successful in change-oriented activities, if they have other
        necessary material, organization, and symbolic resources.

16 The more iterated encounters embedded within corporate and cat-
    egoric units lead to consistent negative emotional arousal among their
    participants, the less likely are individuals to develop commitments to the
    structure and culture of these units; and the more individuals experience
    consistent negative emotional arousal across iterated encounters within
    diverse corporate and categoric units within clearly differentiated insti-
    tutional domains and within clearly differentiated classes and class fac-
    tions of the stratification system, the less will be their commitments to

the structure and culture of macrostructures, and the more likely will their cumulative negative emotional arousal be mobilized in efforts to change the culture and structure of macrostructures.

A The more negative emotional arousal in mesostructures within distributive institutional domains is accompanied by consistent positive emotional arousal in non–distributive institutional domains, the less will be the mobilization potential of cumulative negative emotional arousal in the mesostructures of distributive institutional domains.

B The more individuals experiencing negative emotional arousal in mesostructures within distributive institutional domains make self-attributions for their failures in these domains, the less will be the mobilization potential of cumulative negative emotional arousal.

C The more negative emotional arousal in mesostructures within institutional domains has evoked variants and first-order elaborations of fear, anger, and sadness, the more likely are individuals to have also experienced second–order elaboration of these negative emotions, particularly shame and alienation but also guilt if failures in these domains are evaluated in moral terms.

D The more individuals have experienced shame in mesostructures within distributive institutional domains, the more likely are they to have repressed this shame, particularly if they have been unable to verify self in roles and/or to receive just shares of resources; and the more repressed is this shame as well as other second–order emotions like guilt and alienation, the more likely will the anger component of these second–order elaborations of negative primary emotions surface and be part of external attributions, thereby increasing the level of anger at the structure and culture of mesostructures and macrostructures.

17 The more individuals have experienced diffuse anger, especially anger emerging from repressed second–order elaborations of negative primary emotions, the more likely will they make external attributions to macrostructures; and the more likely will they begin to experience intense first–order elaborations of anger such as righteous anger and vengeance at targets of external attribution.

A The more the connection between negative emotional arousal and the structures and persons causing this arousal become obscured, the more distal will the targets of external attributions become, and the more intense will the emotions accompanying these attributions be.

B The more available are resources – ideological, financial, political – and the more leaders can articulate grievances and use negative ideologies to sustain external attributions to macrostructures and the negative emotions accompanying these attributions, the more likely will intense forms of anger like righteous anger and vengeance be channeled into collective violence.

1   The more local networks and the encounters in them can sustain high levels of positive emotional energy for the planning and implementation of violence against enemies portrayed in negative ideologies, the more likely are individuals to experience and act upon their righteous anger and feelings of vengeance.
2   The more negative emotions can be framed in terms of justice and morality, the more intense will the negative ideologies about the targets of external attributions, and the more likely will local networks and encounters increase the intensity of righteous anger and feelings of vengeance, and the more likely will the goals of the corporate units formed by these networks be viewed in moral absolutes.

Conclusion

There is little more to say, except this: whatever the merits of the theory, *it is a theory* in the sense of stating at a very abstract level the relationships among fundamental properties of the social universe. I have covered a large terrain: the whole social universe. My goal was to explore how generic forms of social organization and how the culture inherent in all patterns of social organization cause the arousal of not just emotional valences along a positive and negative continuum but also specific emotions. Conversely, I have sought to explain how the valence and specific emotions aroused affect not only the dynamics of encounters where they are generated but also larger-scale social structures and their attendant cultures. Emotions are one of the most critical micro-level social forces because they are what hold all levels of social reality together or, in the end, breach encounters or break mesostructures and macrostructures apart. Emotions are, of course, not the only force that has these effects, but emotions are a critical force that, until the last few decades, has been under-theorized in sociology. There are now many interesting theories of emotions in sociology today (see Turner and Stets, 2005, 2007; Stets and Turner, 2006 for reviews), and my efforts in this book have drawn heavily from these theories, with an eye to integrating them into an even more robust sociological theory of emotions. My approach to theorizing is, I realize, not everyone's cup of tea, but even if one does not accept my emphasis on developing scientific principles, some of the ideas that I have put forth may still be useful in other types of conceptual and empirical endeavors. And, as I often emphasize, if this theory is found wanting, then it is incumbent upon the critic to take this "sad song and make it better" or at least compose a better song.

Bibliography

Adolphs, R. and A. R. Damasio. 2001. "The Interaction of Affect and Cognition: A Neurobiological Perspective." In J. P. Forgas, Ed. *Handbook of Affect and Social Cognition*. Mahwah, NJ: Lawrence Erlbaum.

Anderson, J. R. and G. G. Gallup, Jr. 1999. "Self-Recognition in Non-Human Primates: Past and Future Challenges." In M. Haug and R. E. Whalen, Eds. *Animal Models of Human Emotion and Cognition*. Washington, DC: American Psychological Association.

Andrews, P. and L. Martin. 1987. "Cladistic Relationships of Extant and Fossil Hominoids." *Journal of Human Evolution* 16:101–18.

Arieti, S. 1970. "Cognition and Feeling." In M. B. Arnold, Ed. *Feelings and Emotions: The Loyola Symposium on Feelings and Emotions*. New York: Academic Press.

Arnold, M. B. 1960. *Emotion and Personality*. New York: Columbia University Press.

Baker, W. E. and R. R. Faulkner. 1991. "Role as Resource in the Hollywood Film Industry." *American Journal of Sociology* 97:279–309.

Balter, M. and A. Gibbons. 2002. "Were 'Little People' the First to Venture Out of Africa?" *Science* 297:26–7.

Barbalet, J. 1998. *Emotion, Social Theory, and Social Structure: A Macrosociological Approach*. Cambridge: Cambridge University Press.

Bentivoglio, M., K. Kultas-Ilinsky, and I. Ilinsky. 1993. "Limbic Thalamus: Structure, Intrinsic Organization, and Connections." In B. A. Vogt and M. Gabriel, Eds. *Neurobiology of Cingulate Cortex and Limbic Thalamus: A Comprehensive Handbook*. Boston, MA: Birkhäuser.

Berger, J. 1958. "Relations Between Performance, Rewards, and Action-Opportunities in Small Groups." Unpublished PhD dissertation, University of Harvard.

———. 1988. "Directions in Expectation States Research." In M. Webster and M. Foschi, Eds. *Status Generalization: New Theory and Research*. Stanford, CA: Stanford University Press.

Berger, J. and T. L. Conner. 1969. "Performance Expectations and Behavior in Small Groups." *Acta Sociologica* 12:186–98.

Berger, J. and M. Zelditch, Eds. 1985. *Status, Rewards, and Influence*. San Francisco, CA: Jossey-Bass.

———. 1998. *Status, Power and Legitimacy: Strategies and Theories*. New Brunswick, NJ: Transaction.

Berger, J., B. P. Cohen, and M. Zelditch, Jr. 1972. "Status Characteristics and Social Interaction." *American Sociological Review* 37:241–55.

Berger, J., M. H. Fisek, R. Z. Norman, and M. Zelditch, Jr. 1977. *Status Characteristics and Social Interaction: An Expectation-States Approach*. New York: Elsevier.

Berger, J., S. J. Roseholtz, and M. Zelditch, Jr. 1980. "Status Organizing Processes." *Annual Review of Sociology* 6: 479–508.

Berger, J., R. Z. Norman, J. W. Balkwell, and R. F. Smith. 1992. "Status Inconsistency in Task Situations: A Test of Four Status Processing Principles." *American Sociological Review* 57:843–55.

Blau, P. M. 1964. *Exchange and Power in Social Life.* New York: Wiley.

——. 1977. *Inequality and Heterogeneity: A Primitive Theory of Social Structure.* New York: Free Press.

——. 1984. *Distinction: A Social Critique of the Judgment of Taste.* Cambridge, MA: Harvard University Press.

——. 1994. *Structural Context of Opportunities.* Chicago, IL: University of Chicago Press.

Bless, H. 2000. "The Interplay of Affect and Cognition: The Mediating Role of General Knowledge Structures." In J. P. Forgas, Ed. *Feeling and Thinking: The Role of Affect in Social Cognition.* Cambridge: Cambridge University Press.

Bless, H. and N. Schwarz. 1999. "Sufficient and Necessary Conditions in Dual-Process Models: The Case of Mood and Information Processing." In S. Chaiken and Y. Trope, Eds. *Dual-Process Theories in Social Psychology.* New York: Guilford Press.

Boehm, C. n.d. (a) *In Search of Eden.* (Unpublished manuscript under submission to publishers.)

——. n.d. (b) "The Biosocial Evolution of Social Control and Conscience." (Unpublished manuscript.)

Bogen, J. E. and G. M. Bogen. 1969. "The Other Side of the Brain III: The Corpus Callosum and Creativity." *Bulletin of the Los Angeles Neurological Societies* 34:191–220.

Bourdieu, P. 1984. *Distinction: A Social Critique of the Judgment of Taste.* Cambridge, MA: Harvard University Press.

——. 1989. *Language and Symbolic Power.* Cambridge, MA: Harvard University Press.

Bower, G. H. 1991. "Mood Congruity of Social Judgments." In J. P. Forgas, Ed. *Emotion and Social Judgments.* Oxford: Pergamon Press.

Bradshaw, J. L. and N. C. Nettleton. 1983. *Human Cerebral Asymmetry.* Englewood Cliffs, NJ: Prentice-Hall.

Bronson, S. F. and F. B. M. de Waal. 2003. "Fair Refusal by Capuchin Monkeys." *Nature* 437:128–40.

Burke, P. J. 1980. "The Self: Measurement Implications from a Symbolic Interactionist Perspective." *Social Psychology Quarterly* 43:18–29.

——. 1991. "Identity Processes and Social Stress." *American Sociological Review* 56:836–49.

——. 1996. "Social Identities and Psychosocial Stress." In H. B. Kaplan, Ed. *Psychosocial Stress: Perspectives on Structure, Theory, Life Course, and Methods.* Orlando, FL: Academic Press.

Burke, P. J. and J. E. Stets. 1999. "Trust and Commitment Through Self-Verification." *Social Psychology Quarterly* 62:347–66.

Callero, P. L. 1994. "From Role-Playing to Role-Using: Understanding Role as Resource." *Social Psychology Quarterly* 57:228–43.

Cheney, D., R. Seyfarth, and B. Smuts. 1986. "Social Relationships and Social Cognition in Non-Human Primates." *Science* 234:1361–6.

Chomsky, N. 1965. *Aspects of the Theory of Syntax.* Cambridge, MA: MIT Press.

——. 1980. *Rules and Representations.* New York: Columbia University Press.

Collins, R. 1975. *Conflict Sociology: Toward an Explanatory Science.* New York: Academic Press.

——. 1988. *Theoretical Sociology.* San Diego, CA: Harcourt Brace Jovanovich.

——. 1993. "Emotional Energy as the Common Denominator of Rational Action." *Rationality and Society* 5:203–30.

———. 2000. "Situational Stratification: A Micro–Macro Theory of Inequality." *Sociological Theory* 18:17–42.

———. 2004. *Interaction Ritual Chains*. Princeton, NJ: Princeton University Press.

Cooley, C. H. 1902. *Human Nature and the Social Order*. New York: Scribner's.

Damasio, A. R. 1994. *Descartes' Error: Emotion, Reason, and The Human Brain*. New York: G. P. Putnam.

———. 1997. "Towards a Neuropathology of Emotion and Mood." *Nature* 386:769–70.

———. 2003. *Looking for Spinoza: Joy, Sorrow, and the Feeling Brain*. Orlando, FL: Harcourt.

Damasio, A. R., R. Adolphs, and H. Damasio. 2003. "The Contributions of the Lesion Method to the Functional Neuroanatomy of Emotion." In R. J. Davidson, K. R. Scherer, and H. H. Goldsmith, Eds. *Handbook of Affective Sciences*. New York: Oxford University Press.

Darwin, C. 1872. *The Expression of Emotions in Man and Animals*. London: Watts & Co.

Devinski, O. and D. Luciano. 1993. "The Contributions of the Cingulate Cortex to Human Behavior." In B. A. Vogt and M. Gabriel, Eds. *Neurobiology of Cingulate Cortex and Limbic Thalamus: A Comprehensive Handbook*. Boston, MA: Birkhäuser.

Drevets, W. C., J. L. Price, J. R. Simpson, Jr., R. D. Todd, T. Reich, M. Vannier, and M. E. Raichie. 1997. "Subgenual Prefrontal Cortex Abnormalities in Mood Disorders." *Nature* 386 (24 April):824–7.

Durkheim, É. 1997 [1893]. *The Division of Labor in Society*. New York: Free Press.

———. 1951 [1897]. *Suicide: A Study in Sociology*. New York: Free Press.

———. 1965 [1912]. *The Elementary Forms of the Religious Life*. New York: Macmillan.

Eccles, J. C. 1989. *Evolution of the Brain: Creation of Self*. London: Routledge.

Eich, E. and D. Macaulay. 2000. "Fundamental Factors in Mood-Dependent Memory." In J. P. Forgas, Ed. *Feeling and Thinking: The Role of Affect in Social Cognition*. Cambridge: Cambridge University Press.

Eichenbaum, H. 1997. "How Does the Brain Organize Memories?" *Science* 277 (18 July):330–1.

Ekman, P. 1973a. *Darwin and Facial Expression*. New York: Academic Press.

———. 1973b. "Cross-cultural Studies of Facial Expressions." In P. Ekman, Ed. *Darwin and Facial Expression*. New York: Academic Press.

———. 1982. *Emotions in the Human Face*. Cambridge: Cambridge University Press.

———. 1984. "Expression and Nature of Emotion." In K. Scherer and P. Ekman, Eds. *Approaches to Emotion*. Hillsdale, NJ: Lawrence Erlbaum.

———. 1992a. "Are There Basic Emotions?" *Psychological Review* 99:550–3.

———. 1992b. "An Argument for Basic Emotions." *Cognition and Emotion* 6:169–200.

———. 1992c. "Facial Expressions of Emotion: New Findings, New Questions." *Psychological Science* 3:34–8.

Ekman, P. and W. V. Friesen. 1971. "Constants Across Cultures in the Face and Emotion." *Journal of Personality and Social Psychology* 17:124–9.

———. 1975. *Unmasking Face*. Englewood Cliffs, NJ: Prentice-Hall.

Ekman, P., W. V. Friesen, V. Wallace, and P. Ellsworth. 1972. *Emotion in the Human Face*. New York: Pergamon Press.

Emde, R. N. 1980. "Levels of Meaning for Infant Emotions: A Biosocial View." In W. A. Collins, Ed. *Development of Cognition, Affect, and Social Relations: The Minnesota Symposium of Child Psychology*. Hillsdale, NJ: Lawrence Erlbaum.

Enard, W. M., M. Przeworski, S. E. Fisher, C. S. Lai, V. Wiebe, T. Kitano, *et al.* 2002a. "Molecular Evolution of FOXP2, A Gene Involved in Speech and Language." *Nature* 418:896–72.

——. 2002b. "Intra- and Interspecific Variation in Primate Gene Expression Patterns." *Science* 296:340–2.

Epstein, S. 1984. "Controversial Issues in Emotion Theory." In P. Shaver, Ed. *Review of Personality and Social Psychology*, vol. 5. Beverly Hills, CA: Sage.

Falk, D. 2002. Presentation to the American Association of Physical Anthropologists, Buffalo, NY, April 11.

Fehr, B. and J. A. Russell. 1984. "Concept of Emotion Viewed from a Prototype Perspective." *Journal of Experimental Psychology* 113:464–86.

Forbes, J. and J. King. 1982. "Vision: the Dominant Sense Modality." In J. Forbes and J. King, Eds. *Primate Behavior*. New York: Academic Press.

Forgas, J. P. 1992. "Affect in Social Judgments and Decisions: A Multiprocess Model." In M. Zanna, Ed. *Advances in Experimental Social Psychology*, vol. 25. San Diego, CA: Academic Press.

——. 1995. "Mood and Judgment: The Affect Infusion Model (AIM)." *Psychological Bulletin* 117:39–66.

——. 2000. "Affect and Information Processing Strategies: An Interactive Relationship." In J. P. Forgas, Ed. *Feeling and Thinking: The Role of Affect in Social Cognition*. Cambridge: Cambridge University Press.

Forgas, J. P., G. H. Bower, and S. J. Moylan. 1990. "Praise or Blame? Affective Influences on Attributions for Achievement." *Journal of Personality and Social Psychology* 59:809–19.

Frommel, D. K. and C. S. O'Brien. 1982. "A Dimensional Approach to the Circular Ordering of Emotions." *Motivation and Emotion* 6:337–63.

Gallup, G. G., Jr. 1970. "Chimpanzees: Self-Recognition." *Science* 167:86–7.

——. 1979. *Self-Recognition in Chimpanzees and Man: A Developmental and Comparative Perspective*. New York: Plenum Press.

——. 1982. "Self-Awareness and the Emergence of Mind in Primates." *American Journal of Primatology* 2:237–48.

Gamson, W. A. 1992. *Talking Politics*. Cambridge: Cambridge University Press.

Garfinkel, H. 1967. *Studies in Ethnomethodology*. Englewood Cliffs, NJ: Prentice-Hall.

Geschwind, N. 1965a. "Disconnection Syndromes in Animals and Man, Part I." *Brain* 88:237–94.

——. 1965b. "Disconnection Syndromes in Animals and Man, Part II." *Brain* 88:585–644.

——. 1970. "The Organization of Language and the Brain." *Science* 170:940–4.

Geschwind, N. and A. Damasio. 1984. "The Neural Basis of Language." *Annual Review of Neuroscience* 7:127–47.

Gibbons, A. 2004. "Oldest Human Femur Wales into Controversy." *Science* 305:35–7.

Giddens, A. 1984. *The Constitution of Society*. Berkeley and Los Angeles: University of California Press.

Gloor, P. 1997. *The Temporal Lobe and Limbic System*. New York: Oxford University Press.

Goffman, E. 1959. *The Presentation of Self in Everyday Life*. Garden City, NY: Anchor Books.

——. 1961. *Encounters: Two Studies in the Sociology of Interaction*. Indianapolis, IN: Bobbs-Merrill.

——. 1963. *Behavior in Public Places: Notes on the Social Organization of Gatherings*. New York: Free Press.

——. 1967. *Interaction Ritual*. Garden City, NY: Anchor Books.

——. 1971. *Relations in Public: Micro Studies of the Public Order*. New York: Basic Books.

——. 1974. *Frame Analysis: An Essay on the Organization of Experience*. New York: Harper and Row.

——. 1981. *Forms of Talk*. Philadelphia: University of Pennsylvania Press.

——. 1983. "The Interaction Order." *American Sociological Review* 48:1–17.

Goodwin, J. and J. M. Jasper, 2006. "Emotions and Social Movements." In J. E. Stets and J. H. Turner, Eds. *Handbook of the Sociology of Emotions*. New York: Springer.

Gould, D. B. 2001. "Rock the Boat, Don't Rock the Boat, Baby: Ambivalence and the Emergence of Militant AIDS Activism." In J. Goodwin, J. M. Jasper, and F. Polletta, Eds. *Passionate Politics: Emotions and Social Movements*. Chicago, IL: University of Chicago Press.

——. 2002. "Life During Wartime: Emotions and the Development of ACT UP." *Mobilization* 7:177–200.

Gray, J. A. 1982. *The Neuropsychology of Anxiety: An Enquiry into the Functions of the Septo-Hippocampal System*. New York: Oxford University Press.

Greene, J. and J. Haidt. 2002. "How (And Where) Does Moral Judgment Work?" *Trends in Cognitive Sciences* 6:517–23.

Habermas, J. 1970. "Toward a Theory of Communicative Competence." *Inquiry* 13:360–75.

——. 1973. *Legitimation Crisis*. London: Heinemann.

Haidt, J. 2001. "The Emotional Dog and Its Rational Tail: A Social Intuitionist Approach to Moral Judgment." *Psychological Review* 108:814–34.

Hammond, M. 2006. "Evolution and Emotions." In J. E. Stets and J. H. Turner, Eds. *Handbook of the Sociology of Emotions*. New York: Springer.

Hawley, A. 1986. *Human Ecology: A Theoretical Essay*. Chicago, IL: University of Chicago Press.

Heimer, L. 1995. *The Human Brain and Spinal Cord: Functional Neuroanatomy and Dissection Guide*. New York: Springer.

Heise, D. R. 1979. *Understanding Events: Affect and the Construction of Social Action*. Cambridge: Cambridge University Press.

Hewes, G. W. 1973. "Primate Communication and the Gestural Origin of Language." *Current Anthropology* 14:5–12.

Heyes, C. M. 1995. "Self-Recognition in Primates: Further Reflections Create a Hall of Mirrors." *Animal Behavior* 50:1533–42.

——. 1998. "Theory of Mind in Nonhuman Primates." *Behavioral and Brain Sciences* 21:101–34.

Hinde, R. 1983. *Primate Social Relationships*. Oxford: Blackwell.

Hochschild, A. R. 1979. "Emotion Work, Feeling Rules and Social Structure." *American Journal of Sociology* 85:551–75.

——. 1983. *The Managed Heart: Commercialization of Human Feeling*. Berkeley: University of California Press.

Homans, G. C. 1961. *Social Behavior: Its Elementary Forms*. New York: Harcourt Brace Jovanovich.

——. 1974. *Social Behavior: Its Elementary Forms*. Rev. ed. New York: Harcourt Brace Jovanovich.

Honneth, A. 1995. *The Struggle for Recognition: The Moral Grammar of Social Struggles*. Cambridge: Polity Press.

Hyatt, C. W. and W. D. Hopkins. 1994. "Self-Awareness in Bonobos and Chimpanzees: A Comparative Approach." In S. T. Parker, R. W. Mitchell, and M. L. Boccia, Eds. *Self-Awareness in Animals and Humans: Developmental Perspectives*. New York: Cambridge University Press.

Isen, A. 1984. "Towards Understanding the Role of Affect in Cognition." In R. S. Wyer and T. K. Srull, Eds. *Handbook of Social Cognition*, vol. 3. Hillsdale, NJ: Lawrence Erlbaum.

Ito, T. A. and J. T. Caccioppo. 2001 "Affect and Attitudes: A Social Neuroscience Approach." In J. P. Forgas, Ed. *Handbook of Affect and Social Cognition*. Mahwah, NJ: Lawrence Erlbaum.

Izard, C. 1977. *Human Emotions*. New York: Plenum Press.

——. 1992a. "Basic Emotions, Relations Among Emotions, and Emotion-Cognition Relations." *Psychological Review* 99:561–5.

——. 1992b. "Four Systems for Emotion Activation: Cognitive and Noncognitive." *Psychological Review* 100:68–90.

James, W. 1884. "What is an Emotion?" *Mind* 19:188–205.

——. 1890. *The Principles of Psychology*. New York: Holt, Rinehart and Winston.

Jasper, J. M. 1998. "The Emotions of Protest: Affective and Reactive Emotions in and around Social Movements." *Sociological Forum* 13:397–424.

——. 2006a. "Emotions and Motivation." In R. Goodwin and C. Tilly, Eds. *Oxford Handbook of Contextual Political Studies*. Oxford: Oxford University Press.

——. 2006b. *Getting Your Way Home: Strategic Dilemmas in Real Life*. Chicago, IL: University of Chicago Press.

Jasso, G. 1990. "Methods for the Theoretical and Empirical Analysis of Comparison Processes." In C. C. Clogg, Ed. *Sociological Methodology*. Washington, DC: American Sociological Association.

——. 1993. "Choice and Emotion in Comparison Theory." *Rationality and Society* 5: 231–74.

——. 2001. "Comparison Theory." In J. H. Turner, Ed., *Handbook of Sociological Theory*. New York: Kluwer Academic/Plenum.

——. 2006. "Distributive Justice Theory." In J. E. Stets and J. H. Turner, Eds. *Handbook of the Sociology of Emotions*. New York: Springer.

Jeffers, R. and I. Lehiste. 1979. *Principles and Methods for Historical Linguistics*. Cambridge, MA: MIT Press.

Johnson-Laird, P. N. and K. Oatley. 1992. "Basic Emotions, Rationality, and Folk Theory." *Cognition and Emotion* 6:201–23.

Kandel, E. R., J. H. Schwartz, T. M. Jessell. 1995. *Essentials of Neural Science and Behavior*. Norwalk, CN: Appleton and Lange.

Kemper, T. D. 1978. *An Interactional Theory of Emotions*. New York: Wiley.

——. 1987. "How Many Emotions Are There? Wedding the Social and the Autonomic Components." *American Journal of Sociology* 93:263–89.

——. 1990. *Social Structure and Testosterone*. New York: Wiley.

Kemper T. D. and R. Collins. 1990. "Dimensions of Microinteraction." *American Journal of Sociology* 96:32–68.

Kety, S. S. 1972. "Norepinephrine in the Central Nervous System and its Correlations With Behavior." In A. G. Karczman and J. D. Eccles, Eds. *Brain and Behavior*. New York: Springer.

Killcross, S., T. W. Robbins, and B. J. Everitt. 1997. "Different Types of Fear-Conditioned Behaviour Mediated by Separate Nuclei With Amygdala." *Nature* 388 (24 July):377–80.

Kramer, M. S., N. Cutler, J. Feighner, R. Shrivastava, J. Carman, J. J. Sramek, *et al.* 1998. "Distinct Mechanism for Antidepressant Activity by Blockade of Substance P Receptors." *Science* 281:1640–4.

Lawler, E. J. 2001. "An Affect Theory of Social Exchange." *American Journal of Sociology* 107:321–52.

Lawler, E. J. and J. Yoon. 1993. "Power and the Emergence of Commitment Behavior in Negotiated Exchange." *American Sociological Review* 58:465–81.

——. 1996. "Commitment in Exchange Relations: A Test of a Theory of Relational Cohesion." *American Sociological Review* 61:89–108.

——. 1998. "Network Structure and Emotion in Exchange Relations." *American Sociological Review* 63:871–94.

Le Doux, J. E. 1991. "Neuroscience Commentary: Emotion and the Brain." *Journal of NIH Research* 3:49–51.

———. 1993a. "Emotional Networks of the Brain." In M. Lewis and J. M. Haviland, Eds. *Handbook of Emotions*. New York: Guilford Press.

———. 1993b. "Emotional Memory Systems in the Brain." *Behavioural Brain Research* 58:69–79.

———. 1996. *The Emotional Brain: The Mysterious Underpinnings of Emotional Life*. New York: Simon and Schuster.

Lewis, H. 1971. *Shame and Guilt in Neurosis*. New York: International Universities Press.

Lichterman, P. 1996. *The Search for Community: Political Activists Reinventing Commitment*. Cambridge: Cambridge University Press.

Lin, A. C., K. A. Bard, and J. R. Anderson. 1992. "Development of Self-Recognition in Chimpanzees (*Pan troglodytes*)." *Journal of Comparative Psychology* 106:120–7.

Luhmann, N. 1982. *The Differentiation of Society*. Translation by S. Holmes and C. Larmore. New York: Columbia University Press.

———. 1988. *Theory of Action: Towards a New Synthesis Going Beyond Parsons*. London: Routledge.

Maas, P. 1958. *Textual Criticism*. Oxford: Oxford University Press.

McCall, G. J. and J. L. Simmons. 1978. *Identities and Interactions*. New York: Free Press.

McCarthy, J. and M. Zald. 1977. "Resource Mobilization in Social Movements: A Partial Theory." *American Journal of Sociology* 82:1212–39.

MacLean, P. D. 1990. *The Triune Brain in Evolution: Role of Paleocerebral Functions*. New York: Plenum Press.

———. 1993. "Introduction: Perspective on Cingulate Cortex in the Limbic System." In B. A. Vogt and M. Gabriel, Eds. *Neurobiology of Cingulate Cortex and Limbic Thalamus: A Comprehensive Handbook*. Boston, MA: Birkhäuser.

McPherson, J. M. and J. Ranger-Moore. 1991. "Evolution on a Dancing Landscape: Organizations and Networks in Dynamic Blau-Space." *Social Forces* 70:19–42.

Malatesta, C. Z. and J. M. Haviland. 1982. "Learning Display Rules: The Socialization of Emotion Expression in Infancy." *Child Development* 53:991–1003.

Markovsky, B. 1985. "Toward a Multilevel Distributive Justice Theory." *American Sociological Review* 50:822–39.

———. 1988. "Injustice and Arousal." *Social Justice Research* 2:223–33.

Markovsky, B. and E. J. Lawler. 1994. "A New Theory of Group Solidarity." *Advances in Group Processes* 11:113–37.

Maryanski, A. 1986. "African Ape Social Structure: A Comparative Analysis." PhD dissertation, University of California.

———. 1987. "African Ape Social Structure: Is There Strength in Weak Ties?" *Social Networks* 15:191–215.

———. 1992. "The Last Ancestor: An Ecological-Network Model on the Origins of Human Sociality." *Advances in Human Ecology* 2:1–32.

———. 1993. "The Elementary Forms of the First Proto-Human Society: An Ecological/Social Network Approach." *Advances in Human Ecology* 2:215–41.

———. 1994. "Hunting and Gathering Economic Systems." In *Magill's Survey of Social Science: Sociology*. Pasadena, CA: Salem.

———. 1996a. "African Ape Social Networks: A Blueprint for Reconstructing Early Hominid Social Structure." In J. Steele and S. Shennan, Eds. *The Archaeology of Human Ancestry*. London: Routledge.

———. 1996b. "Was Speech an Evolutionary Afterthought?" In B. Velichikovsky and

D. Rumbaugh, Eds. *Communicating Meaning: The Evolution and Development of Language.* Mahwah, NJ: Lawrence Erlbaum.

——. 1997. "Primate Communication and the Ecology of a Language Niche." In U. Segerstrale and Peter Molnar, Eds. *Nonverbal Communication: Where Nature Meets Culture.* Hillsdale, NJ: Lawrence Erlbaum.

——. n.d. "Emile Durkheim and the Totemic Principle: New Data for an Old Theory."

Maryanski, A. and J. H. Turner. 1992. *The Social Cage: Human Nature and the Evolution of Society.* Stanford, CA: Stanford University Press.

Mauss, M. 1925. *The Gift.* Trans. I. Cunnison. New York: Free Press.

Mead, G. H. 1934. *Mind, Self and Society.* Chicago, IL: University of Chicago Press.

Menzel, E. W. 1971. "Communication About the Environment in a Group of Young Chimpanzees." *Folia Primatologica* 15:220–32.

Moreno, J. 1953 [1934]. *Who Shall Survive?* New York: Beacon House.

Mullen, E., 2007. "The Reciprocal Relationship between Affect and Perceptions of Fairness." In K. Tornblom and R. Vermunt, Eds. *Distributive and Procedural Justice: Research and Social Implications.* London: Ashgate.

Mullen, E. and L. J. Skitka. 2006. "Exploring the Psychological Underpinnings of the Moral Mandate Effect: Motivated Reasoning, Group Identification, or Anger?" *Journal of Personality and Social Psychology* 90:629–43.

Needham, C. 1982. *The Principles of Cerebral Dominance: The Evolutionary Significance of the Radical Deduplication of the Human Brain.* Springfield, IL: Thomas.

O'Malley, M. N. and D. K. Davies. 1984. "Equity and Affect: The Effects of Relative Performance and Moods on Resource Allocation." *Basic and Applied Social Psychology* 5:273–82.

Osgood, C. E. 1966. "Dimensionality of the Semantic Space for Communication via Facial Expressions." *Scandinavian Journal of Psychology* 7:1–30.

Panksepp, J. 1982. "Toward a General Psychobiological Theory of Emotions." *Behavioral and Brain Sciences* 5:407–67.

Parsons, T. 1968 [1937]. *The Structure of Social Action.* New York: McGraw-Hill.

——. 1951. *The Social System.* New York: Free Press.

——. 1963a. "On the Concept of Power." *Proceedings of the American Philosophical Society* 107:232–62.

——. 1963b. "On the Concept of Influence." *Public Opinion Quarterly* 27:37–62.

——. 1970. "Some Problems of General Theory." In E. A. Terryakian, Ed. *Theoretical Sociology.* New York: Appleton-Century-Crofts.

——. 1978. *Action Theory and the Human Condition.* New York: Free Press.

Parsons, T. and N. J. Smelser. 1956. *Economy and Society.* New York: Free Press.

Parsons, T., R. F. Bales, and E. A. Shils. 1951. Working Papers in *The Theory of Action.* New York: Harper and Row.

Petty, R. E., D. DeSteno, and D. D. Rucker. 2001. "The Role of Affect in Attitude Change." In J. P. Forgas, Ed. *Handbook of Affect and Social Cognition.* Mahwah, NJ: Lawrence Erlbaum.

Platnick, N. and H. D. Cameron. 1977. "Cladistic Methods in Textual, Linguistic, and Phylogenetic Analysis." *Systematic Zoology* 26:380–5.

Plutchik, R. 1962. *The Emotions: Facts, Theories, and a New Model.* New York: Random House.

——. 1980. *Emotion: A Psychoevolutionary Synthesis.* New York: Harper and Row.

Powers, W. T. 1973. *Behavior: The Control of Perception.* Chicago, IL: Aldine Publishing.

Ridgeway, C. L. 1978. "Conformity, Group-Oriented Motivation, and Status Attainment in Small Groups." *Social Psychology Quarterly* 41:175–88.

——. 1982. "Status in Groups: The Importance of Motivation." *American Sociological Review* 47:76–88.

——. 1994. "Affect." In M. Foschi and E. J. Lawler, Eds. *Group Processes: Sociological Analyses*. Chicago, IL: Nelson-Hall.

——. 2000. "The Formation of Status Beliefs: Improving Status Construction Theory." *Advances in Group Processes* 17:77–102.

——. 2001. "Inequality, Status, and the Construction of Status Beliefs." In J. H. Turner, Ed. *Handbook of Sociological Theory*. New York: Kluwer Academic/Plenum.

——. 2006. "Status and Emotions From an Expectation States Theory." In J. E. Stets and J. H. Turner, Eds. *Handbook of the Sociology of Emotions*. New York: Springer.

Ridgeway, C. L. and C. Johnson. 1990. "What is the Relationship Between Socioemotional Behavior and Status in Task Groups?" *American Journal of Sociology* 95:1189–212.

Ridgeway, C. L. and H. A. Walker. 1995. "Status Structure." In K. S. Cook, G. A. Fine, and J. S. House, Eds. *Sociological Perspectives on Social Psychology*. Boston, MA: Allyn and Bacon.

Ridgeway, C. L. and K. G. Erickson. 2000. "Creating and Spreading Status Beliefs." *American Journal of Sociology* 106:579–615.

Ridgeway, C. L. and S. J. Correll. 2004. "Unpacking the Gender System: A Theoretical Perspective on Cultural Beliefs and Social Relations." *Gender and Society* 18:510–31.

Ridgeway, C. L., E. Boyle, K. Kulpers, and D. Robinson. 1998. "How Do Status Beliefs Develop? The Role of Resources and Interaction." *American Sociological Review* 63:331–50.

Ruff, C. B., E. Trinkaus, and T. W. Holliday. 1997. "Body Mass and Encephalization in Pleistocine Homo." *Nature* 387 (8 May):173–6.

Rupp, L. J. and V. Taylor. 1987. *Survival in the Doldrums: The American Women's Rights Movement, 1945 to the 1960s*. Oxford: Oxford University Press.

Savage-Rumbaugh, S., J. Murphy, R. Seveik, D. Brakke, S. L. Williams, and D. Rumbaugh. 1993. *Language Comprehension in the Ape and Child*, vol. 58 (monographs of the Society for Research in Child Development). Chicago, IL: University of Chicago Press.

Scheff, T. J. 1979. *Catharsis in Healing, Ritual, and Drama*. Berkeley: University of California Press.

——. 1988. "Shame and Conformity: the Deference-Emotion System." *American Sociological Review* 53:395–406.

——. 1990a. *Microsociology: Discourse and Social Structure*. Chicago, IL: University of Chicago Press.

——. 1990b. "Socialization of Emotion: Pride and Shame as Causal Agents." In T. D. Kemper, Ed. *Research Agendas in the Sociology of Emotions*. Albany, NY: SUNY Press.

——. 1997. *Emotions, the Social Bond, and Human Reality*. New York: Cambridge University Press.

Scheff, T. J. and S. M. Retzinger, 1991. *Emotions and Violence: Shame and Rage in Destructive Conflicts*. Lexington, MA: Lexington Books.

Schutz, A. 1967 [1932]. *The Phenomenology of the Social World*. Evanston, IL: Northwestern University Press.

Scott, J. P. 1980. "The Function of Emotions in Behavioral Systems: A Systems Theory Analysis." In R. Plutchik and H. Kellerman Eds. *Emotion: Theory, Research, and Experience*. New York: Academic.

Semendeferi, K., H. Damasio, R. Frank, and G. W. Van Hoesen. 1997. "The Evolution of the Frontal Lobes: A Volumetric Analysis Based on Three-Dimensional Reconstructions of Magnetic Resonance Scans of Human and Ape Brains." *Journal of Human Evolution* 32:375–88.

Shepherd, G. M. 1994. *Neurobiology*, third edition. New York: Oxford University Press.

Simmel, G. 1955 [1890]. *Conflict and the Web of Group Affiliations*. New York: Free Press.

———. 1990 [1907]. *The Philosophy of Money*. Translation by T. Botomore and D. Frisby. Boston, MA: Routledge.

Sinclair, R. C. and M. M. Mark. 1991. "Mood and the Endorsement of Egalitarian Macrojustice Principles versus Equity-Based Microjustice Principles." *Personality and Social Psychology Bulletin* 17:369–75.

———. 1992. "The Influence of Mood State on Judgment and Action: Effects on Persuasion, Categorization, Social Justice, Person Perception, and Judgmental Accuracy." In L. L. Martin and A. Tesser, Eds. *The Construction of Social Judgments*. Hillsdale, NJ: Lawrence Erlbaum.

Singer, T., S. B. Seymour, J. O'Doherty, H. Kavbr, R. J. Dolan, and C. D. Firth. 2004. "Empathy for Pain Involves Affective But Not Sensory Components of Pain." *Science* 303:1157–62.

Skitka, L. J. 2002. "Do the Means Always Justify the Ends, or Do the Ends Sometimes Justify the Means? A Value Protection Model of Justice." *Personality and Social Psychology Bulletin* 18:588–97.

Smith, T. S. and G. T. Stevens. 1997a. "Comfort Regulation As a Morphogenetic Principle." *Advances in Group Processes* 14:113–55.

———. 1997b. "The Architecture of Small Networks: Strong Interaction and Dynamic Organization in Small Social Systems." Paper presented at the American Sociological Association, Toronto, Canada.

Smith-Lovin, L. and D. R. Heise. 1988. *Analyzing Social Interaction: Advances in Affect Control Theory*. New York: Gordon and Breach.

Sperry, R. W. 1982. "Some Effects of Disconnecting the Cerebral Hemispheres." *Science* 217:1223–6.

Sroufe, L. A. 1979. "Socioemotional Development." In J. D. Osofsky, Ed. *Handbook of Infant Development*. New York: Wiley.

Stein, A. 2001. "Revenge of the Shamed: The Christian Right's Emotional Culture War." In J. Goodwin, J. M. Jasper, and F. Polletta, Eds. *Passionate Politics: Emotions and Social Movements*. Chicago, IL: University of Chicago Press.

Stephan, H. 1983. "Evolutionary Trends in Limbic Structures." *Neuroscience and Biobehavioral Reviews* 7:367–74.

Stephan, H. and O. J. Andy. 1969. "Quantitative Comparative Neuroanatomy of Primates: An Attempt at Phylogenetic Interpretation." *Annals of the New York Academy of Science* 167:370–87.

———. 1977. "Quantitative Comparison of the Amygdala in Insectivores and Primates." *Acta Anatomica* 98:130–53.

Stets, J. E. and J. H. Turner, Eds. 2006. *Handbook of the Sociology of Emotions*. New York: Springer.

———. 2007. "The Sociology of Emotions." In M. Lewis, J. M. Haviland-Jones, and L. Feldman Barret, Eds. *Handbook of Emotions*. New York: Guilford.

Stryker, S. 1980. *Symbolic Interactionism: A Social Structural Version*. Menlo Park, CA: Benjamin Cummings.

———. 2004. "Integrating Emotion into Identity Theory." *Advances in Group Processes* 21:1–23.

Tangney, J. P. and R. L. Dearing. 2002. *Shame and Guilt*. New York: Guilford Press.

Tangney, J. P., P. E. Wager, C. Fletcher, and R. Gramzow. 1992. "Shamed into Anger? The Relation of Shame and Guilt to Anger and Self-Reported Aggression." *Journal of Personality and Social Psychology* 62:669–75.

Tangney, J. P., R. S. Miller, L. Flicker, and D. H. Barlow. 1996a. "Are Shame, Guilt, and Embarrassment Distinct Emotions?" *Journal of Personality and Social Psychology* 70:1256–69.

Tangney, J. P., P. E. Wagner, D. H. Barlow, and D. Marschall. 1996b. "The Relation of Shame and Guilt to Constructive vs. Destructive Responses to Anger Across the Lifespan." *Journal of Personality and Social Psychology* 70:797–809.

Tangney, J. P., P. M. Niedenthal, M. V. Covert, and D. H. Barlow. 1998. "Are Shame and Guilt Related to Distinct Self-Discrepancies? A Test of Higgens's (1987) Hypotheses." *Journal of Personality and Social Psychology* 75:256–68.

Taylor, V. 1989. "Social Movement Continuity: The Women's Movement in Abeyance." *American Sociological Review* 54:761–75.

Temerin, A. and J. Cant. 1983. "The Evolutionary Divergence of Old World Monkeys and Apes." *American Naturalist* 122:335–51.

TenHouten, W. S. 1989. "Application of Dual Main Theory to Cross-Cultural Studies of Cognitive Development and Education." *Sociological Perspectives* 32:153–67.

———. 1997. "Neurosociology." Paper presented at the American Sociological Association, Toronto, Canada.

Thamm, R. 1992. "Social Structure and Emotion." *Sociological Perspectives* 35:649–71.

———. 2004. "Towards a Universal Power and Status Theory of Emotion." *Advances in Group Processes* 21:189–222.

———. 2006. "The Classification of Emotions." In J. E. Stets and J. H. Turner, Eds. *Handbook of the Sociology of Emotions*. New York: Springer.

Thibaut, J. W. and H. H. Kelley. 1959. *The Social Psychology of Groups*. New York: Wiley.

Thoits, P. A. 1990. "Emotional Deviance: Research Agendas." In T. D. Kemper, Ed. *Research Agendas in the Sociology of Emotions*. Albany: State University of New York Press.

Tilly, C. 1978. *From Mobilization to Revolution*. Reading, MA: Addison-Wesley.

Tooby, J. and L. Cosmides. 1992. "The Psychological Foundations of Culture." In J. H. Barkow, L. Cosmides, and J. Tooby, Eds. *The Adapted Mind: Evolutionary Psychology and The Generation of Culture*. New York: Oxford University Press.

Trevarthen, C. 1984. "Emotions in Infancy: Regulators of Contact and Relationship with Persons." In K. R. Scherer and P. Ekman, Eds. *Approaches to Emotion*. Hillsdale, NJ: Lawrence Erlbaum.

Turchin, P. 2006. *War and Peace and War: The Life Cycles of Empirical Nations*. New York: Pi Press.

Turner, J. H. 1985. *Societal Stratification: A Theoretical Analysis*. New York: Columbia University Press.

———. 1987. "Toward a Sociological Theory of Motivation." *American Sociological Review* 52:15–27.

———. 1988. *A Theory of Social Interaction*. Stanford, CA: Stanford University Press.

———. 1994a. "Roles and Interaction Processes: Toward a More Robust Theory." In G. Platt and C. Gordon, Eds. *Self, Collective Action, and Society*. Greenwich, CT: JAI Press.

———. 1994b. "A General Theory of Motivation and Emotion in Human Interaction." *Osterreichische Zeitschrift fur Soziologie* 8:20–35.

———. 1995. *Macrodynamics: Toward a Theory on the Organization of Human Populations*. New Brunswick, NJ: Rutgers University Press.

———. 1996a. "The Evolution of Emotions in Humans: A Darwinian-Durkheimian Analysis." *Journal for The Theory of Social Behaviour* 26:1–34.

———. 1996b. "Cognition, Emotion and Interaction in the Big-Brained Primate." In K. M. Kwan, Ed. *Social Processes and Interpersonal Relations*. Greenwich, CT: JAI Press.

——. 1997a. "The Nature and Dynamics of the Social Among Humans." In J. D. Greenwood, Ed. *The Mark of the Social*. New York: Rowman and Littlefield.

——. 1997b. "The Evolution of Emotions: the Nonverbal Basis of Human Social Organization." In U. Segerstrale and P. Molnar, Eds. *Nonverbal Communication: Where Nature Meets Culture*. Mahwah, NJ: Lawrence Erlbaum.

——. 1999a. "The Neurology of Emotion: Implications for Sociological Theories of Interpersonal Behavior." In D. D. Franks and T. S. Smith, Eds. *Mind, Brain, and Society: Toward a Neurosociology of Emotion*. Social Perspectives on Emotion. Vol. 5. Stanford, CT: JAI Press.

——. 1999b. "Toward a General Sociological Theory of Emotions." *Journal for the Theory of Social Behavior* 29:132–62.

——. 2000a. *On the Origins of Human Emotions: A Sociological Inquiry Into the Evolution of Human Affect*. Stanford, CA: Stanford University Press.

——. 2000b. "A Theory of Embedded Encounters." *Advances in Group Processes* 17:283–320.

——. 2002. *Face-to-Face: Toward a Theory of Interpersonal Behavior*. Stanford, CA: Stanford University Press.

——. 2003. *Human Institutions: A Theory of Societal Evolution*. Boulder, CO: Rowman and Littlefield.

——. 2005. *The Sociology of Emotions*. New York: Cambridge University Press.

——. 2006. "Psychoanalytic Sociological Theories of Emotions." In J. E. Stets and J. H. Turner, Eds. *Handbook of the Sociology of Emotions*. New York: Springer.

——. 2007a. "Justice and Emotions." *Social Justice Research*, in press.

——. 2007b. "The Social Psychology of Terrorism." In B. Phillips, Ed. *Understanding Terrorism*. Boulder, CO: Paradigm Press.

——. 2008. "Emotions and Social Structure." In D. Robinson and J. Clay-Warner, eds., Emotions and Social Structure. New York: Elsevier.

Turner, J. H. and R. R. Singleton. 1978. "A Theory of Ethnic Antagonism: Toward a Reintegration of Cultural and Structural Concepts in Ethnic Relations Theory." *Social Forces* 56:1001–19.

Turner, J. H. and D. E. Boyns. 2001. "Expectations, Need-States, and Emotional Arousal in Interaction." In J. Szmatka, K. Wysienska, and M. Lovaglia, Eds. *Theory, Simulation and Experiments*. New York: Praeger.

Turner, J. H. and A. Maryanski. 2005. *Incest: Origins of the Taboo*. Boulder, CO: Paradigm Press.

Turner, J. H. and J. E. Stets. 2005. *The Sociology of Emotions*. New York: Cambridge University Press.

——. 2006. "The Moral Emotions." In J. E. Stets and J. H. Turner, *Handbook of the Sociology of Emotions*. New York: Springer.

——. 2007. "Sociological Theories of Emotions." *Annual Review of Sociology*. Palo Alto, CA: Annual Reviews, Inc.

Turner, J. H., R. R. Singleton, and D. Musick. 1984. *Oppression: A Socio-history of Black–White Relations in America*. Chicago, IL: Nelson-Hall.

Turner, R. H. 1962. "Role Taking: Process Versus Conformity." In A. Rose, Ed. *Human Behavior and Social Processes*. Boston, MA: Houghton Mifflin.

——. 1968. "Roles: Sociological Aspects." *International Encyclopedia of the Social Sciences*. New York: Macmillan.

——. 2001. "Role Theory." In J. H. Turner, Ed. *Handbook of Sociological Theory*. New York: Kluwer Academic Plenum.

——. 2002. "Roles." In J. H. Turner, Ed. *Handbook of Sociological Theory*. New York: Kluwer Academic/Plenum.

Vargha-Khadem, F., D. G. Gadian, K. E. Watkins, A. Connelly, W. Van Paesschen, and M. Mishkin. 1997. "Differential Effects of Early Hippocampal Pathology on Episodic and Semantic Memory." *Science* 277 (18 July):376–80.

Vogt, B. A. 1993. "Structural Organization of Cingulate Cortex." In B. A. Vogt and M. Gabriel, Eds. *Neurobiology of Cingulate Cortex and Limbic Thalamus.* Boston, MA: Birkhäuser.

Volkan, V. 1999. *Bloodlines: From Ethnic Pride to Ethnic Terrorism.* Charlottesville, VA: Pitchstone Press.

———. 2004. *Blind Trust: Large Groups and Their Leaders in Times of Crisis and Terror.* Charlottesville, VA: Pitchstone Press.

———. 2006. *Killing in the Name of Identity: A Study of Bloody Conflicts.* Charlottesville, VA: Pitchstone Press.

Wagner, D. G. and J. Berger. 1997. "Gender and Interpersonal Task Behaviors: Status Expectation Accounts." *Sociological Perspectives* 40:1–32.

Wahlestedt, C. 1998. "Reward for Persistence in Substance Research." *Science* 281:1624–5.

Webster, M. A. and M. Foschi, Eds. 1988. *Status Generalization: New Theory and Research.* Stanford, CA: Stanford University Press.

Webster, M., Jr. and J. M. Whitmeyer. 1999. "A Theory of Second-Order Expectations and Behavior." *Social Psychology Quarterly* 62:17–31.

Weiner, B. 1986. *An Attributional Theory of Motivation and Emotion.* New York: Springer.

———. 2006. *Social Motivation, Justice, and the Moral Emotions: An Attributional Approach.* Mahwah, NJ: Lawrence Erlbaum.

Wentworth, W. M. and J. Ryan. 1992. "Balancing Body, Mind and Culture: The Place of Emotion in Social Life." In D. D. Franks and V. Gecas, Eds. *Social Perspectives on Emotion.* Greenwich, CT: JAI Press.

———. 1994. "Introduction." In D. D. Franks, W. M. Wentworth, and J. Ryan, Eds. *Social Perspectives on Emotion.* Greenwich, CT: JAI Press.

Wentworth, W. M. and D. Yardly. 1994. "Deep Sociality: A Bioevolutionary Perspective on the Sociology of Human Emotions." In D. D. Franks, W. M. Wentworth, and J. Ryan, Eds. *Social Perspectives on Emotion.* Greenwich, CT: JAI Press.

Index

adaptive strategy, emotionality as 27–8, 30–9
Adolphs, R. 116
Affect Control Theory 83, 92, 151, 161
age 68, 69, 79, 80, 84, 129–30, 176
aggression 61–2, 63, 64, 187; *see also* violence
alienation 64, 90, 122, 187, 188, 189, 191, 192, 207; collective experience of 114, 197; and commitments to social structures 190; as elaboration of primary emotions 9, 10–11, 108, 119, 165; from corporate units 114, 117, 125, 137, 148, 203; from institutional domains 125, 137, 180; as quiet expression of anger 11, 121; ritualizing and 171; and roles 136; and social change 188
amygdala 61–2, 63
anatomy 23, 24, 40; brain 34–5, 45–8
Anderson, J.R. 23, 93
Andrews, P. 15
Andy, O.J. 34
anger 62, 84, 90, 95, 108, 109, 122, 125, 187–8, 197, 199, 203, 207; alienation as quiet expression of 11, 121; diffuse 114, 137, 168, 188, 195, 196, 199, 207; and exclusion 120–1; and external attributions 116, 117, 136, 137, 148, 187, 189, 190–1; and justice

assessments 111, 112, 114, 115, 116, 117, 174; and normatization processes 165, 167, 171, 174, 175, 177, 178, 205; as primary emotion 3; as rapid response 63; repressed 96, 197; righteous 115, 117, 188, 189, 191–2, 193, 197, 207, 208
anxiety 90, 165, 167, 191, 192
apes and monkeys 14–27; anatomy 23, 24; brain size 34–5; greeting rituals 25; habitat 22–3, 26–7; last common ancestor 21–2; reciprocity and justice 24–5; self-awareness 23–4, 25; sense of community 25; social structures 15–23, 26–7, 30; social ties 15, 17, 18–23, 28
Arnold, M.B. 4
'as if' feeling 63
associative emotions 62, 63
attention 16, 28; mutual focus of 88, 90
attribution 38–9, 95, 96, 97–100, 108, 116; *see also* external attributions; self-attributions
attunement: interpersonal 32, 33, 41; *see also* role-taking
auditory sense 24, 40
authority 66, 83, 137, 140, 153
autonomic nervous system (ANS) 2, 49–50, 63

Baker, W.E. 132